A HARMONY OF THE GOSPELS FOR STUDENTS

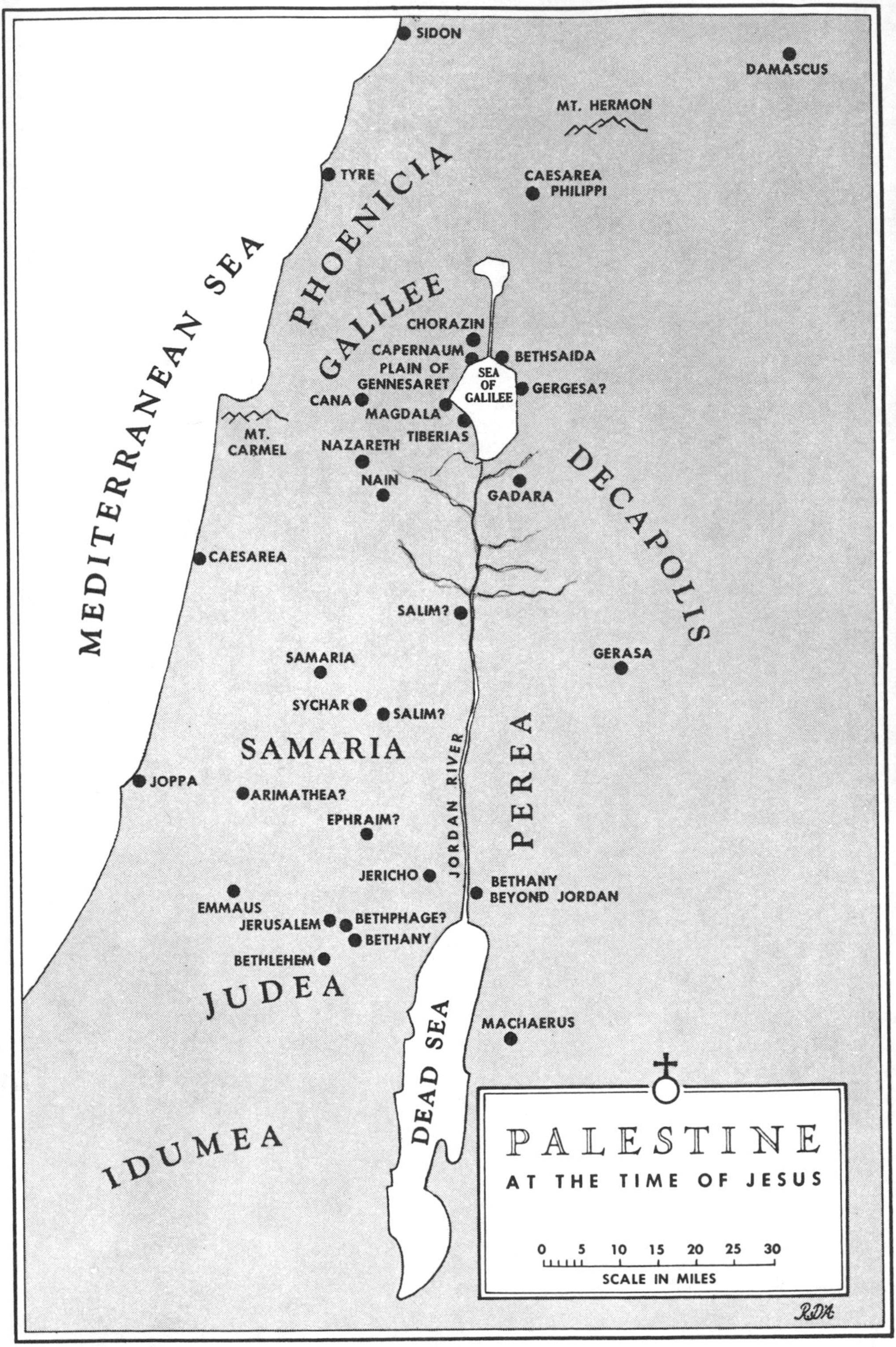
SIDON
DAMASCUS
MT. HERMON
TYRE
PHOENICIA
CAESAREA PHILIPPI
MEDITERRANEAN SEA
GALILEE
CHORAZIN
CAPERNAUM
BETHSAIDA
PLAIN OF GENNESARET
SEA OF GALILEE
GERGESA?
CANA
MAGDALA
TIBERIAS
MT. CARMEL
NAZARETH
NAIN
GADARA
DECAPOLIS
CAESAREA
SALIM?
SAMARIA
GERASA
SYCHAR
SALIM?
SAMARIA
JORDAN RIVER
PEREA
JOPPA
ARIMATHEA?
EPHRAIM?
JERICHO
BETHANY BEYOND JORDAN
EMMAUS
JERUSALEM
BETHPHAGE?
BETHANY
BETHLEHEM
JUDEA
DEAD SEA
MACHAERUS
IDUMEA
PALESTINE
AT THE TIME OF JESUS
0 5 10 15 20 25 30
SCALE IN MILES
RDA

A HARMONY OF THE GOSPELS

FOR STUDENTS

According to the Text of the

REVISED STANDARD VERSION

by

RALPH DANIEL HEIM

FORTRESS PRESS • PHILADELPHIA

Library of Congress Catalog Card Number 47-2807

ISBN 0-8006-1494-1

First paperback edition, fourteenth printing 1974
Twenty-first printing 1989

Printed in the United States of America 1-1494

INTRODUCTION

This HARMONY is designed for the great body of Bible students, not for the smaller group of biblical scholars. High school, college, and seminary students, pastors and parish workers, Sunday and weekday church school teachers and pupils, parents and young people in the home are in view.

The purpose is to help such students consider the Gospel materials on Christ's life and teachings as simply, soundly, and fully as possible, with the utmost clarity of insight into the truth.

As long ago as the second century it was recognized that publications which bring the Gospels into some kind of combination serve that purpose because they enable the student to see and grasp the total record more readily.

This publication has no other aim. It does not mean to make any contribution to the body of scholarly data. It does not argue any particular chronology of events. It would neither urge nor set aside any findings of established scholarship concerning relations of the various records. It means only to be for students of this generation another useful aid in effective study of the biblical truth.

It stresses meaningfulness, simplicity, and utility.

The outline is of itself a short "Life of Christ." It is meant to teach as it proceeds. The headings aim to tell the narrative in the straightforward language of action and disclose the substance of teaching passages as adequately as possible.

The author's classroom experience in twenty years of teaching with hundreds of students has determined a policy of severe simplification as compared with the usual harmonies. The sternest effort has been made to avoid minutiae of all kinds.

It has been deemed enough to show the major parallels, not tearing every possible parallel out of its context, perhaps, to show its relationship to every other. Cross-references are sometimes used but they are kept at a minimum compatible with the average student's needs. Concordances are available for more detailed study.

Transpositions of verses are avoided whenever possible and columns are not regularly broken up and strung out to show exact parallels in an elaborate manner. Continuities of chapters are preserved as fully as possible, and an index is provided for finding passages which have had to be dislocated.

Since an abundance of footnotes is worse than useless, these are reduced to a minimum, excepting those which belong with the text of the Revised Standard Version. All materials appear but once. Throughout, the rule has been to provide a readable book.

It is a four-Gospel harmony because the entire record must be at hand for the study of that which has been called "one Gospel written by four."

More recently there has been a tendency to use a harmony of the synoptic Gospels only and to separate the Gospel of John for isolated study. This book can be used conveniently in that kind of study since John appears in a different type and is presented chiefly in large blocks. At the same time this is a convenient instrument for the study of all four Gospels, the synoptics only, or for any one other as well as John. In each case, all the needful material is at hand for ready reference.

No harmony can be prepared without careful attention to chronology, and it is in that area that many perplexing problems arise. It may be said that this harmony is somewhat experimental at that point. It does not force chronology into the forefront and it does allow literary facts to assume major importance in many issues. For example, in nearly all cases, Matthew's collections of teachings, Luke's interpolations, and John's discourses are left intact. This is accomplished without serious disarrangement of the usual chronology, while it reflects both the current emphasis on literary factors and the present state of uncertainty about chronology. In general, the sequence of events is according to—respectively—Mark, Luke, Matthew, and John in order of decreasing consideration.

Along with the emphasis upon literary considerations and de-emphasis on chronology, it has been possible to make a beginning at stress upon religious content versus topography in the various headings.

The kind permission of The International Council of Religious Education to use the text of the Revised Standard Version and the co-operative spirit of its publishers, Thomas Nelson and Sons, are acknowledged.

There are many persons who deserve expressions of appreciation for their helpfulness during the many years the manuscript has been in preparation. It is possible to mention but one and that shall be a friendly colleague, Dr. Raymond T. Stamm, Professor of New Testament.

The work is dedicated to E, P, H, and M.

RALPH D. HEIM

Gettysburg, Pennsylvania
April 10, 1946

CONTENTS

An Arrangement of the Life and Teachings of Jesus Christ

PART ONE. RECORDS OF CHRIST'S EARLY LIFE

Section A. The Infancy of Christ and of John the Baptist

1. Introduction 3
   a. The prefaces of the synoptic Gospels
      Mt. 1:1; Mk. 1:1; Lk. 1:1-4
   b. The prologue to John's Gospel: the coming of Jesus, the eternal Word in flesh, brings light, truth, and grace to men
      Jn. 1:1-18
   c. The two genealogies of Jesus Christ
      Mt. 1:2-17; Lk. 3:23-38
2. The birth of John the Baptist is promised to Zechariah and Elizabeth . . . 6
   Lk. 1:5-25
3. The virgin, Mary of Nazareth, receives the angel's annunciation of Jesus' birth . 7
   Lk. 1:26-38
4. Mary visits Elizabeth in a city of Judah. The Magnificat 7
   Lk. 1:39-56
5. John the Baptist is born and named. The Benedictus 8
   Lk. 1:57-80
6. Joseph of Nazareth learns of the incarnation; Jesus Christ is born at Bethlehem . 9
   Mt. 1:18-25; Lk. 2:1-7
7. Angels proclaim his birth and shepherds visit him. The Gloria in Excelsis . . 10
   Lk. 2:8-20
8. The circumcision and naming take place on the eighth day 10
   Lk. 2:21
9. The presentation in the temple occurs; Simeon and Anna give thanks. The Nunc Dimittis 10
   Lk. 2:22-40
10. Eastern wise men come to Jerusalem and Bethlehem with gifts; Herod plots to destroy the child 11
    Mt. 2:1-12
11. Joseph and Mary flee into Egypt with Jesus; Herod slaughters the children of Bethlehem and dies; the family returns to Nazareth 12
    Mt. 2:13-23

Section B. Christ's Youth, Early Manhood, and Preparation for His Public Ministry

12. Jesus visits Jerusalem for the Passover when twelve years of age; confers with the teachers in the temple 13
    Lk. 2:41-50

13. At home in Nazareth, Jesus grows in the fourfold way 13
Lk. 2:51, 52

14. John the Baptist preaches and baptizes beside the Jordan until imprisoned . . 13
a. Declares his mission as herald of Jesus
Mt. 3:1-3; Mk. 1:2-4; Lk. 3:1-6
b. Baptizes
Mt. 3:4-6; Mk. 1:5, 6
c. Preaches repentance and righteousness
Mt. 3:7-10; Lk. 3:7-14
d. Announces the Coming One
Mt. 3:11, 12; Mk. 1:7, 8; Lk. 3:15-18
e. Undergoes imprisonment
Lk. 3:19, 20

15. Jesus is baptized by John the Baptist in the Jordan 16
Mt. 3:13-17; Mk. 1:9-11; Lk. 3:21, 22

16. Jesus is tempted in the wilderness 17
Mt. 4:1-11; Mk. 1:12, 13; Lk. 4:1-13

PART TWO. RECORDS OF CHRIST'S PUBLIC MINISTRY

Section C. Christ's Early Work, Especially in Judea and Samaria, According to John[1]

17. John the Baptist declares the pre-eminence of Jesus; announces the Lamb of God . 21
Jn. 1:19-34

18. Jesus wins five disciples including Andrew, Simon, Philip, and Nathanael . . 21
Jn. 1:35-51

19. Jesus gives a sign at a marriage at Cana in Galilee; sojourns with disciples and family in Capernaum 22
Jn. 2:1-12

20. In Jerusalem for the Passover, Jesus drives trade out of the temple 23
Jn. 2:13-25
(See also article 109)

21. Nicodemus visits Jesus by night; they discuss new birth and salvation . . . 23
Jn. 3:1-21

22. Jesus baptizes in Judea; John exalts him at Aenon 24
Jn. 3:22-36

23. Jesus teaches at Sychar in Samaria 25
a. Telling the woman about the water of life
Jn. 4:1-15
b. Discussing true worship
Jn. 4:16-26
c. Directing the disciples to the food of service
Jn. 4:27-38
d. Winning believers in Sychar
Jn. 4:39-42

24. Jesus arrives in Galilee 26
Jn. 4:43-45

25. An official's son in Capernaum is healed 26
Jn. 4:46-54

[1] Section C includes the materials which pertain to what is often designated *Christ's Earlier Judean Ministry.*

Section D. Christ's Early Teaching, Preaching, and Healing in Galilee, According to Matthew, Mark, and Luke [2]

26. After John's imprisonment, Jesus preaches repentance, the kingdom's coming, and belief in the Gospel 27
Mt. 4:12-17; Mk. 1:14, 15; Lk. 4:14, 15

27. Jesus speaks in the synagogue at Nazareth, and is rejected 28
Lk. 4:16-30
(See also article 49)

28. Peter, Andrew, James, and John are called as disciples following a great catch of fish 28
Mt. 4:18-22; Mk. 1:16-20; Lk. 5:1-11

29. Jesus teaches, heals, and preaches in Capernaum and elsewhere in Galilee . . 30
a. Teaching in the Capernaum synagogue
Mk. 1:21, 22; Lk. 4:31, 32
b. Healing a man with an unclean spirit
Mk. 1:23-28; Lk. 4:33-37
c. Healing Simon Peter's mother-in-law and others
Mt. 8:14-17; Mk. 1:29-34; Lk. 4:38-41
d. Leaving Capernaum to preach in other cities
Mt. 4:23-25; Mk. 1:35-39; Lk. 4:42-44
e. Cleansing a leper
Mt. 8:1-4; Mk. 1:40-45; Lk. 5:12-16

Section E. Christ's Popularity among the People and the Rise of Opposition by Jewish Leaders

30. Jesus in Capernaum heals a paralytic carried by four friends; scribes and Pharisees charge blasphemy 33
Mt. 9:1-8; Mk. 2:1-12; Lk. 5:17-26

31. Levi (Matthew), a tax collector, is called as a disciple; Jesus attends the feast while scribes and Pharisees find fault 35
Mt. 9:9-13; Mk. 2:13-17; Lk. 5:27-32

32. Jesus answers a question about fasting; tells of old and new cloth and garments, wine and wineskins 36
Mt. 9:14-17; Mk. 2:18-22; Lk. 5:33-39

33. Jesus heals an invalid man at the pool of Bethzatha in Jerusalem; Jews cite Sabbath laws and dispute his equality with the Father 37
Jn. 5:1-18

34. Jesus discourses on his gift of eternal life and the testimony concerning himself . 37
Jn. 5:19-47

35. The Pharisees censure the disciples for plucking grain on the Sabbath; Jesus gives a principle of Sabbath observance 38
Mt. 12:1-8; Mk. 2:23-28; Lk. 6:1-5

36. Jesus heals a man with a withered hand on the Sabbath; the scribes and Pharisees determine to destroy him 40
Mt. 12:9-14; Mk. 3:1-6; Lk. 6:6-11

37. Many seek Jesus as he speaks and heals by the lake 40
Mt. 12:15-21; Mk. 3:7-12

[2] Sections D—I include the materials which pertain to what is usually designated *Christ's Galilean Ministry.*

Section F. Christ's Choice of the Twelve, His Sermon on the Mount, and the Beelzebub Controversy

38. The twelve are appointed to be disciples and apostles 41
Mk. 3:13-19a; Lk. 6:12-19

39. In his "Sermon on the Mount" Jesus deals with the duties and privileges of citizens of the kingdom of God 42
a. Their ways to happiness and their destinies. The Beatitudes
Mt. 5:1-12; Lk. 6:20-26
b. Their purposes in the world
Mt. 5:13-16
c. Their use of the law and the prophets
Mt. 5:17-19
d. Their better righteousness: perfect morality versus obedience to law alone
Mt. 5:20-48; Lk. 6:27-36
e. Their better righteousness: sincere religion versus profession. The Lord's Prayer
Mt. 6:1-18
(See also Lk. 11:1-4, article 80)
f. Their highest good: God's kingdom and righteousness
Mt. 6:19-34
(See also article 83c)
g. Their principle of similar returns. The Golden Rule
Mt. 7:1-12; Lk. 6:37-42
h. Their deeds
Mt. 7:13-23; Lk. 6:43-45
i. Their help
Mt. 7:24-29; Lk. 6:46-49

40. Jesus heals the centurion's slave in Capernaum 50
Mt. 8:5-13; Lk. 7:1-10

41. Jesus raises a widow's only son at Nain 51
Lk. 7:11-17

42. John the Baptist sends disciples to ask a last question; Jesus replies 51
a. Showing his works; commending John
Mt. 11:2-15; Lk. 7:18-30
b. Condemning the wickedness of the generation
Mt. 11:16-19; Lk. 7:31-35
c. Upbraiding three impenitent cities
Mt. 11:20-24
(See also Lk. 10:13-15, article 77)
d. Returning thanks for knowledge of God; inviting the weary to rest in him
Mt. 11:25-30
(See also Lk. 10:21, 22, article 77)

43. Jesus, anointed by a penitent woman, gives a parable of the creditor who forgave two debtors 54
Lk. 7:36-50

44. Jesus and the twelve, with women ministering, engage in a preaching tour . . 54
Lk. 8:1-3

45. Jesus withstands friends, enemies, and relatives seeking to restrain him . . . 55
a. Is charged with madness
Mk. 3:19b-21

b. Heals a blind and dumb demoniac; denies alliance with Beelzebub
Mt. 12:22-30; Mk. 3:22-27

c. Discusses the eternal sin—blasphemy against the Holy Spirit, the seeking of signs, and other evils
Mt. 12:31-45; Mk. 3:28-30
(See also article 81)

d. Designates his true relatives
Mt. 12:46-50; Mk. 3:31-35; Lk. 8:19-21

Section G. Christ's Parables of the Kingdom and His Journey into the Country of the Gerasenes

46. Jesus gives nine parables of the kingdom of God 58

a. The soils
Mt. 13:1-9; Mk. 4:1-9; Lk. 8:4-8

b. The reason for using parables and the explanation of the soils
Mt. 13:10-23; Mk. 4:10-25; Lk. 8:9-18

c. The weeds, with explanation
Mt. 13:24-30, 36-43

d. The virile seed and the fertile earth
Mk. 4:26-29

e. The mustard seed; the leaven
Mt. 13:31-33; Mk. 4:30-32
(See also article 86)

f. Jesus' custom of using parables
Mt. 13:34, 35; Mk. 4:33, 34

g. The hidden treasure; the pearl of great value; the net; treasures old and new
Mt. 13:44-52

47. Jesus calms the storm on the Sea of Galilee 63
Mt. 8:18, 23-27; Mk. 4:35-41; Lk. 8:22-25

48. Jesus heals and helps many 64

a. The Gerasene demoniac
Mt. 8:28-34; Mk. 5:1-20; Lk. 8:26-39

b. Jairus' daughter and the woman with hemorrhage
Mt. 9:18-26; Mk. 5:21-43; Lk. 8:40-56

c. Two blind men, and a dumb demoniac
Mt. 9:27-34

49. Jesus returns to Nazareth and is not honored 70
Mt. 13:53-58; Mk. 6:1-6a
(See also article 27)

Section H. Christ's Sending Forth of the Twelve and His Journey into Phoenicia

50. The twelve are instructed and sent out to minister 71

a. The plight of the people; the sending of the twelve
Mt. 9:35—10:4; Mk. 6:6b, 7; Lk. 9:1, 2

b. Instructions for the journey
Mt. 10:5-15; Mk. 6:8-11; Lk. 9:3-5

c. The persecution of the disciples and their fearless witness
Mt. 10:16-33

d. The cost and rewards of discipleship and service
Mt. 10:34—11:1; Mk. 6:12, 13; Lk. 9:6
(See also article 77)

51. John the Baptist is martyred by Herod and Herodias 75
Mt. 14:1-12; Mk. 6:14-29; Lk. 9:7-9

52. Five thousand are fed after the twelve return to Jesus 77
Mt. 14:13-21; Mk. 6:30-44; Lk. 9:10-17; Jn. 6:1-14
(See also article 58)

53. Jesus refuses a crown; prays; walks on the sea; returns to Gennesaret . . . 79
Mt. 14:22-36; Mk. 6:45-56; Jn. 6:15-24

54. Jesus discourses on the Bread of Life; the Jews debate; many disciples fall away . 81
Jn. 6:25-71

55. Jesus condemns the traditionalism of the elders; declares that the source of evil is within 83
Mt. 15:1-20; Mk. 7:1-23

56. Jesus journeys toward Tyre and Sidon; a Syrophoenician woman's daughter is healed 85
Mt. 15:21-28; Mk. 7:24-30

57. Jesus returns through the region of the Decapolis; heals a deaf mute 86
Mt. 15:29-31; Mk. 7:31-37

58. Four thousand are fed; Christ departs to the region of Magadan 86
Mt. 15:32-39; Mk. 8:1-10
(See also article 52)

59. Pharisees and Sadducees ask for a sign; Jesus warns the disciples to beware of their spirit 87
Mt. 16:1-12; Mk. 8:11-21

60. A blind man is healed near Bethsaida 89
Mk. 8:22-26

Section I. Christ's Journey to Caesarea Philippi and His Transfiguration

61. Peter confesses Jesus' Messiahship 89
Mt. 16:13-20; Mk. 8:27-30; Lk. 9:18-20

62. Jesus foretells his suffering, death, and resurrection; rebukes Peter's remonstrance 90
Mt. 16:21-23; Mk. 8:31-33; Lk. 9:21, 22

63. Jesus speaks of cross-bearing and finding one's life 91
Mt. 16:24-28; Mk. 8:34—9:1; Lk. 9:23-27

64. The transfiguration takes place; Elijah's second coming is discussed 91
Mt. 17:1-13; Mk. 9:2-13; Lk. 9:28-36

65. The epileptic boy is healed 93
Mt. 17:14-21; Mk. 9:14-29; Lk. 9:37-43a

66. Jesus foretells his death and resurrection a second time 95
Mt. 17:22, 23; Mk. 9:30-32; Lk. 9:43b-45

67. The half-shekel tax is found in the mouth of a fish 95
Mt. 17:24-27

68. The disciples dispute about rank; Jesus teaches childlike humility, self-denial, and concern for the young and the lowly 96
Mt. 18:1-14; Mk. 9:33-50; Lk. 9:46-50
(See also article 91a)

69. Jesus deals with reconciliation and forgiveness; gives the parable of the unforgiving servant 98
Mt. 18:15-35

Section J. Christ's Attendance at the Feasts of Tabernacles and Dedication

70. Jesus attends the feast of Tabernacles; meets hostility 99
a. Goes privately to the feast
Jn. 7:1-15
b. Faces enemies
Jn. 7:16-24
c. Is considered and denied as the Christ
Jn. 7:25-52

71. Jesus debates with Jews in the temple 101
a. On the Son as light of the world
Jn. 8:12-30
b. On spiritual freedom
Jn. 8:31-38
c. On sons of Abraham and the Son of God
Jn. 8:39-59

72. Jesus heals the man born blind 103
Jn. 9:1-41

73. The good shepherd is portrayed in an allegory 104
Jn. 10:1-21

74. Jesus attends the feast of Dedication in Jerusalem; returns beyond Jordan . . 105
Jn. 10:22-42

Section K. Christ's Further Work as Reported Largely by Luke Alone[3]

75. Jesus departs from Galilee through Samaria to Judea beyond the Jordan . . . 106
Mt. 19:1, 2; Mk. 10:1; Lk. 9:51-56

76. Jesus sets tests for three hesitant disciples 107
Mt. 8:19 22; Lk. 9.57-62

77. Seventy, instructed and sent out to minister, return 107
Lk. 10:1-24
(See also articles 42c, d, and 50)

78. Jesus tells the parable of the good Samaritan 108
Lk. 10:25-37

79. Jesus visits the home of Martha and Mary in Bethany 109
Lk. *10:38-42*

80. Jesus teaches his disciples how to prevail in prayer; speaks parable of the friend calling at midnight. The Lord's Prayer 109
Lk. 11:1-13
(See also Mt. 6:9-15, article 39e)

81. Jesus discusses casting out demons by Beelzebub, the sign of Jonah, and inner light 110
Lk. 11:14-36
(See also article 45)

82. At a Pharisee's table Jesus pronounces woes upon Pharisees and lawyers . . . 111
Lk. 11:37-54
(See also article 113)

83. Jesus talks to the disciples on trust and watchfulness 111
a. God's care of the confessor
Lk. 12:1-12
b. The parable of the foolish rich man
Lk. 12:13-21

[3] Sections K and L include the materials which pertain to what is often called *Christ's Perean Ministry.*

c. Trust in God's providence
Lk. 12:22-34
(See also article 39f)
d. The parable of the watchful servants
Lk. 12:35-48
e. Interpreting the signs of the times
Lk. 12:49-59

84. Disasters of Galileans teach urgency of repentance; Jesus speaks the parable of the unfruitful fig tree 114
Lk. 13:1-9

85. Jesus heals a stooped woman on the sabbath; meets criticism 114
Lk. 13:10-17

86. Jesus likens the kingdom to mustard seed and leaven 115
Lk. 13:18-21
(See also article 46e)

87. Jesus discusses the question whether but few are saved 115
Lk. 13:22-30

88. Jesus replies to the warning that Herod will kill him; laments over Jerusalem . . 115
Lk. 13:31-35
(See also Mt. 23:37-39, article 113)

89. Jesus dines with a chief Pharisee; heals a dropsical man; teaches humility; gives a parable of the great banquet 116
Lk. 14:1-24
(See also article 111c)

90. Jesus discusses the cost of discipleship 117
Lk. 14:25-35

91. Three parables on grace and two parables on wealth are given 117
a. The lost sheep
Lk. 15:1-7
(See also Mt. 18:10-14, article 68)
b. The lost coin
Lk. 15:8-10
c. The lost son
Lk. 15:11-32
d. The dishonest steward
Lk. 16:1-18
e. The rich man and Lazarus
Lk. 16:19-31

92. Jesus discusses forgiveness, faith, and service 120
Lk. 17:1-10

93. Ten lepers are healed; one returns to thank Jesus 120
Lk. 17:11-19

94. Jesus discusses the nature of the kingdom's coming 121
Lk. 17:20-37
(See also article 116a)

95. Jesus gives parables of the widow and the judge and of the Pharisee and the tax collector 121
Lk. 18:1-14

Section L. Christ's Final Approach to Jerusalem [4]

96. Jesus speaks concerning marriage and divorce 122
Mt. 19:3-12; Mk. 10:2-12

[4] Section L includes the materials which pertain to what is sometimes designated *Christ's Later Judaean Ministry.*

97. Jesus blesses little children 123
Mt. 19:13-15; Mk. 10:13-16; Lk. 18:15-17

98. A rich young ruler refuses discipleship; Jesus cites dangers of wealth 124
Mt. 19:16-30; Mk. 10:17-31; Lk. 18:18-30

99. Jesus gives a parable about the payment of laborers in a vineyard 126
Mt. 20:1-16

100. Jesus foretells his death and resurrection the third time 126
Mt. 20:17-19; Mk. 10:32-34; Lk. 18:31-34

101. The ambition of James, John, and their mother is corrected 127
Mt. 20:20-28; Mk. 10:35-45

102. Blind Bartimaeus is healed near Jericho 128
Mt. 20:29-34; Mk. 10:46-52; Lk. 18:35-43

103. Zacchaeus, a tax collector in Jericho, receives Jesus 129
Lk. 19:1-10

104. Jesus gives the parable of the pounds; draws near to Jerusalem 129
Lk. 19:11-28

105. Lazarus is raised at Bethany 130
Jn. 11:1-44

106. Jesus is condemned by the council; withdraws into Ephraim 132
Jn. 11:45-57

PART THREE. RECORDS OF CHRIST'S PASSION AND RESURRECTION

Section M. Christ's Passion Week: His Triumphal Entry and Conflict in Jerusalem

107. Jesus enters Jerusalem with acclaim 135
Mt. 21:1-11; Mk. 11:1-11; Lk. 19:29-44; Jn. 12:12-19

108. Jesus puts a curse upon an unfruitful fig tree, which withers; he declares the power of faith 137
Mt. 21:18-22; Mk. 11:12-14, 20-25

109. Jesus cleanses the temple and heals there; children praise him 138
Mt. 21:12-17; Mk. 11:15-19; Lk. 19:45-48
(See also article 20)

110. Chief priests, scribes, and elders question the authority of Jesus 139
Mt. 21:23-27; Mk. 11:27-33; Lk. 20:1-8

111. Three parables on Israel's unfruitfulness are given 140

a. Two sons
Mt. 21:28-32

b. Wicked tenants
Mt. 21:33-46; Mk. 12:1-12; Lk. 20:9-19

c. Guests at the wedding feast of the king's son
Mt. 22:1-14

(See also Lk. 14:15-24, article 89)

112. Scheming leaders put three questions; Jesus asks one 143

a. The Pharisees and Herodians: about paying taxes to Caesar
Mt. 22:15-22; Mk. 12:13-17; Lk. 20:20-26

b. The Sadducees: about the resurrection
Mt. 22:23-33; Mk. 12:18-27; Lk. 20:27-38

c. The scribes: about the great commandment
Mt. 22:34-40; Mk. 12:28-34; Lk. 20:39, 40

d. Jesus: about the Messiah's ancestry
Mt. 22:41-46; Mk. 12:35-37; Lk. 20:41-44

113. Jesus pronounces woes upon the scribes and Pharisees as hypocrites 147
Mt. 23:1-39; Mk. 12:38-40; Lk. 20:45-47
(See also articles 82 and 88)

114. Jesus comments on the widow's offering of two coins 150
Mk. 12:41-44; Lk. 21:1-4

115. Certain Greeks seek Jesus; the Jews reject him 151
Jn. 12:20-50

116. Jesus discourses on the destruction of Jerusalem, the close of the age, the coming of the Son of Man, and the judgment 152

a. Times and signs
Mt. 24:1-51; Mk. 13:1-37; Lk. 21:5-38
(See also article 94)

b. The parables of the ten maidens and of the talents
Mt. 25:1-30

c. The great separation
Mt. 25:31-46

117. For thirty pieces of silver Judas Iscariot conspires with the rulers against Jesus . 160
Mt. 26:1-5, 14-16; Mk. 14:1, 2, 10, 11; Lk. 22:1-6

118. A woman of Bethany anoints Jesus; she is censured 161
Mt. 26:6-13; Mk. 14:3-9; Jn. 12:1-11

Section N. Christ's Passion Week: His Last Supper, Trial, and Crucifixion

119. Jesus and the twelve have the last supper together 162

a. Preparation for the passover
Mt. 26:17-19; Mk. 14:12-16; Lk. 22:7-13

b. The washing of the disciples' feet
Jn. 13:1-20

c. The meal and the betrayer
Mt. 26:20-25; Mk. 14:17-21; Jn. 13:21-35

d. The institution of the Lord's Supper
Mt. 26:26-29; Mk. 14:22-25; Lk. 22:14-23

e. Contention as to the greatest disciple
Lk. 22:24-30

f. The forewarning of Peter and the other disciples
Mt. 26:30-35; Mk. 14:26-31; Lk. 22:31-38; Jn. 13:36-38

120. Jesus gives his farewell discourses and intercessory prayer 168

a. Discussion of faith, hope, love, and obedience
Jn. 14:1-15

b. Promise of the Counselor's coming
Jn. 14:16-31

c. Allegory of the vine and the branches; the command to love one another
Jn. 15:1-17

d. Warning of persecution for his witnesses
Jn. 15:18—16:4a

e. Words of comfort for the disciples concerning his going
Jn. 16:4b-33

f. Prayer for his own
Jn. 17:1-26

121. Jesus prays in Gethsemane; is betrayed and arrested 173
Mt. 26:36-56; Mk. 14:32-52; Lk. 22:39-53; Jn. 18:1-12

122. Jesus is tried and condemned; Peter denies; Judas dies 176
a. Investigation before the Jewish authorities; arraignment before Annas and Caiaphas; Peter's denial; condemnation of Jesus
Mt. 26:57—27:1; Mk. 14:53-72; Lk. 22:54-71; Jn. 18:13-27
b. Beginning of trial before Pilate; the charge and examination
Mt. 27:2, 11-14; Mk. 15:1-5; Lk. 23:1-5; Jn. 18:28-38a
c. Judas' suicide
Mt. 27:3-10
d. Mockery before Herod
Lk. 23:6-12
e. Continuation of trial before Pilate; the tumult of the people; the release of Barabbas
Mt. 27:15-26; Mk. 15:6-15; Lk. 23:13-25; Jn. 18:38b-40
f. Conclusion of trial before Pilate; the mocking of Jesus; his final condemnation
Mt. 27:27-31; Mk. 15:16-20; Jn. 19:1-16

123. Jesus is crucified on Golgotha. The "seven words" 186
Mt. 27:32-56; Mk. 15:21-41; Lk. 23:26-49; Jn. 19:17-37

124. Joseph and Nicodemus bury Jesus in the tomb of Joseph of Arimathea; soldiers seal and guard the burial place 190
Mt. 27:57-66; Mk. 15:42-47; Lk. 23:50-56; Jn. 19:38-42

Section O. Christ's Resurrection, Subsequent Appearances, and Ascension

125. Jesus arises 192
a. The women visit the tomb and find it empty
Mt. 28:1-7; Mk. 16:1-8; Lk. 24:1-12; Jn. 20:1, 2
b. Peter and another disciple run to the tomb
Jn. 20:3-10
c. Mary Magdalene and the other women see and hear the risen Lord
Mt. 28:8-10; Jn. 20:11-18
d. The guard reports
Mt. 28:11-15

126. Jesus appears to Cleopas and a companion walking to Emmaus 195
Lk. 24:13-35

127. Jesus appears to the disciples in Jerusalem, Thomas being absent 196
Jn. 20:19-25

128. Jesus appears to Thomas with the other disciples 196
Lk. 24:36-49; Jn. 20:26-29

129. Seven disciples see Jesus by the Sea of Tiberias; have large catch of fish; Peter expresses his love and is restored to favor 197
Jn. 21:1-23

130. Jesus appears to the eleven on a mountain in Galilee; gives the "great commission" 199
Mt. 28:16-20

131. Jesus ascends 199
Lk. 24:50-53

132. The purpose and the conclusion of John's Gospel 199
Jn. 20:30, 31; 21:24, 25

INDEXES 201

PART ONE

RECORDS OF CHRIST'S EARLY LIFE

Section A. The Infancy of Christ and of John the Baptist

§ 1. Introduction

a. The prefaces of the synoptic Gospels

Mt. 1:1

1 The book of the genealogy of Jesus Christ, the son of David, the son of Abraham.

Mk. 1:1

1 The beginning of the gospel of Jesus Christ, the Son of God.[a]

Lk. 1:1-4

1 Inasmuch as many have undertaken to compile a narrative of the things which have been accomplished among us, 2 just as they were delivered to us by those who from the beginning were eyewitnesses and ministers of the word, 3 it seemed good to me also, having followed all things closely[b] for some time past, to write an orderly account for you, most excellent Theophilus, 4 that you may know the truth concerning the things of which you have been informed.

John

b. The prologue to John's Gospel: the coming of Jesus, the eternal Word in flesh, brings light, truth, and grace to men

Jn. 1:1-18

1 In the beginning was the Word, and the Word was with God, and the Word
was God. 2 He was in the beginning with God; 3 all things were made through him,
and without him was not anything made that was made. 4 In him was life,[c] and the
life was the light of men. 5 The light shines in the darkness, and the darkness has
not overcome it.

6 There was a man sent from God, whose name was John. 7 He came for testi-

[a] Some ancient authorities omit *the son of God.*
[b] Or *accurately.*
[c] Or *was not anything made. That which has been made was life in him.*

mony, to bear witness to the light, that all might believe through him. 8 He was
not the light, but came to bear witness to the light.
9 The true light that enlightens every man was coming into the world; 10 he was
in the world, and the world was made through him, yet the world knew him not;
11 he came to his own home, and his own people received him not. 12 But to all who
received him, who believed in his name, he gave power to become children of God;
13 who were born, not of blood nor of the will of the flesh nor of the will of man,
but of God.
14 And the Word became flesh and dwelt among us, full of grace and truth; we
have beheld his glory, glory as of the only Son from the Father. (15 John bore
witness to him, and cried, "This was he of whom I said, 'He who comes after me
ranks before me, for he was before me.' ") 16 And from his fullness have we all
received, grace upon grace. 17 For the law was given through Moses; grace and
truth came through Jesus Christ. 18 No one has ever seen God; the only Son, who
is in the bosom of the Father, he has made him known.

c. The two genealogies of Jesus Christ

Mt. 1:2-17

2 Abraham was the father of
Isaac, and Isaac the father of
Jacob, and Jacob the father of
Judah and his brothers, 3 and
Judah the father of Perez and
Zerah by Tamar, and Perez the
father of Hezron, and Hezron
the father of Ram,[d] 4 and Ram[d]
the father of Amminadab, and
Amminadab the father of Nahshon, and Nahshon the father of
Salmon, 5 and Salmon the father
of Boaz by Rahab, and Boaz the
father of Obed by Ruth, and
Obed the father of Jesse, 6 and
Jesse the father of David the
king.
And David was the father of
Solomon by the wife of Uriah,
7 and Solomon the father of Rehoboam, and Rehoboam the
father of Abijah, and Abijah the
father of Asa,[f] 8 and Asa[f] the

Mark

Lk. 3:23-38

23 Jesus, when he began his
ministry, was about thirty years
of age, being the son (as was
supposed) of Joseph, the son of
Heli, 24 the son of Matthat, the
son of Levi, the son of Melchi,
the son of Jannai, the son of
Joseph, 25 the son of Mattathias,
the son of Amos, the son of
Nahum, the son of Esli, the
son of Naggai, 26 the son of
Maath, the son of Mattathias,
the son of Semein,
the son of Josech, the son of
Joda, 27 the son of Joanan, the
son of Rhesa, the son of Zerubbabel, the son of Shealtiel,[e] the
son of Neri, 28 the son of
Melchi, the son of Addi, the son
of Cosam, the son of Elmadam,
the son of Er, 29 the son of
Jesus, the son of Eliezer, the son
of Jorim, the son of Matthat, the

John

[d] Greek *Aram.*
[e] Greek *Salathiel.*
[f] Greek *Asaph.*

Mt. 1:2-17 | Mark | Lk. 3:23-38 | John

father of Jehoshaphat, and Jehoshaphat the father of Joram, and Joram the father of Uzziah, [9] and Uzziah the father of Jotham, and Jotham the father of Ahaz, and Ahaz the father of Hezekiah, [10] and Hezekiah the father of Manasseh, and Manasseh the father of Amon,[g] and Amon[g] the father of Josiah, [11] and Josiah the father of Jechoniah and his brothers, at the time of the deportation to Babylon.

[12] And after the deportation to Babylon: Jechoniah was the father of Shealtiel,[k] and Shealtiel[k] the father of Zerubbabel, [13] and Zerubbabel the father of Abiud, and Abiud the father of Eliakim, and Eliakim the father of Azor, [14] and Azor the father of Zadok, and Zadok the father of Achim, and Achim the father of Eliud, [15] and Eliud the father of Eleazar, and Eleazar the father of Matthan, and Matthan the father of Jacob, [16] and Jacob the father of Joseph the husband of Mary, of whom Jesus was born, who is called Christ.

[17] So all the generations from Abraham to David were fourteen generations, and from David to the deportation to Babylon fourteen generations, and from the deportation to Babylon to the Christ fourteen generations.

son of Levi, [30] the son of Symeon, the son of Judas, the son of Joseph, the son of Jonam, the son of Eliakim, [31] the son of Melea, the son of Menna, the son of Mattatha, the son of Nathan, the son of David, [32] the son of Jesse, the son of Obed, the son of Boaz, the son of Salmon,[h] the son of Nahshon, [33] the son of Amminadab,[i] the son of Arni,[j] the son of Hezron, the son of Perez, the son of Judah, [34] the son of Jacob, the son of Isaac, the son of Abraham, the son of Terah, the son of Nahor, [35] the son of Serug, the son of Reu, the son of Peleg, the son of Eber, the son of Shelah, [36] the son of Cainan, the son of Arphaxad, the son of Shem, the son of Noah, the son of Lamech, [37] the son of Methuselah, the son of Enoch, the son of Jared, the son of Mahalaleel, the son of Cainan, [38] the son of Enos, the son of Seth, the son of Adam, the son of God.

[g] Some authorities read *Amos.*
[h] Some ancient authorities read *Sala.*
[i] Many ancient authorities insert *son of Admin* or *son of Aram.*
[j] Some ancient authorities read *Aram.*
[k] Greek *Salathiel.*

§ 2. The birth of John the Baptist is promised to Zechariah and Elizabeth

Lk. 1:5-25

5 In the days of Herod, king of Judea, there was a priest named Zechariah,[1] of the
division of Abijah; and he had a wife of the daughters of Aaron, and her name was
Elizabeth. 6 And they were both righteous before God, walking in all the commandments and ordinances of the Lord blameless. 7 But they had no child, because Elizabeth
was barren, and both were advanced in years.

8 Now while he was serving as priest before God when his division was on duty,
9 according to the custom of the priesthood, it fell to him by lot to enter the temple
of the Lord and burn incense. 10 And the whole multitude of the people were praying
outside at the hour of incense. 11 And there appeared to him an angel of the Lord
standing on the right side of the altar of incense. 12 And Zechariah was troubled when
he saw him, and fear fell upon him. 13 But the angel said to him, "Do not be afraid,
Zechariah, for your prayer is heard, and your wife Elizabeth will bear you a son, and
you shall call his name John.

> 14 And you will have joy and gladness,
> and many will rejoice at his birth;
> 15 for he will be great before the Lord,
> and he shall drink no wine nor strong drink,
> and he will be filled with the Holy Spirit,
> even from his mother's womb.
> 16 And he will turn many of the sons of Israel to the Lord their God,
> 17 and he will go before him in the spirit and power of Elijah,
> to turn the hearts of the fathers to the children,
> and the disobedient to the wisdom of the just,
> to make ready for the Lord a people prepared."

18 And Zechariah said to the angel, "How shall I know this? For I am an old man,
and my wife is advanced in years." 19 And the angel answered him, "I am Gabriel,
who stand in the presence of God; and I was sent to speak to you, and to bring you
this good news. 20 And behold, you will be silent and unable to speak until the day
that these things come to pass, because you did not believe my words, which will be
fulfilled in their time." 21 And the people were waiting for Zechariah, and they
wondered at his delay in the temple. 22 And when he came out, he could not speak
to them, and they perceived that he had seen a vision in the temple; and he made
signs to them and remained dumb. 23 And when his time of service was ended, he
went to his home.

24 After these days his wife Elizabeth conceived, and for five months she hid herself,
saying, 25 "Thus the Lord has done to me in the days when he looked on me, to take
away my reproach among men."

[1] Greek *Zacharias.*

§ 3. The virgin, Mary of Nazareth, receives the angel's annunciation of Jesus' birth

Lk. 1:26-38

26 In the sixth month the angel Gabriel was sent from God to a city of Galilee
named Nazareth, 27 to a virgin betrothed to a man whose name was Joseph, of the
house of David; and the virgin's name was Mary. 28 And he came to her and said,
"Hail, O favored one, the Lord is with you!"[m] 29 But she was greatly troubled at the
saying, and considered in her mind what sort of greeting this might be. 30 And the
angel said to her, "Do not be afraid, Mary, for you have found favor with God. 31 And
behold, you will conceive in your womb and bear a son, and you shall call his name
Jesus.

> 32 He will be great, and will be called the Son of the Most High;
> and the Lord God will give to him the throne of his father David,
> 33 and he will reign over the house of Jacob forever;
> and of his kingdom there will be no end."

34 And Mary said to the angel, "How can this be, since I have no husband?" 35 And
the angel said to her,

> "The Holy Spirit will come upon you,
> and the power of the Most High will overshadow you;
> therefore the child to be born[n] will be called holy,
> the Son of God.

36 And behold, your kinswoman Elizabeth in her old age has also conceived a son;
and this is the sixth month with her who was called barren. 37 For with God nothing
will be impossible." 38 And Mary said, "Behold I am the handmaid of the Lord; let
it be to me according to your word." And the angel departed from her.

§ 4. Mary visits Elizabeth in a city of Judah. The Magnificat

Lk. 1:39-56

39 In those days Mary arose and went with haste into the hill country, to a city
of Judah, 40 and she entered the house of Zechariah and greeted Elizabeth. 41 And
when Elizabeth heard the greeting of Mary, the babe leaped in her womb; and
Elizabeth was filled with the Holy Spirit 42 and she exclaimed with a loud cry,
"Blessed are you among women, and blessed is the fruit of your womb! 43 And why
is this granted me, that the mother of my Lord should come to me? 44 For behold,
when the voice of your greeting came to my ears, the babe in my womb leaped for
joy. 45 And blessed is she who believed that there would be[o] a fullfillment of what
was spoken to her from the Lord." 46 And Mary said,

> "My soul magnifies the Lord,
> 47 and my spirit rejoices in God my Savior,
> 48 for he has regarded the low estate of his handmaiden.

[m] Some ancient authorities add *Blessed are you among women.*
[n] Some ancient authorities add *of you.*
[o] Or *believed, for there will be.*

For behold, henceforth all generations will call me blessed;
49 for he who is mighty has done great things for me,
and holy is his name.
50 And his mercy is on those who fear him
from generation to generation.
51 He has shown strength with his arm,
he has scattered the proud in the imagination of their hearts,
52 he has put down the mighty from their thrones,
and exalted those of low degree;
53 he has filled the hungry with good things,
and the rich he has sent empty away.
54 He has helped his servant Israel,
in remembrance of his mercy,
55 as he spoke to our fathers,
to Abraham and to his posterity forever."

56 And Mary remained with her about three months, and returned to her home.

§ 5. John the Baptist is born and named. The Benedictus

Lk. 1:57-80

57 Now the time came for Elizabeth to be delivered, and she gave birth to a son.
58 And her neighbors and kinsfolk heard that the Lord had shown great mercy to her,
and they rejoiced with her. 59 And on the eighth day they came to circumcise the
child; and they would have named him Zechariah after his father, 60 but his mother
said, "Not so; he shall be called John." 61 And they said to her, "None of your
kindred is called by this name." 62 And they made signs to his father, inquiring what
he would have him called. 63 And he asked for a writing tablet, and wrote, "His
name is John." And they all marveled. 64 And immediately his mouth was opened
and his tongue loosed, and he spoke, blessing God. 65 And fear came on all their
neighbors. And all these things were talked about through all the hill country of
Judea; 66 and all who heard them laid them up in their hearts, saying, "What then
will this child be?" For the hand of the Lord was with him.
67 And his father Zechariah was filled with the Holy Spirit, and prophesied, saying,

68 "Blessed be the Lord God of Israel,
for he has visited and redeemed his people,
69 and has raised up a horn of salvation for us
in the house of his servant David,
70 as he spoke by the mouth of his holy prophets from old,
71 that we should be saved from our enemies,
and from the hand of all who hate us;
72 to perform the mercy promised to our fathers,
and to remember his holy covenant,
73 the oath which he swore to our father Abraham, 74 to grant us

that we, being delivered from the hand of our enemies,
might serve him without fear,
75 in holiness and righteousness before him all the days of our life.
76 And thou, child, shalt be called the prophet of the Most High;
for thou shalt go before the Lord to prepare his ways,
77 to give knowledge of salvation to his people
in the forgiveness of their sins,
78 through the tender mercy of our God,
when the day shall dawn upon[p] us from on high
79 to give light to those who sit in darkness and in the shadow of death,
to guide our feet into the way of peace."

80 And the child grew and became strong in spirit, and he was in the wilderness till the day of his manifestation to Israel.

§ 6. Joseph of Nazareth learns of the incarnation; Jesus Christ is born at Bethlehem

Mt. 1:18-25

18 Now the birth of Jesus Christ[q] took place in this way. When his mother Mary had been betrothed to Joseph, before they came together she was found to be with child of the Holy Spirit; 19 and her husband Joseph, being a just man and unwilling to put her to shame, resolved to divorce her quietly. 20 But as he considered this, behold, an angel of the Lord appeared to him in a dream, saying, "Joseph, son of David, do not fear to take Mary your wife, for that which is conceived in her is of the Holy Spirit; 21 she will bear a son, and you shall call his name Jesus, for he will save his people from their sins." 22 All this took place to fulfill what the Lord had spoken by the prophet:

23 "Behold, a virgin shall conceive and bear a son,
and his name shall be

Mark

Lk. 2:1-7

1 In those days a decree went out from Caesar Augustus that all the world should be enrolled.
2 This was the first enrollment, when Quirinius was governor of Syria. 3 And all went to be enrolled, each to his own city.
4 And Joseph also went up from Galilee, from the city of Nazareth, to Judea, to the city of David, which is called Bethlehem, because he was of the house and lineage of David, 5 to be enrolled with Mary, his betrothed, who was with child.
6 And while they were there, the time came for her to be delivered. 7 And she gave birth to her first-born son and wrapped him in swaddling cloths, and laid him in a manger, because there was no place for them in the inn.

John

[p] Or *whereby the dayspring will visit.* Many ancient authorities read *since the dayspring has visited.*
[q] Some ancient authorities read *of the Christ.*

Mt. 1:18-25	Mark	Lk. 2	John
called Emmanuel" (which means, God with us). [24] When Joseph woke from sleep, he did as the angel of the Lord commanded him; he took his wife, [25] but knew her not until she had borne a son; and he called his name Jesus.			

§ 7. Angels proclaim his birth and shepherds visit him. The Gloria in Excelsis

Lk. 2:8-20

[8] And in that region there were shepherds out in the field, keeping watch over their
flock by night. [9] And an angel of the Lord appeared to them, and the glory of the
Lord shone around them, and they were filled with fear. [10] And the angel said to them,
"Be not afraid; for behold, I bring you good news of a great joy which will come to
all the people; [11] for to you is born this day in the city of David a Savior, who is
Christ the Lord. [12] And this will be a sign for you: you will find a babe wrapped in
swaddling cloths and lying in a manger." [13] And suddenly there was with the angel
a multitude of the heavenly host praising God and saying,

[14] "Glory to God in the highest,
and on earth peace among men with whom he is pleased!"[r]

[15] When the angels went away from them into heaven, the shepherds said to one
another, "Let us go over to Bethlehem and see this thing that has happened, which the
Lord has made known to us." [16] And they went with haste, and found Mary and
Joseph, and the babe lying in a manger. [17] And when they saw it they made known
the saying which had been told them concerning this child; [18] and all who heard it
wondered at what the shepherds told them. [19] But Mary kept all these things, ponder-
ing them in her heart. [20] And the shepherds returned, glorifying and praising God
for all they had heard and seen, as it had been told them.

§ 8. The circumcision and naming take place on the eighth day

Lk. 2:21

[21] And at the end of eight days, when he was circumcised, he was called Jesus, the
name given by the angel before he was conceived in the womb.

§ 9. The presentation in the temple occurs; Simeon and Anna give thanks. The Nunc Dimittis

Lk. 2:22-40

[22] And when the time came for their purification according to the law of Moses,
they brought him up to Jerusalem to present him to the Lord [23] (as it is written in

[r] Some ancient authorities read *peace, goodwill among men.*

the law of the Lord, "Every male that opens the womb shall be called holy to the
Lord") 24 and to offer a sacrifice according to what is said in the law of the Lord,
"a pair of turtledoves, or two young pigeons." 25 Now there was a man in Jerusalem,
whose name was Simeon, and this man was righteous and devout, looking for the
consolation of Israel, and the Holy Spirit was upon him. 26 And it had been revealed
to him by the Holy Spirit that he should not see death before he had seen the Lord's
Christ. 27 And inspired by the Spirit[a] he came into the temple; and when the parents
brought in the child Jesus, to do for him according to the custom of the law, 28 he
took him up in his arms and blessed God and said,

> 29 "Lord, now lettest thou thy servant depart in peace,
> according to thy word;
> 30 for mine eyes have seen thy salvation
> 31 which thou hast prepared in the presence of all peoples,
> 32 a light for revelation to the Gentiles,
> and for glory to thy people Israel."

33 And his father and his mother marveled at what was said about him; 34 and
Simeon blessed them and said to Mary his mother,

> "Behold, this child is set for the fall and rising of many in Israel,
> and for a sign that is spoken against
> 35 (and a sword will pierce through your own soul also),
> that thoughts out of many hearts may be revealed."

36 And there was a prophetess, Anna, the daughter of Phanuel, of the tribe of
Asher; she was of a great age, having lived with her husband seven years from her
virginity, 37 and as a widow till she was eighty-four. She did not depart from the
temple, worshiping with fasting and prayer night and day. 38 And coming up at that
very hour she gave thanks to God, and spoke of him to all who were looking for the
redemption of Jerusalem.

39 And when they had performed everything according to the law of the Lord,
they returned into Galilee, to their own city, Nazareth. 40 And the child grew and
became strong, filled with wisdom; and the favor of God was upon him.

§ 10. Eastern wise men come to Jerusalem and Bethlehem with gifts; Herod plots to destroy the child

Mt. 2:1-12

1 Now when Jesus was born in Bethlehem of Judea in the days of Herod the king,
behold, wise men from the East came to Jerusalem, saying, 2 "Where is he who has
been born king of the Jews? For we have seen his star in the East, and have come to
worship him." 3 When Herod the king heard this, he was troubled, and all Jerusalem
with him; 4 and assembling all the chief priests and scribes of the people, he inquired
of them where the Christ was to be born. 5 They told him, "In Bethlehem of Judea;
for so it is written by the prophet:

[a] Or *in the Spirit*.

[6] 'And thou Bethlehem, in the land of Judah,
art by no means least among the rulers of Judah;
for from thee shall come a ruler
who will govern my people Israel.' "

[7] Then Herod summoned the wise men secretly and ascertained from them what
time the star appeared; [8] and he sent them to Bethlehem, saying, "Go and search
diligently for the child, and when you have found him bring me word, that I too may
come and worship him." [9] When they had heard the king they went their way; and
lo, the star which they had seen in the East went before them, till it came to rest over
the place where the child was. [10] When they saw the star, they rejoiced exceedingly
with great joy; [11] and going into the house they saw the child with Mary his mother,
and they fell down and worshiped him. Then, opening their treasures, they offered
him gifts, gold and frankincense and myrrh. [12] And being warned in a dream not
to return to Herod, they departed to their own country by another way.

§ 11. Joseph and Mary flee into Egypt with Jesus; Herod slaughters the children of Bethlehem and dies; the family returns to Nazareth

Mt. 2:13-23

[13] Now when they had departed, behold, an angel of the Lord appeared to Joseph
in a dream and said, "Rise, take the child and his mother, and flee to Egypt, and
remain there till I tell you; for Herod is about to search for the child, to destroy him."
[14] And he rose and took the child and his mother by night, and departed to Egypt,
[15] and remained there until the death of Herod. This was to fulfill what the Lord
had spoken by the prophet, "Out of Egypt have I called my son."

[16] Then Herod, when he saw that he had been tricked by the wise men, was in a
furious rage, and he sent and killed all the male children in Bethlehem and in all that
region who were two years old or under, according to the time which he had
ascertained from the wise men. [17] Then was fulfilled what was spoken by the prophet
Jeremiah:

[18] "A voice was heard in Ramah,
wailing and loud lamentation,
Rachel weeping for her children;
she refused to be consoled,
because they were no more."

[19] But when Herod died, behold, an angel of the Lord appeared in a dream to
Joseph in Egypt, saying, [20] "Rise, take the child and his mother, and go to the land
of Israel, for those who sought the child's life are dead." [21] And he rose and took the
child and his mother, and went to the land of Israel. [22] But when he heard that
Archelaus reigned over Judea in place of his father Herod, he was afraid to go there,
and being warned in a dream he withdrew to the district of Galilee. [23] And he went
and dwelt in a city called Nazareth, that what was spoken by the prophets might be
fulfilled, "He shall be called a Nazarene."

Section B. Christ's Youth, Early Manhood, and Preparation for His Public Ministry

§ 12. Jesus visits Jerusalem for the Passover when twelve years of age; confers with the teachers in the temple

Lk. 2:41-50

41 Now his parents went to Jerusalem every year at the feast of the Passover. 42 And
when he was twelve years old, they went up according to custom; 43 and when the
feast was ended, as they were returning, the boy Jesus stayed behind in Jerusalem.
His parents did not know it, 44 but supposing him to be in the company they went
a day's journey, and they sought him among their kinsfolk and acquaintances; 45 and
when they did not find him, they returned to Jerusalem, seeking him. 46 After three
days they found him in the temple, sitting among the teachers, listening to them and
asking them questions; 47 and all who heard him were amazed at his understanding
and his answers. 48 And when they saw him they were astonished; and his mother
said to him, "Son, why have you treated us so? Behold, your father and I have been
looking for you anxiously." 49 And he said to them, "How is it that you sought me?
Did you not know that I must be in my Father's house?" 50 And they did not understand the saying which he spoke to them.

§ 13. At home in Nazareth, Jesus grows in the fourfold way

Lk. 2:51, 52

51 And he went down with them and came to Nazareth, and was obedient to them;
and his mother kept all these things in her heart.

52 And Jesus increased in wisdom and in stature,[a] and in favor with God and man.

§ 14. John the Baptist preaches and baptizes beside the Jordan until imprisoned

a. Declares his mission as herald of Jesus

Mt. 3:1-3

1 In those days came John the Baptist, preaching in the wilderness of Judea, 2 "Repent, for the kingdom of heaven is at hand."
3 For this is he who was spoken of by the prophet Isaiah when he said,
"The voice of one crying in the wilderness:

Mk. 1:2-4

2 As it is written in Isaiah the prophet,[b]
"Behold, I send my messenger before thy face,
who shall prepare thy way;
3 the voice of one crying in the wilderness:
Prepare the way of the Lord,

Lk. 3:1-6

1 In the fifteenth year of the reign of Tiberius Caesar, Pontius Pilate being governor of Judea, and Herod being tetrarch of Galilee, and his brother Philip tetrarch of the region of Ituraea and Trachonitis, and Lysanias tetrarch of Abilene, 2 in the high-priesthood of

John

[a] Or *years.*
[b] Some ancient authorities read *in the prophets.*

Mt. 3:1-3

Prepare the way of the Lord,
make his paths straight."

Mk. 1:2-4

make his paths straight—"
[4] John the baptizer appeared in the wilderness, preaching a baptism of repentance for the forgiveness of sins.

Lk. 3:1-6

Annas and Caiaphas, the word of God came to John the son of Zechariah in the wilderness; [3] and he went into all the region about the Jordan, preaching a baptism of repentance for the forgiveness of sin. [4] As it is written in the book of the words of Isaiah the prophet,
"The voice of one crying in the wilderness:
Prepare the way of the Lord,
make his paths straight.
[5] Every valley shall be filled,
and every mountain and hill shall be brought low,
and the crooked shall be made straight,
and the rough ways shall be made smooth;
[6] and all flesh shall see the salvation of God."

John

b. Baptizes

Mt. 3:4-6

[4] Now John wore a garment of camel's hair, and a leather girdle around his waist; and his food was locusts and wild honey. [5] Then went out to him Jerusalem and all Judea and all the region about the Jordan, [6] and

Mk. 1:5, 6

[5] And there went out to him all the country of Judea, and all the people of Jerusalem; and they were baptized by him in the river Jordan, confessing their sins. [6] Now John was clothed with camel's hair, and had a

Luke

John

Mt. 3:4-6

they were baptized by him in the river Jordan, confessing their sins.

Mk. 1:5,6

leather girdle around his waist, and ate locusts and wild honey.

Luke

John

c. Preaches repentance and righteousness

Mt. 3:7-10

[7] But when he saw many of the Pharisees and Sadducees coming for baptism, he said to them, "You brood of vipers. Who warned you to flee from the wrath to come? [8] Bear fruit that befits repentance, [9] and do not presume to say to yourselves, 'We have Abraham as our father'; for I tell you, God is able from these stones to raise up children to Abraham. [10] Even now the ax is laid to the root of the trees; every tree therefore that does not bear good fruit is cut down and thrown into the fire.

Mark

Lk. 3:7-14

[7] He said therefore to the multitudes that came out to be baptized by him, "You brood of vipers. Who warned you to flee from the wrath to come? [8] Bear fruits that befit repentance, and do not begin to say to yourselves, 'We have Abraham as our father'; for I tell you, God is able from these stones to raise up children to Abraham. [9] Even now the ax is laid to the root of the trees; every tree therefore that does not bear good fruit is cut down and thrown into the fire."

[10] And the multitudes asked him, "What then shall we do?" [11] And he answered them, "He who has two coats, let him share with him who has none; and he who has food, let him do likewise." [12] Tax collectors also came to be baptized, and said to him, "Teacher, what shall we do?" [13] And he said to them, "Collect no more than is appointed you." [14] Soldiers also asked him, "And we, what shall we do?" And he said to them, "Rob no one by violence or by false accusation, and be content with your wages."

John

d. Announces the Coming One

Mt. 3:11, 12

11 "I baptize you with water for repentance, but he who is coming after me is mightier than I, whose sandals I am not worthy to carry; he will baptize you with the Holy Spirit and with fire. 12 His winnowing fork is in his hand, and he will clear his threshing floor and gather his wheat into the granary, but the chaff he will burn with unquenchable fire."

Mk. 1:7, 8

7 And he preached, saying, "After me comes he who is mightier than I, the thong of whose sandals I am not worthy to stoop down and untie. 8 I have baptized you with water; but he will baptize you with the Holy Spirit."

Lk. 3:15-18

15 As the people were in expectation, and all men questioned in their hearts concerning John, whether perhaps he were the Christ, 16 John answered them all, "I baptize you with water; but he who is mightier than I is coming, the thong of whose sandals I am not worthy to untie; he will baptize you with the Holy Spirit and with fire. 17 His winnowing fork is in his hand, to clear his threshing floor, and to gather the wheat into his granary, but the chaff he will burn with unquenchable fire."

18 So, with many other exhortations, he preached good news to the people.

John

e. Undergoes imprisonment

Lk. 3:19, 20

19 But Herod the tetrarch, who had been reproved by him for Herodias, his brother's wife, and for all the evil things that Herod had done, 20 added this to them all, that he shut up John in prison.

§ 15. Jesus is baptized by John the Baptist in the Jordan

Mt. 3:13-17

13 Then Jesus came from Galilee to the Jordan to John, to be baptized by him. 14 John would have

Mk. 1:9-11

9 In those days Jesus came from Nazareth of Galilee and was baptized by John in the Jordan. 10 And when

Lk. 3:21, 22

21 Now when all the people were baptized, and when Jesus also had been baptized and was praying, the heaven

John

Mt. 3:13-17

prevented him, saying, "I need to be baptized by you, and do you come to me?" [15] But Jesus answered him, "Let it be so now; for thus it is fitting for us to fulfill all righteousness." Then he consented. [16] And when Jesus was baptized, he went up immediately from the water, and behold, the heavens were opened[f] and he saw the Spirit of God descending like a dove and alighting on him; [17] and lo, a voice from heaven, saying, "This is my beloved Son,[g] with whom I am well pleased."

Mk. 1:9-11

he came up out of the water, immediately he saw the heavens opened and the Spirit descending upon him like a dove; [11] and a voice came from heaven, "Thou art my beloved Son;[e] with thee I am well pleased."

Lk. 3:21, 22

was opened, [22] and the Holy Spirit descended upon him in bodily form, as a dove, and a voice came from heaven, "Thou art my beloved Son;[c] with thee I am well pleased."[d]

John

§ 16. Jesus is tempted in the wilderness

Mt. 4:1-11

[1] Then Jesus was led up by the Spirit into the wilderness to be tempted by the devil. [2] And he fasted forty days and forty nights, and afterward he was hungry. [3] And the tempter came and said to him, "If you are the Son of God, command these stones to become loaves of bread." [4] But

Mk. 1:12, 13

[12] The Spirit immediately drove him out into the wilderness. [13] And he was in the wilderness forty days, tempted by Satan; and he was with the wild beasts; and the angels ministered to him.

Lk. 4:1-13

[1] And Jesus, full of the Holy Spirit, returned from the Jordan, and was led by the Spirit [2] for forty days in the wilderness, tempted by the devil. And he ate nothing in those days; and when they were ended, he was hungry. [3] The devil said to him, "If you are the Son of God, com-

John

[c] Or *my Son, my* (or *the*) *Beloved.*
[d] Some ancient authorities read *today have I begotten thee.*
[e] Or *my Son, my* (or *the*) *Beloved.*
[f] Some ancient authorities add *to him.*
[g] Or *my Son, my* (or *the*) *Beloved.*

Mt. 4:1-11

he answered, "It is written,
'Man shall not live by bread
alone,
but by every word that proceeds from the mouth of
God.' "
5 Then the devil took him to
the holy city, and set him on the
pinnacle of the temple, 6 and
said to him, "If you are the Son
of God, throw yourself down;
for it is written,
'He will give his angels charge
of you,'
and
'On their hands they will bear
you up,
lest you strike your foot
against a stone.' "
7 Jesus said to him, "Again it
is written, 'You shall not tempt
the Lord your God.' " 8 Again,
the devil took him to a very
high mountain, and showed him
all the kingdoms of the world
and the glory of them; 9 and he
said to him, "All these I will
give you, if you will fall down
and worship me."
10 Then Jesus said to him,
"Begone, Satan! for it is written,
'You shall worship the Lord
your God, and him only shall
you serve.' "
11 Then the devil left him,
and behold, angels came and
ministered to him.

Mk. 1

Lk. 4:1-13

mand this stone to become
bread." 4 And Jesus answered
him, "It is written, 'Man shall
not live by bread alone.' " 5 And
the devil took him up, and
showed him all the kingdoms
of the world in a moment of
time, 6 and said to him, "To you
I will give all this authority and
their glory; for it has been delivered to me, and I give it to
whom I will. 7 If you, then, will
worship me, it shall all be
yours." 8 And Jesus answered
him, "It is written,
'You shall worship the Lord
your God, and him only shall
you serve.' "
9 And he took him to Jerusalem, and set him on the pinnacle
of the temple, and said to him,
"If you are the Son of God,
throw yourself down from here;
10 for it is written,
'He will give his angels
charge of you, to guard you,'
11 and
'On their hands they will bear
you up,
lest you strike your foot
against a stone.' "
12 And Jesus answered him,
"It is said, 'You shall not tempt
the Lord your God.' " 13 And
when the devil had ended every
temptation, he departed from
him until an opportune time.

John

PART TWO

RECORDS OF CHRIST'S PUBLIC MINISTRY

Section C. Christ's Early Work, Especially in Judea and Samaria, According to John*

§ 17. John the Baptist declares the pre-eminence of Jesus; announces the Lamb of God

Jn. 1:19-34

19 And this is the testimony of John, when the Jews sent priests and Levites from
Jerusalem to ask him, "Who are you?" 20 He confessed, he did not deny, but
confessed, "I am not the Christ." 21 And they asked him, "What then? Are you
Elijah?" He said, "I am not." "Are you the prophet?" And he answered, "No."
22 They said to him then, "Who are you? Let us have an answer for those who sent
us. What do you say about yourself?" 23 He said, "I am the voice of one crying
in the wilderness, 'Make straight the way of the Lord,' as the prophet Isaiah said."
24 Now they had been sent from the Pharisees. 25 They asked him, "Then why
are you baptizing, if you are neither the Christ, nor Elijah, nor the prophet?"
26 John answered them, "I baptize with water; but among you stands one whom
you do not know, 27 even he who comes after me, the thong of whose sandal I
am not worthy to untie." 28 This took place in Bethany beyond the Jordan, where
John was baptizing.
29 The next day he saw Jesus coming toward him, and said, "Behold, the Lamb
of God, who takes away the sin of the world! 30 This is he of whom I said, 'After
me comes a man who ranks before me, for he was before me.' 31 I myself did not
know him; but for this I came baptizing with water, that he might be revealed to
Israel." 32 And John bore witness, "I saw the Spirit descend as a dove from heaven,
and it remained on him. 33 I myself did not know him; but he who sent me to
baptize with water said to me, 'He on whom you see the Spirit descend and remain,
this is he who baptizes with the Holy Spirit.' 34 And I have seen and have borne
witness that this is the Son of God."

§ 18. Jesus wins five disciples including Andrew, Simon, Philip and Nathanael

Jn. 1:35-51

35 The next day again John was standing with two of his disciples; 36 and he
looked at Jesus as he walked, and said, "Behold, the Lamb of God!" 37 The two
disciples heard him say this, and they followed Jesus. 38 Jesus turned, and saw them
following, and said to them, "What do you seek?" And they said to him, "Rabbi
(which means Teacher), where are you staying?" 39 He said to them, "Come and
see." They came and saw where he was staying; and they stayed with him that

* Section C includes the materials which pertain to what is often designated *Christ's Earlier Judean Ministry.*

day, for it was about the tenth hour. 40 One of the two who heard John speak, and
followed him, was Andrew, Simon Peter's brother. 41 He first found his brother
Simon, and said to him, "We have found the Messiah" (which means Christ). 42 He
brought him to Jesus. Jesus looked at him, and said, "So you are Simon the son of
John? You shall be called Cephas" (which means Rock[a]).
43 The next day Jesus decided to go to Galilee. And he found Philip and said
to him, "Follow me." 44 Now Philip was from Bethsaida, the city of Andrew and
Peter. 45 Philip found Nathanael, and said to him, "We have found him of whom
Moses in the law and also the prophets wrote, Jesus of Nazareth, the son of
Joseph." 46 Nathanael said to him, "Can anything good come out of Nazareth?"
Philip said to him, "Come and see." 47 Jesus saw Nathanael coming to him, and
said of him, "Behold, an Israelite indeed, in whom is no guile!" 48 Nathanael said
to him, "How do you know me?" Jesus answered him, "Before Philip called you,
when you were under the fig tree, I saw you." 49 Nathanael answered him, "Rabbi,
you are the Son of God! You are the King of Israel!" 50 Jesus answered him,
"Because I said to you, I saw you under the fig tree, do you believe? You shall see
greater things than these." 51 And he said to him, "Truly, truly, I say to you, you
will see heaven opened, and the angels of God ascending and descending upon the
Son of man."

§ 19. Jesus gives a sign at a marriage at Cana in Galilee; sojourns with disciples and family in Capernaum

Jn. 2:1-12

1 On the third day there was a marriage at Cana in Galilee, and the mother of
Jesus was there; 2 Jesus also was invited to the marriage, with his disciples. 3 When
the wine failed, the mother of Jesus said to him, "They have no wine." 4 And
Jesus said to her, "O woman, what have you to do with me? My hour has not yet
come." 5 His mother said to the servants, "Do whatever he tells you." 6 Now six
stone jars were standing there, for the Jewish rites of purification, each holding two
or three measures.[b] 7 Jesus said to them, "Fill the jars with water." And they
filled them up to the brim. 8 He said to them, "Now draw some out, and take it
to the steward of the feast." So they took it. 9 When the steward of the feast
tasted the water now become wine, and did not know where it came from (though
the servants who had drawn the water knew), the steward of the feast called the
bridegroom 10 and said to him, "Every man serves the good wine first; and when
men have drunk freely, then the poor wine; but you have kept the good wine until
now." 11 This, the first of his signs, Jesus did at Cana in Galilee, and manifested
his glory; and his disciples believed in him.
12 After this he went down to Capernaum, with his mother and his brothers and
his disciples; and there they stayed for a few days.

[a] Greek *Peter*.
[b] That is, about twenty or thirty gallons.

§ 20. In Jerusalem for the Passover, Jesus drives trade out of the temple *

Jn. 2:13-25

13 The Passover of the Jews was at hand, and Jesus went up to Jerusalem. 14 In
the temple he found those who were selling oxen and sheep and pigeons, and the
money-changers at their business. 15 And making a whip of cords, he drove them
all, with the sheep and oxen, out of the temple; and he poured out the coins of the
money-changers and overturned their tables. 16 And he told those who sold the
pigeons, "Take these things away; you shall not make my Father's house a house of
trade." 17 His disciples remembered that it was written, "Zeal for thy house will
consume me." 18 The Jews then said to him, "What sign have you to show us for
doing this?" 19 Jesus answered them, "Destroy this temple, and in three days I
will raise it up." 20 The Jews then said, "It has taken forty-six years to build this
temple, and will you raise it up in three days?" 21 But he spoke of the temple of
his body. 22 When therefore he was raised from the dead, his disciples remembered that he had said this; and they believed the scripture and the word which
Jesus had spoken.

23 Now when he was in Jerusalem at the Passover feast, many believed in his
name when they saw his signs which he did; 24 but Jesus did not trust himself to
them, 25 because he knew all men and needed no one to bear witness of man; for
he himself knew what was in man.

(See also article 109)

§ 21. Nicodemus visits Jesus by night; they discuss new birth and salvation

Jn. 3:1-21

1 Now there was a man of the Pharisees, named Nicodemus, a ruler of the Jews.
2 This man came to Jesus[c] by night and said to him, "Rabbi, we know that you are
a teacher come from God; for no one can do these signs that you do, unless God
is with him." 3 Jesus answered him, "Truly, truly, I say to you, unless one is born
anew, he cannot see the kingdom of God." 4 Nicodemus said to him, "How can
a man be born when he is old? Can he enter a second time into his mother's
womb and be born?" 5 Jesus answered, "Truly, truly, I say to you, unless one is
born of water and the Spirit, he cannot enter the kingdom of God. 6 That which
is born of the flesh is flesh, and that which is born of the Spirit is spirit.[d] 7 Do not
marvel that I said to you, 'You must be born anew.' 8 The wind[d] blows where it
wills, and you hear the sound of it, but you do not know whence it comes or whither
it goes; so it is with every one who is born of the Spirit." 9 Nicodemus said to him,
"How can this be?" 10 Jesus answered him, "Are you a teacher of Israel, and yet
you do not understand this? 11 Truly, truly, I say to you, we speak of what we know,

[c] Greek *him.*
[d] The same Greek word means both *wind* and *spirit.*

* Many authorities hold that there was but one cleansing and that this is John's version of the incident recorded in Matt. 21:12-17, Mark 11:15-19, and Luke 19:45-48.

and bear witness to what we have seen; but you do not receive our testimony.
[12] If I have told you earthly things and you do not believe, how can you believe if I
tell you heavenly things? [13] No one has ascended into heaven but he who descended
from heaven, the Son of man.[e] [14] And as Moses lifted up the serpent in the wilderness, so must the Son of man be lifted up, [15] that whoever believes in him may
have eternal life."

[16] For God so loved the world that he gave his only Son, that whoever believes
in him should not perish but have eternal life. [17] For God sent the Son into the
world, not to condemn the world, but that the world might be saved through him.
[18] He who believes in him is not condemned; he who does not believe is condemned
already, because he has not believed in the name of the only Son of God. [19] And
this is the judgment, that the light has come into the world, and men loved darkness
rather than light, because their deeds were evil. [20] For every one who does evil
hates the light, and does not come to the light, lest his deeds should be exposed.
[21] But he who does what is true comes to the light, that it may be clearly seen that
his deeds have been wrought in God.

§ 22. Jesus baptizes in Judea; John exalts him at Aenon

Jn. 3:22-36

[22] After this Jesus and his disciples went into the land of Judea; there he
remained with them and baptized. [23] John also was baptizing at Aenon near Salim,
because there was much water there; and people came and were baptized. [24] For
John had not yet been put in prison.

[25] Now a discussion arose between John's disciples and a Jew over purifying.
[26] And they came to John, and said to him, "Rabbi, he who was with you beyond
the Jordan, to whom you bore witness, here he is, baptizing, and all are going to
him." [27] John answered, "No one can receive anything except what is given him
from heaven. [28] You yourselves bear me witness, that I said, I am not the Christ,
but I have been sent before him. [29] He who has the bride is the bridegroom; the
friend of the bridegroom, who stands and hears him, rejoices greatly at the bridegroom's voice; therefore this joy of mine is now full. [30] He must increase, but I must
decrease."

[31] He who comes from above is above all; he who is of the earth belongs to the
earth, and of the earth he speaks; he who comes from heaven is above all. [32] He
bears witness to what he has seen and heard, yet no one receives his testimony;
[33] he who receives his testimony sets his seal to this, that God is true. [34] For he
whom God has sent utters the words of God, for it is not by measure that he gives
the Spirit; [35] the Father loves the Son, and has given all things into his hand. [36] He
who believes in the Son has eternal life; he who does not obey the Son shall not see
life, but the wrath of God rests upon him.

e Some ancient authorities add *who is in heaven.*

§ 23. Jesus teaches at Sychar in Samaria

a. Telling the woman about the water of life

Jn. 4:1-15

1 Now when the Lord knew that the Pharisees had heard that Jesus was making
and baptizing more disciples than John 2(although Jesus himself did not baptize,
but only his disciples), 3 he left Judea and departed again to Galilee.
4 He had to pass through Samaria. 5 So he came to a city of Samaria, called
Sychar, near the field that Jacob gave to his son Joseph. 6 Jacob's well was there,
and so Jesus, wearied as he was with his journey, sat down beside the well. It was
about the sixth hour.
7 There came a woman of Samaria to draw water. Jesus said to her, "Give me
a drink." 8 For his disciples had gone away into the city to buy food. 9 The
Samaritan woman said to him, "How is it that you, a Jew, ask a drink of me, a
woman of Samaria?" For Jews have no dealings with Samaritans. 10 Jesus
answered her, "If you knew the gift of God, and who it is that is saying to you,
'Give me a drink,' you would have asked him, and he would have given you living
water." 11 The woman said to him, "Sir, you have nothing to draw with, and the
well is deep; where do you get that living water? 12 Are you greater than our
father Jacob, who gave us the well, and drank from it himself, and his sons, and his
cattle?" 13 Jesus said to her, "Every one who drinks of this water will thirst again,
14 but whoever drinks of the water that I shall give him will never thirst; the water
that I shall give him will become in him a spring of water welling up to eternal
life." 15 The woman said to him, "Sir, give me this water, that I may not thirst, nor
come here to draw."

b. Discussing true worship

Jn. 4:16-26

16 Jesus said to her, "Go, call your husband, and come here." 17 The woman
answered him, "I have no husband." Jesus said to her, "You are right in saying,
'I have no husband'; 18 for you have had five husbands, and he whom you now have
is not your husband; this you said truly." 19 The woman said to him, "Sir, I perceive
that you are a prophet. 20 Our fathers worshiped on this mountain; and you say
that in Jerusalem is the place where men ought to worship." 21 Jesus said to her,
"Woman, believe me, the hour is coming when neither on this mountain nor in
Jerusalem will you worship the Father. 22 You worship what you do not know; we
worship what we know, for salvation is from the Jews. 23 But the hour is coming,
and now is, when the true worshipers will worship the Father in spirit and truth, for
such the Father seeks to worship him. 24 God is spirit, and those who worship him
must worship in spirit and truth." 25 The woman said to him, "I know that Messiah
is coming (he who is called Christ); when he comes, he will show us all things."
26 Jesus said to her, "I who speak to you am he."

c. Directing the disciples to the food of service

Jn. 4:27-38

27 Just then his disciples came. They marveled that he was talking with a woman,
but none said, "What do you wish?" or, "Why are you talking with her?" 28 So
the woman left her water jar, and went away into the city, and said to the
people, 29 "Come, see a man who told me all that I ever did. Can this be the
Christ?" 30 They went out of the city and were coming to him.
31 Meanwhile the disciples besought him, saying, "Rabbi, eat." 32 But he said
to them, "I have food to eat of which you do not know." 33 So the disciples said
to one another, "Has any one brought him food?" 34 Jesus said to them, "My
food is to do the will of him who sent me, and to accomplish his work. 35 Do you
not say, 'There are yet four months, then comes the harvest'? I tell you, lift up your
eyes, and see how the fields are already white for harvest. 36 He who reaps
receives wages, and gathers fruit for eternal life, so that sower and reaper may
rejoice together. 37 For here the saying holds true, 'One sows and another reaps.'
38 I sent you to reap that for which you did not labor; others have labored, and you
have entered into their labor."

d. Winning believers in Sychar

Jn. 4:39-42

39 Many Samaritans from that city believed in him because of the woman's
testimony, "He told me all that I ever did." 40 So when the Samaritans came to
him, they asked him to stay with them; and he stayed there two days. 41 And
many more believed because of his word. 42 They said to the woman, "It is no
longer because of your words that we believe, for we have heard for ourselves,
and we know that this is indeed the Savior of the world."

§ 24. Jesus Arrives in Galilee

Jn. 4:43-45

43 After the two days he departed to Galilee. 44 For Jesus himself testified that
a prophet has no honor in his own country. 45 So when he came to Galilee, the
Galileans welcomed him, having seen all that he had done in Jerusalem at the
feast, for they too had gone to the feast.

§ 25. An official's son in Capernaum is healed

Jn. 4:46-54

46 So he came again to Cana in Galilee, where he had made the water wine.
And at Capernaum there was an official whose son was ill. 47 When he heard that
Jesus had come from Judea to Galilee, he went and begged him to come down
and heal his son, for he was at the point of death. 48 Jesus therefore said to him,
"Unless you see signs and wonders you will not believe." 49 The official said to him,

"Sir, come down before my child dies." 50 Jesus said to him, "Go; your son will
live." The man believed the word that Jesus spoke to him and went his way. 51 As
he was going down, his servants met him and told him that his son was living. 52 So
he asked them the hour when he began to mend, and they said to him, "Yesterday
at the seventh hour the fever left him." 53 The father knew that was the hour when
Jesus had said to him, "Your son will live"; and he himself believed, and all his
household. 54 This was now the second sign that Jesus did when he had come from
Judea to Galilee.

Section D. Christ's Early Teaching, Preaching, and Healing in Galilee According to Matthew, Mark, and Luke*

§ 26. After John's imprisonment, Jesus preaches repentance, the kingdom's coming, and belief in the Gospel

Mt. 4:12-17

12 Now when he heard that John had been arrested, he withdrew into Galilee; 13 and leaving Nazareth he went and dwelt in Capernaum by the sea, in the territory of Zebulun and Naphtali, 14 that what was spoken by the prophet Isaiah might be fulfilled:

15 "The land of Zebulun and the land of Naphtali,
toward the sea, across the Jordan,
Galilee of the Gentiles—
16 the people who sat in darkness
have seen a great light,
and for those who sat in the region and shadow of death
light has dawned."

17 From that time Jesus began to preach, saying, "Repent, for the kingdom of heaven is at hand."

Mk. 1:14, 15

14 Now after John was arrested, Jesus came into Galilee, preaching the gospel of God, 15 and saying, "The time is fulfilled, and the kingdom of God is at hand; repent, and believe in the gospel."

Lk. 4:14, 15

14 And Jesus returned in the power of the Spirit into Galilee, and a report concerning him went out through all the surrounding country. 15 And he taught in their synagogues, being glorified by all.

John

---

* Sections D-I include the materials which pertain to what is usually designated *Christ's Galilean Ministry.*

§ 27. Jesus speaks in the synagogue at Nazareth and is rejected*

Lk. 4:16-30

16 And he came to Nazareth, where he had been brought up; and he went to the
synagogue, as his custom was, on the sabbath day. And he stood up to read; 17 and
there was given to him the book of the prophet Isaiah. He opened the book, and
found the place where it was written,

18 "The Spirit of the Lord is upon me,
because he has anointed me to preach good news to the poor.
He has sent me to proclaim release to the captives
and recovering of sight to the blind,
to set at liberty those who are oppressed,
19 to proclaim the acceptable year of the Lord."

20 And he closed the book, and gave it back to the attendant, and sat down; and the
eyes of all in the synagogue were fixed on him. 21 And he began to say to them,
"Today this scripture has been fulfilled in your hearing." 22 And all spoke well of
him, and wondered at the gracious words which proceeded out of his mouth; and
they said, "Is not this Joseph's son?" 23 And he said to them, "Doubtless you will
quote to me this proverb, 'Physician, heal yourself; what we have heard you did at
Capernaum, do here also in your own country.' " 24 And he said, "Truly, I say to you,
no prophet is acceptable in his own country. 25 But in truth, I tell you, there were
many widows in Israel in the days of Elijah, when the heaven was shut up three years
and six months, when there came a great famine over all the land; 26 and Elijah was
sent to none of them but only to Zarephath, in the land of Sidon, to a woman who
was a widow. 27 And there were many lepers in Israel in the time of the prophet
Elisha; and none of them was cleansed, but only Naaman the Syrian." 28 When they
heard this, all in the synagogue were filled with wrath. 29 And they rose up and put
him out of the city, and led him to the brow of the hill on which their city was
built, that they might throw him down headlong. 30 But passing through the midst
of them he went away.

(See also article 49)

§ 28. Peter, Andrew, James, and John are called as disciples following a great catch of fish

Mt. 4:18-22

18 As he walked by the sea of Galilee, he saw two brothers, Simon who is called Peter and Andrew his brother, casting a net into the sea; for they

Mk. 1:16-20

16 And passing along by the sea of Galilee, he saw Simon and Andrew the brother of Simon casting a net in the sea; for they were fishermen. 17 And Jesus

Lk. 5:1-11

1 While the people pressed upon him to hear the word of God, he was standing by the lake of Gennesaret.
2 And he saw two boats by the lake; but the

John

* Many authorities hold that there was but one rejection and that this is Luke's version of the incident recorded in Matt. 13:53-58 and Mark 6:1-6a.

Mt. 4:18-22

were fishermen. 19 And he said to them, "Follow me, and I will make you fishers of men." 20 Immediately they left their nets and followed him. 21 And going on from there he saw two other brothers, James the son of Zebedee and John his brother, in the boat with Zebedee their father, mending their nets, and he called them. 22 Immediately they left the boat and their father, and followed him.

Mk. 1:16-20

said to them, "Follow me and I will make you become fishers of men." 18 And immediately they left their nets and followed him. 19 And going on a little farther, he saw James the son of Zebedee and John his brother, who were in their boat mending the nets. 20 And immediately he called them; and they left their father Zebedee in the boat with the hired servants, and followed him.

Lk. 5:1-11

fishermen had gone out of them and were washing their nets. 3 Getting into one of the boats, which was Simon's, he asked him to put out a little from the land. And he sat down and taught the people from the boat. 4 And when he had ceased speaking, he said to Simon, "Put out into the deep and let down your nets for a catch." 5 And Simon answered, "Master, we toiled all night and took nothing! But at your word I will let down the nets." 6 And when they had done this, they enclosed a great shoal of fish; and as their nets were breaking, 7 they beckoned to their partners in the other boat to come and help them. And they came and filled both the boats, so that they began to sink. 8 But when Simon Peter saw it, he fell down at Jesus' knees, saying, "Depart from me, for I am a sinful man, O Lord." 9 For he was astonished, and all that were with him, at the catch of fish which they had taken; 10 and so also were James and

John

Mt. 4 | Mk. 1 | Lk. 5:1-11 | John

John, sons of Zebedee, who were partners with Simon. And Jesus said to Simon, "Do not be afraid; henceforth you will be catching men." [11] And when they had brought their boats to land, they left everything and followed him.

§ 29. Jesus teaches, heals, and preaches in Capernaum and elsewhere in Galilee

a. Teaching in the Capernaum synagogue

Matt. | Mk. 1:21, 22 | Lk. 4:31, 32 | John

Mk. 1:21, 22

[21] And they went into Capernaum; and immediately on the sabbath he entered the synagogue and taught. [22] And they were astonished at his teaching, for he taught them as one who had authority, and not as the scribes.

Lk. 4:31, 32

[31] And he went down to Capernaum, a city of Galilee. And he was teaching them on the sabbath; [32] and they were astonished at his teaching, for his word was with authority.

b. Healing a man with an unclean spirit

Matt. | Mk. 1:23-28 | Lk. 4:33-37 | John

Mk. 1:23-28

[23] And immediately there was in their synagogue a man with an unclean spirit; [24] and he cried out, "What have you to do with us, Jesus of Nazareth? Have you come to destroy us? I know who you are, the Holy One of God." [25] But Jesus rebuked him, saying, "Be silent, and come out of him!" [26] And the unclean spirit, convulsing him and crying with a loud voice, came out of him. [27] And they were all amazed, so that they questioned among themselves, saying,

Lk. 4:33-37

[33] And in the synagogue there was a man who had the spirit of an unclean demon; and he cried out with a loud voice, [34] "Ah![a] What have you to do with us, Jesus of Nazareth? Have you come to destroy us? I know who you are, the Holy One of God." [35] But Jesus rebuked him, saying, "Be silent, and come out of him." And when the demon had thrown him down in the midst, he came out of him, having done him no harm. [36] And they were all amazed and said to

[a] Or *let us alone.*

Matt.	Mk. 1:23-28	Lk. 4:33-37	John
	"What is this? A new teaching! With authority he commands even the unclean spirits, and they obey him." 28 And at once his fame spread everywhere throughout all the surrounding region of Galilee.	one another, "What is this word? For with authority and power he commands the unclean spirits, and they come out." 37 And reports of him went into every place in the surrounding region.	

c. Healing Simon Peter's mother-in-law and others

Mt. 8:14-17	Mk. 1:29-34	Lk. 4:38-41	John
14 And when Jesus entered Peter's house, he saw his mother-in-law lying sick with a fever; 15 he touched her hand, and the fever left her, and she rose and served him. 16 That evening they brought to him many who were possessed with demons; and he cast out the spirits with a word, and healed all who were sick. 17 This was to fulfill what was spoken by the prophet Isaiah, "He took our infirmities and bore our diseases."	29 And immediately he[b] left the synagogue, and entered the house of Simon and Andrew, with James and John. 30 Now Simon's mother-in-law lay sick with a fever, and immediately they told him of her. 31 And he came and took her by the hand and lifted her up, and the fever left her; and she served them. 32 That evening, at sundown, they brought to him all who were sick or possessed with demons. 33 And the whole city was gathered together about the door. 34 And he healed many who were sick with various diseases, and cast out many demons; and he would not permit the demons to speak, because they knew him.	38 And he arose and left the synagogue, and entered Simon's house. Now Simon's mother-in-law was ill with a high fever, and they besought him for her. 39 And he stood over her and rebuked the fever, and it left her; and immediately she rose and served them. 40 Now when the sun was setting, all those who had any that were sick with various diseases brought them to him; and he laid his hands on every one of them and healed them. 41 And demons also came out of many, crying, "You are the Son of God!" But he rebuked them, and would not allow them to speak, because they knew that he was the Christ.	

[b] Many ancient authorities read *they*.

d. Leaving Capernaum to preach in other cities

Mt. 4:23-25

23 And he went about all Galilee, teaching in their synagogues and preaching the gospel of the kingdom and healing every disease and every infirmity among the people. 24 So his fame spread throughout all Syria, and they brought him all the sick, those afflicted with various diseases and pains, demoniacs, epileptics, and paralytics, and he healed them. 25 And great crowds followed him from Galilee and the Decapolis and Jerusalem and Judea and from beyond the Jordan.

Mk. 1:35-39

35 And in the morning, a great while before day, he rose and went out to a lonely place, and there he prayed. 36 And Simon and those who were with him followed him, 37 and they found him and said to him, "Every one is searching for you." 38 And he said to them, "Let us go on to the next towns, that I may preach there also; for that is why I came out." 39 And he went throughout all Galilee, preaching in their synagogues and casting out demons.

Lk. 4:42-44

42 And when it was day he departed and went into a lonely place. And the people sought him and came to him, and would have kept him from leaving them; 43 but he said to them, "I must preach the good news of the kingdom of God to the other cities also; for I was sent for this purpose." 44 And he was preaching in the synagogues of Judea.[c]

John

e. Cleansing a leper

Mt. 8:1-4

1 When he came down from the mountain, great crowds followed him; 2 and behold, a leper came to him and knelt before him, saying, "Lord, if you will, you can make me clean." 3 And he stretched out his hand and touched him, saying, "I will; be clean." And immediately his leprosy was cleansed.

Mk. 1:40-45

40 And a leper came to him beseeching him, and kneeling said to him, "If you will, you can make me clean." 41 And being moved with pity, he stretched out his hand and touched him, and said to him, "I will; be clean." 42 And immediately the leprosy left him, and he was made clean. 43 And he

Lk. 5:12-16

12 While he was in one of the cities, there came a man full of leprosy; and when he saw Jesus, he fell on his face and besought him, "Lord, if you will, you can make me clean." 13 And he stretched out his hand, and touched him, saying, "I will; be clean." And immediately the leprosy left him. 14 And he

John

c Some ancient authorities read *Galilee.*

Mt. 8:1-4

[4] And Jesus said to him, "See that you say nothing to any one; but go, show yourself to the priest, and offer the gift that Moses commanded for a proof to the people." [d]

Mk. 1:40-45

sternly charged him, and sent him away at once, [44] and said to him, "See that you say nothing to any one; but go, show yourself to the priest, and offer for your cleansing what Moses commanded, for a proof to the people." [d]
[45] But he went out and began to talk freely about it, and to spread the news, so that Jesus[e] could no longer openly enter a town, but was out in the country; and people came to him from every quarter.

Lk. 5:12-16

charged him to tell no one; but "go and show yourself to the priest, and make an offering for your cleansing, as Moses commanded, for a proof to the people." [d]
[15] But so much the more the report went abroad concerning him; and great multitudes gathered to hear and to be healed of their infirmities. [16] But he withdrew to the wilderness and prayed.

John

d Greek *to them.*
e Greek *he.*

Section E. Christ's Popularity Among the People and the Rise of Opposition by Jewish Leaders

§ 30. Jesus in Capernaum heals a paralytic carried by four friends; scribes and Pharisees charge blasphemy

Mt. 9:1-8

[1] And getting into a boat he crossed over and came to his own city. [2] And behold, they brought to him a paralytic, lying on his bed; and when Jesus saw their faith he said to the paralytic, "Take heart, my son; your sins are forgiven."
[3] And behold, some of the scribes said to themselves, "This man

Mk. 2:1-12

[1] And when he returned to Capernaum after some days, it was reported that he was at home. [2] And many were gathered together, so that there was no longer room for them, not even about the door; and he was preaching the word to them.
[3] And they came, bringing to him a paralytic carried by four men.

Lk. 5:17-26

[17] On one of those days, as he was teaching, there were Pharisees and teachers of the law sitting by, who had come from every town of Galilee and Judea and from Jerusalem; and the power of the Lord was with him to heal.[a] [18] And behold, men were bringing on a bed a man who was paralyzed,

John

a Some ancient authorities read *was present to heal them.*

Mt. 9:1-8

is blaspheming." 4 But Jesus, knowing[b] their thoughts, said, "Why do you think evil in your hearts? 5 For which is easier, to say, 'Your sins are forgiven,' or to say, 'Rise and walk'? 6 But that you may know that the Son of man has authority on earth to forgive sins"—he then said to the paralytic—"Rise, take up your bed and go home." 7 And he rose and went home. 8 When the crowds saw it, they were afraid, and they glorified God, who had given such authority to men.

Mk. 2:1-12

4 And when they could not get near him because of the crowd, they removed the roof above him; and when they had made an opening, they let down the pallet on which the paralytic lay. 5 And when Jesus saw their faith, he said to the paralytic, "My son, your sins are forgiven." 6 Now some of the scribes were sitting there, questioning in their hearts, 7 "Why does this man speak thus? It is blasphemy! Who can forgive sins but God alone?" 8 And immediately Jesus, perceiving in his spirit that they thus questioned within themselves, said to them, "Why do you question thus in your hearts? 9 Which is easier, to say to the paralytic, 'Your sins are forgiven'; or to say, 'Rise, take up your pallet and walk'? 10 But that you may know that the Son of man has authority on earth to forgive sins"—he said to the paralytic—11 "I say to you, rise, take up your pallet and

Lk. 5:17-26

and they sought to bring him in and lay him before Jesus;[c] 19 but finding no way to bring him in, because of the crowd, they went up on the roof and let him down with his bed through the tiles into the midst before Jesus. 20 And when he saw their faith he said, "Man, your sins are forgiven you." 21 And the scribes and the Pharisees began to question, saying, "Who is this that speaks blasphemies? Who can forgive sins but God only?" 22 When Jesus perceived their questionings, he answered them, "Why do you question in your hearts? 23 Which is easier, to say, 'Your sins are forgiven you,' or to say, 'Rise and walk'? 24 But that you may know that the Son of man has authority on earth to forgive sins"—he said to the man who was paralyzed—"I say to you, rise, take up your bed and go home." 25 And immediately he rose before them, and

John

[b] Many ancient authorities read *seeing.*
[c] Greek *him.*

Mt. 9	Mk. 2:1-12	Lk. 5:17-26	John
	go home." [12] And he rose, and immediately took up the pallet and went out before them all; so that they were all amazed and glorified God, saying, "We never saw anything like this!"	took up that on which he lay, and went home, glorifying God. [26] And amazement seized them all, and they glorified God and were filled with awe, saying, "We have seen strange things today."	

§ 31. Levi (Matthew), a tax collector, is called as a disciple; Jesus attends the feast while scribes and Pharisees find fault

Mt. 9:9-13	Mk. 2:13-17	Lk. 5:27-32	John
[9] As Jesus passed on from there, he saw a man called Matthew sitting at the tax office; and he said to him, "Follow me." And he rose and followed him. [10] And as he sat at table[d] in the house, behold, many tax collectors and sinners came and sat down with Jesus and his disciples. [11] And when the Pharisees saw this, they said to his disciples, "Why does your master eat with tax collectors and sinners?" [12] But when he heard it, he said, "Those who are well have no need of a physician, but those who are sick. [13] Go and learn what this means, 'I desire mercy, and not sacrifice.' For	[13] He went out again beside the sea; and all the crowd gathered about him, and he taught them. [14] And as he passed on, he saw Levi the son of Alphaeus sitting at the tax office, and he said to him, "Follow me." And he rose and followed him. [15] And as he sat at table in his house, many tax collectors and sinners were sitting with Jesus and his disciples; for there were many who followed him. [16] And the scribes of[f] the Pharisees, when they saw that he was eating with sinners and tax collectors, said to his disciples, "Why does he eat and drink[g] with tax collectors and	[27] After this he went out, and saw a tax collector, named Levi, sitting at the tax office; and he said to him, "Follow me." [28] And he left everything, and rose and followed him. [29] And Levi made him a great feast in his house; and there was a large company of tax collectors and others sitting at table[e] with them. [30] And the Pharisees and their scribes murmured against his disciples, saying, "Why do you eat and drink with tax collectors and sinners?" [31] And Jesus answered them, "Those who are well have no need of a physician, but those who are sick; [32] I have not come to call the righteous, but	

[d] Greek *reclined.*
[e] Greek *reclining.*
[f] Some ancient authorities read *and.*
[g] Some ancient authorities omit *and drink.*

Mt. 9:9-13

I came not to call the righteous, but sinners."

Mk. 2:13-17

sinners?" [17] And when Jesus heard it, he said to them, "Those who are well have no need of a physician, but those who are sick; I came not to call the righteous, but sinners."

Lk. 5:27-32

sinners to repentance."

John

§ 32. Jesus answers a question about fasting; tells of old and new cloth and garments, wine and wineskins

Mt. 9:14-17

[14] Then the disciples of John came to him, saying, "Why do we and the Pharisees fast,[a] but your disciples do not fast?" [15] And Jesus said to them, "Can the wedding guests mourn as long as the bridegroom is with them? The days will come, when the bridegroom is taken away from them, and then they will fast. [16] And no one puts a piece of unshrunk cloth on an old garment, for the patch tears away from the garment, and a worse tear is made. [17] Neither is new wine put into old wineskins; if it is, the skins burst, and the wine is spilled, and the skins are destroyed; but new wine is put into fresh wineskins, and so both are preserved."

Mk. 2:18-22

[18] Now John's disciples and the Pharisees were fasting; and people came and said to him, "Why do John's disciples and the disciples of the Pharisees fast, but your disciples do not fast?" [19] And Jesus said to them, "Can the wedding guests fast while the bridegroom is with them? As long as they have the bridegroom with them, they cannot fast. [20] The days will come, when the bridegroom is taken away from them, and then they will fast on that day. [21] No one sews a piece of unshrunk cloth on an old garment; if he does, the patch tears away from it, the new from the old, and a worse tear is made. [22] And no one puts new

Lk. 5:33-39

[33] And they said to him, "The disciples of John fast often and offer prayers, and so do the disciples of the Pharisees, but yours eat and drink." [34] And Jesus said to them, "Can you make wedding guests fast while the bridegroom is with them? [35] The days will come, when the bridegroom is taken away from them, and then they will fast in those days." [36] He told them a parable also: "No one tears a piece from a new garment and puts it upon an old garment; if he does, he will tear the new, and the piece from the new will not match the old. [37] And no one puts new wine into old wineskins; if he does, the new wine will

John

[a] Many ancient authorities add *much* or *often*.

Mt. 9	Mk. 2:18-22	Lk. 5:33-39	John
	wine into old wine-skins; if he does, the wine will burst the skins, and the wine is lost, and so are the skins."[i]	burst the skins and it will be spilled, and the skins will be destroyed. 38 But new wine must be put into fresh wine-skins. 39 And no one after drinking old wine desires new; for he says, 'The old is good.'"[j]	

§ 33. Jesus heals an invalid man at the pool of Bethzatha in Jerusalem; Jews cite Sabbath laws and dispute his equality with the Father

Jn. 5:1-18

1 After this there was a feast of the Jews, and Jesus went up to Jerusalem.
2 Now there is in Jerusalem by the sheep gate a pool, in Hebrew called Bethzatha,[k] which has five porticoes. 3 In these lay a multitude of invalids, blind, lame,
paralyzed. 5 One man was there, who had been ill for thirty-eight years. 6 When
Jesus saw him and knew that he had been lying there a long time, he said to him,
"Do you want to be healed?" 7 The sick man answered him, "Sir, I have no man
to put me into the pool when the water is troubled, and while I am going another
steps down before me." 8 Jesus said to him, "Rise, take up your pallet, and walk."
9 And at once the man was healed, and took up his pallet and walked.
Now that day was the sabbath. 10 So the Jews said to the man who was cured,
"It is the sabbath, it is not lawful for you to carry your pallet." 11 But he answered
them, "The man who healed me said to me, 'Take up your pallet, and walk.' "
12 They asked him, "Who is the man who said to you, 'Take up your pallet, and
walk'?" 13 Now the man who had been healed did not know who it was, for Jesus
had withdrawn, as there was a crowd in the place. 14 Afterward, Jesus found him in
the temple, and said to him, "See, you are well! Sin no more, that nothing worse
befall you." 15 The man went away and told the Jews that it was Jesus who had
healed him. 16 And this was why the Jews persecuted Jesus, because he did this on
the sabbath. 17 But Jesus answered them, "My Father is working still, and I am
working." 18 This was why the Jews sought all the more to kill him, because he
not only broke the sabbath but also called God his Father, making himself equal
with God.

§ 34. Jesus discourses on his gift of eternal life and the testimony concerning himself

Jn. 5:19-47

19 Jesus said to them, "Truly, truly, I say to you, the Son can do nothing of his
own accord, but only what he sees the Father doing; for whatever he does, that
the Son does likewise. 20 For the Father loves the Son, and shows him all that he

[i] Some ancient authorities add *but new wine is for fresh skins.*
[j] Many ancient authorities read *better.*
[k] Some ancient authorities read *Bethesda,* others *Bethsaida.*

himself is doing; and greater works than these will he show him, that you may
marvel. 21 For as the Father raises the dead and gives them life, so also the Son
gives life to whom he will. 22 The Father judges no one, but has given all judgment
to the Son, that all may honor the Son, 23 even as they honor the Father. He who
does not honor the Son does not honor the Father who sent him. 24 Truly, truly,
I say to you, he who hears my word and believes him who sent me, has eternal life;
he does not come into judgment, but has passed from death to life.

25 "Truly, truly, I say to you, the hour is coming, and now is, when the dead will
hear the voice of the Son of God, and those who hear will live. 26 For as the Father
has life in himself, so he has granted the Son also to have life in himself, 27 and has
given him authority to execute judgment, because he is the Son of man. 28 Do not
marvel at this; for the hour is coming when all who are in the tombs will hear his
voice 29 and come forth, those who have done good, to the resurrection of life,
and those who have done evil, to the resurrection of judgment.

30 "I can do nothing on my own authority; as I hear, I judge; and my judgment
is just, because I seek not my own will but the will of him who sent me. 31 If I bear
witness to myself, my testimony is not true; 32 there is another who bears witness to
me, and I know that the testimony which he bears to me is true. 33 You sent to
John, and he has borne witness to the truth. 34 Not that the testimony which I
receive is from man; but I say this that you may be saved. 35 He was a burning
and shining lamp, and you were willing to rejoice for a while in his light. 36 But
the testimony which I have is greater than that of John; for the works which the
Father has granted me to accomplish, these very works which I am doing, bear me
witness that the Father has sent me. 37 And the Father who sent me has himself
borne witness to me. His voice you have never heard, his form you have never
seen; 38 and you do not have his word abiding in you, for you do not believe him
whom he has sent. 39 You search the scriptures, because you think that in them you
have eternal life; and it is they that bear witness to me; 40 yet you refuse to come
to me that you may have life. 41 I do not receive glory from men. 42 But I know
that you have not the love of God within you. 43 I have come in my Father's name,
and you do not receive me; if another comes in his own name, him you will receive.
44 How can you believe, who receive glory from one another and do not seek the
glory that comes from the only God? 45 Do not think that I shall accuse you to the
Father; it is Moses who accuses you, on whom you set your hope. 46 If you believed
Moses, you would believe me, for he wrote of me. 47 But if you do not believe his
writings, how will you believe my words?"

§ 35. The Pharisees censure the disciples for plucking grain on the Sabbath; Jesus gives a principle of Sabbath observance

Mt. 12:1-8

1 At that time Jesus
went through the grain-

Mk. 2:23-28

23 One sabbath he
was going through the

Lk. 6:1-5

1 On a sabbath,[ι]
while he was going

John

[ι] Many ancient authorities read *On the second first sabbath* (on the second sabbath after the first).

Mt. 12:1-8

fields on the sabbath;
his disciples were
hungry, and they began
to pluck ears of grain
and to eat. 2 But when
the Pharisees saw it,
they said to him, "Look,
your disciples are doing
what is not lawful to
do on the sabbath."
3 He said to them,
"Have you not read
what David did, when
he was hungry, and
those who were with
him: 4 how he en-
tered the house of God
and ate the bread of
the Presence, which it
was not lawful for him
to eat nor for those
who were with him,
but only for the
priests? 5 Or have you
not read in the law
how on the sabbath the
priests in the temple
profane the sabbath,
and are guiltless? 6 I
tell you, something
greater than the temple
is here. 7 And if you
had known what this
means, 'I desire mercy,
and not sacrifice,' you
would not have con-
demned the guiltless.
8 For the Son of man is
lord of the sabbath."

Mk. 2:23-28

grainfields; and as they
made their way his dis-
ciples began to pluck
ears of grain. 24 And
the Pharisees said to
him, "Look, why are
they doing what is not
lawful on the sabbath?"
25 And he said to them,
"Have you never read
what David did, when
he was in need and was
hungry, he and those
who were with him:
26 how he entered the
house of God, when
Abiathar was high
priest, and ate the
bread of the Presence,
which it is not lawful
for any but the priests
to eat, and also gave it
to those who were with
him?" 27 And he said
to them, "The sabbath
was made for man, not
man for the sabbath;
28 so the Son of man is
lord even of the sab-
bath."

Lk. 6:1-5

through the grainfields,
his disciples plucked
and ate some ears of
grain, rubbing them in
their hands. 2 But
some of the Pharisees
said, "Why are you
doing what is not law-
ful to do on the sab-
bath?" 3 And Jesus
answered, "Have you
not read what David
did when he was
hungry, he and those
who were with him:
4 how he entered the
house of God, and took
and ate the bread of
the Presence, which it
is not lawful for any
but the priests to eat,
and also gave it to
those with him?"
5 And he said to them,
"The Son of man is
lord of the sabbath."

John

§ 36. Jesus heals a man with a withered hand on the Sabbath; the scribes and Pharisees determine to destroy him

Mt. 12:9-14

9 And he went on from there, and entered their synagogue. 10 And behold, there was a man with a withered hand. And they asked him, "Is it lawful to heal on the sabbath?" so that they might accuse him. 11 He said to them, "What man of you, if he has one sheep and it falls into a pit on the sabbath, will not lay hold of it and lift it out? 12 Of how much more value is a man than a sheep! So it is lawful to do good on the sabbath." 13 Then he said to the man, "Stretch out your hand." And the man stretched it out, and it was restored, whole like the other. 14 But the Pharisees went out and took counsel against him, how to destroy him.

Mk. 3:1-6

1 Again he entered the synagogue, and a man was there who had a withered hand. 2 And they watched him, to see whether he would heal him on the sabbath, so that they might accuse him. 3 And he said to the man who had the withered hand, "Come here." 4 And he said to them, "Is it lawful on the sabbath to do good or to do harm, to save life or to kill?" But they were silent. 5 And he looked around at them with anger, grieved at their hardness of heart, and said to the man, "Stretch out your hand." He stretched it out, and his hand was restored. 6 The Pharisees went out, and immediately held counsel with the Herodians against him, how to destroy him.

Lk. 6:6-11

6 On another sabbath, when he entered the synagogue and taught, a man was there whose right hand was withered. 7 And the scribes and the Pharisees watched him, to see whether he would heal on the sabbath, so that they might find an accusation against him. 8 But he knew their thoughts, and he said to the man who had the withered hand, "Come and stand here." And he rose and stood there. 9 And Jesus said to them, "I ask you, is it lawful on the sabbath to do good or to do harm, to save life or to destroy it?" 10 And he looked around on them all, and said to him, "Stretch out your hand." And he did so, and his hand was restored. 11 But they were filled with fury and discussed with one another what they might do to Jesus.

John

§ 37. Many seek Jesus as he speaks and heals by the lake

Mt. 12:15-21

15 Jesus, aware of this, withdrew from there. And many followed him, and he healed

Mk. 3:7-12

7 Jesus withdrew with his disciples to the sea, and a great multitude from Galilee fol-

Luke

John

Mt. 12:15-21

them all, [16] and ordered them not to make him known. [17] This was to fulfill what was spoken by the prophet Isaiah:

[18] "Behold, my servant whom I have chosen,
my beloved with whom my soul is well pleased.
I will put my Spirit upon him,
and he shall proclaim justice to the Gentiles.
[19] He will not wrangle or cry aloud,
nor will any one hear his voice in the streets;
[20] he will not break a bruised reed
or quench a smoldering wick,
till he brings justice to victory;
[21] and in his name will the Gentiles hope."

Mk. 3:7-12

lowed; also from Judea [8] and Jerusalem and Idumea and from beyond the Jordan and from about Tyre and Sidon a great multitude, hearing all that he did, came to him. [9] And he told his disciples to have a boat ready for him because of the crowd, lest they should crush him; [10] for he had healed many, so that all who had diseases pressed upon him to touch him. [11] And whenever the unclean spirits beheld him, they fell down before him and cried out, "You are the Son of God." [12] And he strictly ordered them not to make him known.

Luke

John

Section F. Christ's Choice of the Twelve, His Sermon on the Mount, and the Beelzebub Controversy

§ 38. The twelve are appointed to be disciples and apostles

Matt.

Mk. 3:13-19a

[13] And he went up into the hills, and called to him those whom he desired; and they came to him. [14] And he appointed twelve,[a] to be with him, and to be sent out to preach [15] and have authority to cast out demons: [16] Simon whom he surnamed Peter; [17] James the son of Zebedee and John the brother

Lk. 6:12-19

[12] In these days he went out into the hills to pray; and all night he continued in prayer to God. [13] And when it was day, he called his disciples, and chose from them twelve, whom he named apostles; [14] Simon, whom he named Peter, and Andrew his brother, and James and John, and Philip, and Batholomew,

John

[a] Some ancient authorities add *whom also he named apostles.*

Matt.	Mk. 3:13-19a	Lk. 6:12-19	John
	of James, whom he surnamed Boanerges, that is, sons of thunder; 18 Andrew, and Philip, and Bartholomew, and Matthew, and Thomas, and James the son of Alphaeus, and Thaddaeus, and Simon the Cananaean, 19a and Judas Iscariot, who betrayed him.	15 and Matthew, and Thomas, and James the son of Alphaeus, and Simon who was called the Zealot, 16 and Judas the son[b] of James, and Judas Iscariot, who became a traitor. 17 And he came down with them and stood on a level place, with a great crowd of his disciples and a great multitude of people from all Judea and Jerusalem and the seacoast of Tyre and Sidon, who came to hear him and to be healed of their diseases; 18 and those who were troubled with unclean spirits were cured. 19 And all the crowd sought to touch him, for power came forth from him and healed them all.	

§ 39. In his "Sermon on the Mount" Jesus deals with the duties and privileges of citizens of the kingdom of God*

a. Their ways to happiness and their destinies. The Beatitudes

Mt. 5:1-12	Mark	Lk. 6:20-26	John
1 Seeing the crowds, he went up on the mountain, and when he sat down his disciples came to him. 2 And he opened his mouth and taught them, saying: 3 "Blessed are the poor in spirit, for theirs is the kingdom of heaven. 4 "Blessed are those who mourn, for they shall be comforted. 5 "Blessed are the meek, for they shall inherit the earth. 6 "Blessed are those who		20 And he lifted up his eyes on his disciples, and said: "Blessed are you poor, for yours is the kingdom of God. 21 "Blessed are you that hunger now, for you shall be satisfied. "Blessed are you that weep now, for you shall laugh. 22 "Blessed are you when men hate you, and when they exclude you and revile you, and cast out your name as evil, on account of the Son of man! 23 Rejoice in	

[b] Or *brother*.

* Luke 6:20b-49 is often called The Sermon on the Plain.

Mt. 5:1-12	Mark	Lk. 6:20-26	John
hunger and thirst for righteousness, for they shall be satisfied. 7 "Blessed are the merciful, for they shall obtain mercy. 8 "Blessed are the pure in heart, for they shall see God. 9 "Blessed are the peacemakers, for they shall be called sons of God. 10 "Blessed are those who are persecuted for righteousness' sake, for theirs is the kingdom of heaven. 11 "Blessed are you when men revile you and persecute you and utter all kinds of evil against you falsely on my account. 12 "Rejoice and be glad, for your reward is great in heaven, for so men persecuted the prophets who were before you."		that day, and leap for joy, for behold, your reward is great in heaven; for so their fathers did to the prophets. 24 "But woe to you that are rich, for you have received your consolation. 25 "Woe to you that are full now, for you shall hunger. "Woe to you that laugh now, for you shall mourn and weep. 26 "Woe to you, when all men speak well of you, for so their fathers did to the false prophets."	

b. Their purposes in the world

Mt. 5:13-16

13 "You are the salt of the earth; but if salt has lost its taste, how can its saltness be restored? It is no longer good for anything except to be thrown out and trodden under foot by men.

14 "You are the light of the world. A city set on a hill cannot be hid. 15 Nor do men light a lamp and put it under a bushel, but on a stand, and it gives light to all in the house. 16 Let your light so shine before men, that they may see your good works and give glory to your Father who is in heaven.

c. Their use of the law and the prophets

Mt. 5:17-19

17 "Think not that I have come to abolish the law and the prophets; I have come not to abolish them but to fulfill them. 18 For truly, I say to you, till heaven and earth pass away, not an iota, not a dot, will pass from the law until all is accomplished. 19 Whoever then relaxes one of the least of these commandments and teaches men so, shall be called least in the kingdom of heaven; but he who does them and teaches them shall be called great in the kingdom of heaven."

d. Their better righteousness: perfect morality versus obedience to law alone

Mt. 5:20-48	Mark	Lk. 6	John

20 "For I tell you, unless your righteousness exceeds that
of the scribes and Pharisees, you will never enter the kingdom of heaven.
21 "You have heard that it was said to the men of old,
'You shall not kill; and whoever kills shall be liable to
judgment.' 22 But I say to you that every one who is angry
with his brother[c] shall be liable to judgment; whoever
insults[d] his brother shall be liable to the council, and whoever says, 'You fool!' shall be liable to the hell[e] of fire.
23 So if you are offering your gift at the altar, and there
remember that your brother has something against you,
24 leave your gift there before the altar and go; first be
reconciled to your brother, and then come and offer your
gift. 25 Make friends quickly with your accuser, while you
are going with him to court, lest your accuser hand you
over to the judge, and the judge to the guard, and you be
put in prison; 26 truly, I say to you, you will never get out
till you have paid the last penny.
27 "You have heard that it was said, 'You shall not commit adultery.' 28 But I say to you that every one who looks
at a woman lustfully has already committed adultery with
her in his heart. 29 If your right eye causes you to sin,
pluck it out and throw it away; it is better that you lose
one of your members than that your whole body be thrown
into hell.[e] 30 And if your right hand causes you to sin, cut
it off and throw it away; it is better that you lose one of
your members than that your whole body go into hell.[e]
31 "It was also said, 'Whoever divorces his wife, let him
give her a certificate of divorce.' 32 But I say to you that
every one who divorces his wife, except on the ground of
unchastity, makes her an adulteress; and whoever marries
a divorced woman commits adultery.
33 "Again you have heard that it was said to the men of
old, 'You shall not swear falsely, but shall perform to the
Lord what you have sworn.' 34 But I say to you, Do not
swear at all, either by heaven, for it is the throne of God,
35 or by the earth, for it is his footstool, or by Jerusalem,
for it is the city of the great King. 36 And do not swear
by your head, for you cannot make one hair white or
black. 37 Let what you say be simply 'Yes' or 'No'; anything

c Many ancient authorities insert *without cause*.
d Greek *says Raca to* (an obscure term of abuse).
e Greek *Gehenna*.

Mt. 5:20-48

more than this comes from evil.[f]

38 "You have heard that it was said, 'An eye for an eye and a tooth for a tooth.' 39 But I say to you, Do not resist one who is evil. But if any one strikes you on the right cheek, turn to him the other also; 40 and if any one would sue you and take your coat, let him have your cloak as well; 41 and if any one forces you to go one mile, go with him two miles. 42 Give to him who begs from you, and do not refuse him who would borrow from you.

43 "You have heard that it was said, 'You shall love your neighbor and hate your enemy.' 44 But I say to you, Love your enemies and pray for those who persecute you, 45 so that you may be sons of your Father who is in heaven; for he makes his sun rise on the evil and on the good, and sends rain on the just and on the unjust. 46 For if you love those who love you, what reward have you? Do not even the tax collectors do the same? 47 And if you salute only your brethren, what more are you doing than others? Do not even the Gentiles do the same? 48 You, therefore, must be perfect, as your heavenly Father is perfect."

Mark

Lk. 6:27-36

27 "But I say to you that hear, Love your enemies, do good to those who hate you, 28 bless those who curse you, pray for those who abuse you. 29 To him who strikes you on the cheek, offer the other also; and from him who takes away your cloak do not withhold your coat as well. 30 Give to every one who begs from you; and of him who takes away your goods, do not ask them again. 31 And as you wish that men would do to you, do so to them.

32 "If you love those who love you, what credit is that to you? For even sinners love those who love them. 33 And if you do good to those who do good to you, what credit is that to you? For even sinners do the same. 34 And if you lend to those from whom you hope to receive, what credit is that to you? Even sinners lend to sinners, to receive as much again. 35 But love your enemies, and do good, and lend, expecting nothing in return;[g] and your reward will be great, and you will be sons of the Most High; for he is kind to the ungrateful and the selfish. 36 Be merciful, even as your Father is merciful."

John

e. Their better righteousness: sincere religion versus profession. The Lord's Prayer

Mt. 6:1-18

1 "Beware of practicing your piety before men in order to be seen by them; for then you will have no reward from your Father who is in heaven.

f Or *the evil one.*
g Some ancient authorities read *despairing of no man.*

2 "Thus, when you give alms, sound no trumpet before you, as the hypocrites do
in the synagogues and in the streets, that they may be praised by men. Truly, I say to
you, they have their reward. 3 But when you give alms, do not let your left hand
know what your right hand is doing 4 so that your alms may be in secret; and your
Father who sees in secret will reward you.

5 "And when you pray, you must not be like the hypocrites; for they love to stand
and pray in the synagogues and at the street corners, that they may be seen by men.
Truly, I say to you, they have their reward. 6 But when you pray, go into your room
and shut the door and pray to your Father who is in secret; and your Father who sees
in secret will reward you.

7 "And in praying do not heap up empty phrases as the Gentiles do; for they think
that they will be heard for their many words. 8 Do not be like them, for your Father
knows what you need before you ask him. 9 Pray then like this:

'Our Father who art in heaven,
Hallowed be thy name.
10 Thy kingdom come,
Thy will be done,
On earth as it is in heaven.
11 Give us this day our daily bread;[h]
12 And forgive us our debts,
As we also have forgiven our debtors;
13 And lead us not into temptation,
But deliver us from evil.'[i]

14 "For if you forgive men their trespasses, your heavenly Father also will forgive
you;15 but if you do not forgive men their trespasses, neither will your Father forgive
your trespasses.

16 "And when you fast, do not look dismal, like the hypocrites, for they disfigure
their faces that their fasting may be seen by men. Truly, I say to you, they have their
reward. 17 But when you fast, anoint your head and wash your face, 18 that your
fasting may not be seen by men but by your Father who is in secret; and your Father
who sees in secret will reward you."

(See also Luke 11:1-4, article 80)

f. Their highest good: God's kingdom and righteousness

Mt. 6:19-34

19 "Do not lay up for yourselves treasures on earth, where moth and rust[j] consume
and where thieves break in and steal, 20 but lay up for yourselves treasures in heaven,
where neither moth nor rust[j] consumes and where thieves do not break in and steal;
21 for where your treasure is, there will your heart be also.

22 "The eye is the lamp of the body. So, if your eye is sound, your whole body

[h] Or *our bread for the morrow.*
[i] Or *the evil one.* Many ancient authorities add, in some form, *For thine is the Kingdom and the power and the glory, forever. Amen.*
[j] Or *worm.*

will be full of light; 23 but if your eye is not sound, your whole body will be full of
darkness. If then the light in you is darkness, how great is the darkness!
24 "No one can serve two masters; for either he will hate the one and love the
other, or he will be devoted to the one and despise the other. You cannot serve God
and mammon.
25 "Therefore I tell you, do not be anxious about your life, what you shall eat or
what you shall drink, nor about your body, what you shall put on. Is not life more
than food, and the body more than clothing? 26 Look at the birds of the air: they
neither sow nor reap nor gather into barns, and yet your heavenly Father feeds them.
Are you not of more value than they? 27 And which of you by being anxious can
add one cubit to his span of life?* 28 And why be anxious about clothing? Consider
the lilies of the field, how they grow; they neither toil nor spin; 29 yet I tell you, even
Solomon in all his glory was not arrayed like one of these. 30 But if God so clothes
the grass of the field, which today is alive and tomorrow is thrown into the oven, will
he not much more clothe you, O men of little faith? 31 Therefore do not be anxious,
saying, 'What shall we eat?' or 'What shall we drink?' or 'What shall we wear?' 32 For
the Gentiles seek all these things; and your heavenly Father knows that you need
them all. 33 But seek first his kingdom and his righteousness, and all these things
shall be yours as well.
34 "Therefore do not be anxious about tomorrow, for tomorrow will be anxious for
itself. Let the day's own trouble be sufficient for the day."

(See also article 83c)

g. Their principle of similar returns. The Golden Rule

Mt. 7:1-12

1 "Judge not, that you be not
judged. 2 For with the judgment
you pronounce you will be
judged, and the measure you
give will be the measure you get.
3 Why do you see the speck that
is in your brother's eye, but do
not notice the log that is in your
own eye? 4 Or how can you say
to your brother, 'Let me take the
speck out of your eye,' when
there is the log in your own
eye? 5 You hypocrite, first take
the log out of your own eye, and
then you will see clearly to take
the speck out of your brother's
eye.

Mark

Lk. 6:37-42

37 "Judge not and you will not
be judged; condemn not and
you will not be condemned;
forgive and you will be forgiven; 38 give, and it will be
given to you; good measure,
pressed down, shaken together,
running over, will be put into
your lap. For the measure you
give will be the measure you get
back."
39 He also told them a parable: "Can a blind man lead a
blind man? Will they not both
fall into a pit? 40 A disciple is
not above his teacher, but every
one when he is fully taught will

John

* Or *to his stature.*

Mt. 7:1-12	Mark	Lk. 6:37-42	John
6 "Do not give dogs what is holy; and do not throw your pearls before swine, lest they trample them underfoot and turn to attack you.		be like his teacher. 41 Why do you see the speck that is in your brother's eye, but do not notice the log that is in your own eye? 42 Or how can you say to your brother, 'Brother, let me take out the speck that is in your eye,' when you yourself do not see the log that is in your own eye? You hypocrite, first take the log out of your own eye, and then you will see clearly to take out the speck that is in your brother's eye."	
7 "Ask, and it will be given you; seek, and you will find; knock, and it will be opened to you. 8 For every one who asks receives, and he who seeks finds, and to him who knocks it will be opened. 9 Or what man of you, if his son asks him for a loaf, will give him a stone? 10 Or if he asks for a fish, will give him a serpent? 11 If you then, who are evil, know how to give good gifts to your children, how much more will your Father who is in heaven give good things to those who ask him? 12 So whatever you wish that men would do to you, do so to them, for this is the law and the prophets."			

b. Their deeds

Mt. 7:13-23	Mark	Lk. 6:43-45	John
13 "Enter by the narrow gate; for the gate is wide and the way is easy,[l] that leads to destruction, and those who enter by it are many. 14 For the gate is narrow and the way is hard, that leads to life, and those who find it are few.		43 "For no good tree bears bad fruit, nor again does a bad tree bear good fruit; 44 for each tree is known by its own fruit. For figs are not gathered from thorns, nor are grapes picked from a bramble bush. 45 The good man out of the good treasure of his heart produces good, and the evil man out of his evil treasure produces evil; for out of the abundance of the heart his mouth speaks."	
15 "Beware of false prophets, who come to you in sheep's clothing but inwardly are ravenous wolves. 16 You will know them by their fruits. Are grapes			

[l] Some ancient authorities read *for the way is wide and easy.*

Mt. 7:13-23 | Mark | Lk. 6 | John

gathered from thorns, or figs
from thistles? 17 So, every sound
tree bears good fruit, but the
bad tree bears evil fruit. 18 A
sound tree cannot bear evil fruit,
nor can a bad tree bear good
fruit. 19 Every tree that does not
bear good fruit is cut down and
thrown into the fire. 20 Thus
you will know them by their
fruits.

21 "Not every one who says to
me, 'Lord, Lord,' shall enter the
kingdom of heaven, but he who
does the will of my Father who
is in heaven. 22 On that day
many will say to me, 'Lord,
Lord, did we not prophesy in
your name, and cast out demons
in your name, and do many
mighty works in your name?'
23 And then will I declare to
them, 'I never knew you; depart
from me, you evil-doers.' "

i. Their help

Mt. 7:24-29 | Mark | Lk. 6:46-49 | John

24 "Every one then who hears
these words of mine and does
them will be like a wise man
who built his house upon the
rock; 25 and the rain fell, and
the floods came, and the winds
blew and beat upon that house,
but it did not fall, because it had
been founded on the rock.
26 And every one who hears
these words of mine and does
not do them will be like a
foolish man who built his house
upon the sand; 27 and the rain

Lk. 6:46-49

46 "Why do you call me Lord
and not do what I tell you?
47 Every one who comes to me
and hears my words and does
them, I will show you what he is
like: 48 he is like a man build-
ing a house, who dug deep, and
laid the foundation upon rock;
and when a flood arose, the
stream broke against that house,
and could not shake it, because it
had been well built.[m] 49 But he
who hears and does not do them
is like a man who built a house

[m] Some ancient authorities read *founded upon the rock.*

Mt. 7:24-29 | Mark | Lk. 6:46-49 | John

fell, and the floods came, and the winds blew and beat against that house, and it fell; and great was the fall of it."

[28] And when Jesus finished these sayings, the crowds were astonished at his teaching, [29] for he taught them as one who had authority, and not as their scribes.

on the ground without a foundation; against which the stream broke, and immediately it fell, and the ruin of that house was great."

§ 40. Jesus heals the centurion's slave in Capernaum

Mt. 8:5-13 | Mark | Lk. 7:1-10 | John

[5] As he entered Capernaum, a centurion came forward to him, beseeching him [6] and saying, "Lord, my servant is lying paralyzed at home, in terrible distress." [7] And he said to him, "I will come and heal him." [8] But the centurion answered him, "Lord, I am not worthy to have you come under my roof; but only say the word, and my servant will be healed. [9] For I am a man under authority, with soldiers under me; and I say to one, 'Go,' and he goes, and to another, 'Come,' and he comes, and to my slave, 'Do this,' and he does it." [10] When Jesus heard him, he marveled, and said to those who followed him, "Truly, I say to you, not even[o] in Israel have I found such faith. [11] I tell you, many will come from east and west and sit at table with Abraham, Isaac, and Jacob in the kingdom of heaven, [12] while the sons of the king-

[1] After he had ended all his sayings in the hearing of the people he entered Capernaum. [2] Now a centurion had a slave who was dear[n] to him, who was sick and at the point of death. [3] When he heard of Jesus, he sent to him elders of the Jews, asking him to come and heal his slave. [4] And when they came to Jesus, they besought him earnestly, saying, "He is worthy to have you do this for him, [5] for he loves our nation, and he built us our synagogue." [6] And Jesus went with them. When he was not far from the house, the centurion sent friends to him, saying to him, "Lord, do not trouble yourself, for I am not worthy to have you come under my roof; [7] therefore I did not presume to come to you. But say the word, and let my servant be healed. [8] For I am a man set under authority, with soldiers under me: and I say to one, 'Go,'

[n] Or *valuable*.
[o] Some ancient authorities read *with no one*.

Mt. 8:5-13	Mark	Lk. 7:1-10	John
dom will be thrown into the outer darkness; there men will weep and gnash their teeth." [13] And to the centurion Jesus said, "Go; be it done for you as you have believed." And the servant was healed at that very moment.		and he goes; and to another, 'Come,' and he comes; and to my slave, 'Do this,' and he does it." [9] When Jesus heard this he marveled at him, and turned and said to the multitude that followed him, "I tell you, not even in Israel have I found such faith." [10] And when those who had been sent returned to the house, they found the slave well.	

§ 41. Jesus raises a widow's only son at Nain

Lk. 7:11-17

[11] Soon afterward[p] he went to a city called Nain, and his disciples and a great crowd
went with him. [12] As he drew near to the gate of the city, behold, a man who had
died was being carried out, the only son of his mother, and she was a widow; and a
large crowd from the city was with her. [13] And when the Lord saw her, he had
compassion on her and said to her, "Do not weep." [14] And he came and touched the
bier, and the bearers stood still. And he said, "Young man, I say to you, arise." [15] And
the dead man sat up, and began to speak. And he gave him to his mother. [16] Fear
seized them all; and they glorified God, saying, "A great prophet has arisen among us!"
and "God has visited his people!" [17] And this report concerning him spread through
the whole of Judea and all the surrounding country.

§ 42. John the Baptist sends disciples to ask a last question; Jesus replies

a. Showing his works; commending John

Mt. 11:2-15	Mark	Lk. 7:18-30	John
[2] Now when John heard in prison about the deeds of the Christ, he sent word by his disciples [3] and said to him, "Are you he who is to come, or shall we look for another?" [4] And Jesus answered them, "Go and tell John what you hear and see: [5] the blind receive their sight and the lame walk, lepers are cleansed and the deaf hear, and the dead are raised up, and the poor have good news preached		[18] The disciples of John told him of all these things. [19] And John, calling to him two of his disciples, sent them to the Lord, saying, "Are you he who is to come, or shall we look for another?" [20] And when the men had come to him, they said, "John the Baptist has sent us to you, saying, 'Are you he who is to come, or shall we look for another?' " [21] In that hour he cured many of diseases and	

[p] Many ancient authorities read *next day.*

Mt. 11:2-15 | Mark | Lk. 7:18-30 | John

to them. 6 And blessed is he who takes no offense at me."

7 As they went away, Jesus began to speak to the crowds concerning John: "What did you go out into the wilderness to behold? A reed shaken by the wind? 8 Why then did you go out? To see a man[q] clothed in soft raiment? Behold, those who wear soft raiment are in kings' houses. 9 Why then did you go out? To see a prophet?[r] Yes, I tell you, and more than a prophet. 10 This is he of whom it is written,

'Behold, I send my messenger
before thy face,
who shall prepare thy way
before thee.'

11 "Truly, I say to you, among those born of women there has risen no one greater than John the Baptist; yet he who is least in the kingdom of heaven is greater than he. 12 From the days of John the Baptist until now the kingdom of heaven has suffered violence,[s] and men of violence take it by force. 13 For all the prophets and the law prophesied until John; 14 and if you are willing to accept it, he is Elijah who is to come. 15 He who has ears to hear,[t] let him hear."

plagues and evil spirits, and on many that were blind he bestowed sight. 22 And he answered them, "Go and tell John what you have seen and heard: the blind receive their sight, the lame walk, lepers are cleansed, and the deaf hear, the dead are raised up, the poor have good news preached to them. 23 And blessed is he who takes no offense at me!"

24 When the messengers of John had gone, he began to speak to the crowds concerning John: "What did you go out into the wilderness to behold? A reed shaken by the wind? 25 What then did you go out to see? A man clothed in soft raiment? Behold, those who are gorgeously appareled and live in luxury are in kings' courts. 26 What then did you go out to see? A prophet? Yes, I tell you, and more than a prophet. 27 This is he of whom it is written,

'Behold, I send my messenger
before thy face,
who shall prepare thy way
before thee.'

28 "I tell you, among those born of women none is greater than John; yet he who is least in the kingdom of God is greater than he." 29 (When they heard this all the people and the tax collectors justified God, having been baptized with the

[q] Or *What then did you go out to see? A man.*
[r] Many ancient authorities read *What then did you go out to see? A prophet?*
[s] Or *has been coming violently.*
[t] Some ancient authorities omit *to hear.*

Mt. 11	Mark	Lk. 7:18-30	John
		baptism of John; [30] but the Pharisees and the lawyers rejected the purpose of God for themselves, not having been baptized by him.)	

b. Condemning the wickedness of the generation

Mt. 11:16-19	Mark	Lk. 7:31-35	John
[16] "But to what shall I compare this generation? It is like children sitting in the market places and calling to their playmates, [17] 'We piped to you, and you did not dance; we wailed, and you did not mourn.' [18] For John came neither eating nor drinking, and they say, 'He has a demon'; [19] the Son of man came eating and drinking, and they say, 'Behold, a glutton and a drunkard, a friend of tax collectors and sinners!' Yet wisdom is justified by her deeds."*		[31] "To what then shall I compare the men of this generation, and what are they like? [32] They are like children sitting in the market place and calling to one another, 'We piped to you, and you did not dance; we wailed, and you did not weep.' [33] For John the Baptist has come eating no bread and drinking no wine; and you say, 'He has a demon.' [34] The Son of man has come eating and drinking; and you say, 'Behold, a glutton and a drunkard, a friend of tax collectors and sinners!' [35] Yet wisdom is justified by all her children."	

c. Upbraiding three impenitent cities

Mt. 11:20-24

[20] Then he began to upbraid the cities where most of his mighty works had been done, because they did not repent. [21] "Woe to you, Chorazin! woe to you, Bethsaida! for if the mighty works done in you had been done in Tyre and Sidon, they would have repented long ago in sackcloth and ashes. [22] But I tell you, it shall be more tolerable on the day of judgment for Tyre and Sidon than for you. [23] And you, Capernaum, will you be exalted to heaven? You shall be brought down to Hades. For if the mighty works done in you had been done in Sodom, it would have remained until this day. [24] But I tell you that it shall be more tolerable on the day of judgment for the land of Sodom than for you."

(See also Luke 10:13-15, article 77)

* Many ancient authorities read *children* (Luke 7:35).

d. Returning thanks for knowledge of God; inviting the weary to rest in him

Mt. 11:25-30

25 At that time Jesus declared, "I thank thee, Father, Lord of heaven and earth, that
thou hast hidden these things from the wise and understanding and revealed them to
babes; 26 yea, Father, for such was thy gracious will.* 27 All things have been delivered
to me by my Father; and no one knows the Son except the Father, and no one knows
the Father except the Son and any one to whom the Son chooses to reveal him.
28 Come to me, all who labor and are heavy-laden, and I will give you rest. 29 Take
my yoke upon you, and learn from me; for I am gentle and lowly in heart, and you
will find rest for your souls. 30 For my yoke is easy, and my burden is light."

(See also Luke 10:21, 22, article 77)

§ 43. Jesus, anointed by a penitent woman, gives a parable of the creditor who forgave two debtors

Lk. 7:36-50

36 One of the Pharisees asked him to eat with him, and he went into the Pharisee's
house, and sat at table. 37 And behold, a woman of the city, who was a sinner, when
she learned that he was sitting at table in the Pharisee's house, brought an alabaster
flask of ointment, 38 and standing behind him at his feet, weeping, she began to wet
his feet with her tears, and wiped them with the hair of her head, and kissed his feet,
and anointed them with the ointment. 39 Now when the Pharisee who had invited
him saw it, he said to himself, "If this man were a prophet, he would have known who
and what sort of woman this is who is touching him, for she is a sinner." 40 And
Jesus answering said to him, "Simon, I have something to say to you." And he
answered, "What is it, Teacher?" 41 "A certain creditor had two debtors; one owed
five hundred denarii, and the other fifty. 42 When they could not pay, he forgave
them both. Now which of them will love him more?" 43 Simon answered, "The one,
I suppose, to whom he forgave more." And he said to him, "You have judged rightly."
44 Then turning toward the woman he said to Simon, "Do you see this woman? I
entered your house, you gave me no water for my feet, but she has wet my feet with
her tears and wiped them with her hair. 45 You gave me no kiss, but from the time
I came in she has not ceased to kiss my feet. 46 You did not anoint my head with
oil, but she has anointed my feet with ointment. 47 Therefore I tell you, her sins,
which are many, are forgiven, for she loved much; but he who is forgiven little, loves
little." 48 And he said to her, "Your sins are forgiven." 49 Then those who were at
table with him began to say among themselves, "Who is this, who even forgives
sins?" 50 And he said to the woman, "Your faith has saved you: go in peace."

§ 44. Jesus and the twelve, with women ministering, engage in a preaching tour

Lk. 8:1-3

1 Soon afterward he went on through cities and villages, preaching and bringing
the good news of the kingdom of God. And the twelve were with him, 2 and also

* Or *so it was well-pleasing before thee.*

some women who had been healed of evil spirits and infirmities: Mary, called Magdalene, from whom seven demons had gone out, 3 and Joanna, the wife of Chuza, Herod's steward, and Susanna, and many others, who provided for them[w] out of their means.

§ 45. Jesus withstands friends, enemies, and relatives seeking to restrain him

a. Is charged with madness

Mk. 3:19b-21

19b Then he went home; 20 and the crowd came together again, so that they could not even eat. 21 And when his friends heard it, they went out to seize him, for they said, "He is beside himself."

b. Heals a blind and dumb demoniac; denies alliance with Beelzebub

Mt. 12:22-30

22 Then a blind and dumb demoniac was brought to him, and he healed him, so that the dumb man spoke and saw. 23 And all the people were amazed, and said, "Can this be the Son of David?" 24 But when the Pharisees heard it they said, "It is only by Beelzebub,[a] the prince of demons, that this man casts out demons." 25 Knowing their thoughts, he said to them, "Every kingdom divided against itself is laid waste, and no city or house divided against itself will stand; 26 and if Satan casts out Satan, he is divided against himself; how then will his kingdom stand? 27 And if I cast out demons by Beelzebub,[a] by whom do your sons cast them out? Therefore they shall be your judges. 28 But if it is by the Spirit of God that I cast out demons, then the kingdom of God has come upon you. 29 Or

Mk. 3:22-27

22 And the scribes who came down from Jerusalem said, "He is possessed by Beelzebub,[a] and by the prince of demons he casts out the demons." 23 And he called them to him, and said to them in parables, "How can Satan cast out Satan? 24 If a kingdom is divided against itself, that kingdom cannot stand. 25 And if a house is divided against itself, that house will not be able to stand. 26 And if Satan has risen up against himself and is divided, he cannot stand, but is coming to an end. 27 But no one can enter a strong man's house and plunder his goods, unless he first binds the strong man; then indeed he may plunder his house."

Luke

John

[w] Some ancient authorities read *him*.
[a] Greek *Beelzebul*.

Mt. 12:22-30	Mk. 3	Luke	John
how can one enter a strong man's house and plunder his goods, unless he first binds the strong man? Then indeed he may plunder his house. [30] He who is not with me is against me, and he who does not gather with me scatters."			

c. Discusses the eternal sin—blasphemy against the Holy Spirit, the seeking of signs, and other evils

Mt. 12:31-45	Mk. 3:28-30	Luke	John
[31] "Therefore I tell you, every sin and blasphemy will be forgiven men, but the blasphemy against the Spirit will not be forgiven. [32] And whoever says a word against the Son of man will be forgiven; but whoever speaks against the Holy Spirit will not be forgiven, either in this age or in the age to come. [33] "Either make the tree good, and its fruit good; or make the tree bad, and its fruit bad; for the tree is known by its fruit. [34] You brood of vipers! how can you speak good, when you are evil? For out of the abundance of the heart the mouth speaks. [35] The good man out of his good treasure brings forth good, and the evil man out of his evil treasure brings forth evil. [36] I tell you, on the day of judgment men will render account for every careless word they utter, [37] for by your words you will be justified, and by your words you will be condemned."	[28] "Truly, I say to you, all sins will be forgiven the sons of men, and whatever blasphemies they utter; [29] but whoever blasphemes against the Holy Spirit never has forgiveness, but is guilty of an eternal sin"— [30] for they had said, "He has an unclean spirit."		

Mt. 12:31-45 | Mk. 3 | Luke | John

[38] Then some of the scribes and Pharisees said to him, "Teacher, we wish to see a sign from you." [39] But he answered them, "An evil and adulterous generation seeks a sign; but no sign shall be given to it except the sign of the prophet Jonah. [40] For as Jonah was three days and three nights in the belly of the whale, so will the Son of man be three days and three nights in the heart of the earth. [41] The men of Nineveh will arise at the judgment with this generation and condemn it; for they repented at the preaching of Jonah, and behold, something greater than Jonah is here. [42] The queen of the South will arise at the judgment with this generation and condemn it; for she came from the ends of the earth to hear the wisdom of Solomon; and behold, something greater than Solomon is here.

[43] "When the unclean spirit has gone out of a man, he passes through waterless places seeking rest, but he finds none. [44] Then he says, 'I will return to my house from which I came.' And when he comes he finds it empty, swept, and put in order. [45] Then he goes and brings with him seven other spirits more evil than himself, and they enter and dwell there; and the last state of that man becomes worse than the first. So shall it be also with this evil generation."

(See also article 81)

d. Designates his true relatives

Mt. 12:46-50

[46] While he was still speaking to the people, behold, his mother and his brothers stood outside, asking to speak to him.[y] [48] But he replied to the man who told him, "Who is my mother, and who are my brothers?" [49] And stretching out his hand toward his disciples, he

Mk. 3:31-35

[31] And his mother and his brothers came; and standing outside they sent to him and called him. [32] And a crowd was sitting about him; and they said to him, "Your mother and your brothers[z] are outside, asking for you." [33] And he answered, "Who are my mother

Lk. 8:19-21

[19] Then his mother and his brothers came to him, but they could not reach him for the crowd. [20] And he was told, "Your mother and your brothers are standing outside, desiring to see you." [21] But he said to them, "My mother and my brothers are those who

John

[y] Some ancient authorities insert verse 47: *Some one told him, "Your mother and your brothers are standing outside, asking to speak to you."*

[z] Some early authorities add *and your sisters.*

Mt. 12:46-50

said, "Here are my mother and my brothers! [50] For whoever does the will of my Father in heaven is my brother, and sister, and mother."

Mk. 3:31-35

and my brothers?" [34] And looking around on those who sat about him, he said, "Here are my mother and my brothers! [35] Whoever does the will of God is my brother, and sister, and mother."

Lk. 8:19-21

hear the word of God and do it."

John

Section G. Christ's Parables of the Kingdom and His Journey into the Country of the Gerasenes

§ 46. Jesus gives nine parables of the kingdom of God

a. The soils

Mt. 13:1-9

[1] That same day Jesus went out of the house and sat beside the sea. [2] And great crowds gathered about him, so that he got into a boat and sat there; and the whole crowd stood on the beach. [3] And he told them many things in parables, saying: "A sower went out to sow. [4] And as he sowed, some seeds fell along the path, and the birds came and devoured them. [5] Other seeds fell on rocky ground, where they had not much soil, and immediately they sprang up, since they had no depth of soil, [6] but when the sun rose they were

Mk. 4:1-9

[1] Again he began to teach beside the sea. And a very large crowd gathered about him, so that he got into a boat and sat in it on the sea; and the whole crowd was beside the sea on the land. [2] And he taught them many things in parables, and in his teaching he said to them: [3] "Listen! A sower went out to sow. [4] And as he sowed, some seed fell along the path, and the birds came and devoured it. [5] Other seed fell on rocky ground, where it had not much soil, and immediately it sprang up, since it had no depth of soil; [6] and

Lk. 8:4-8

[4] And when a great crowd came together and people from town after town came to him, he said in a parable: [5] "A sower went out to sow his seed; and as he sowed, some fell along the path, and was trodden under foot, and the birds of the air devoured it. [6] And some fell on the rock; and as it grew up, it withered away, because it had no moisture. [7] And some fell among thorns; and the thorns grew with it and choked it. [8] And some fell into good soil and grew, and yielded a hundredfold." As he said this, he called out, "He who has

John

Mt. 13:1-9

scorched; and since they had no root they withered away. [7] Other seeds fell upon thorns, and the thorns grew up and choked them. [8] Other seeds fell on good soil and brought forth grain, some a hundredfold, some sixty, some thirty. [9] He who has ears,[a] let him hear."

Mk. 4:1-9

when the sun rose it was scorched, and since it had no root it withered away. [7] Other seed fell among thorns and the thorns grew up and choked it, and it yielded no grain. [8] And other seeds fell into good soil and brought forth grain, growing up and increasing and yielding thirtyfold and sixtyfold and a hundredfold." [9] And he said, "He who has ears to hear, let him hear."

Lk. 8:4-8

ears to hear, let him hear."

John

b. The reason for using parables and the explanation of the soils

Mt. 13:10-23

[10] Then the disciples came and said to him, "Why do you speak to them in parables?" [11] And he answered them, "To you it has been given to know the secrets of the kingdom of heaven, but to them it has not been given. [12] For to him who has will more be given, and he will have abundance; but from him who has not, even what he has will be taken away. [13] This is why I speak to them in parables, because seeing they do not see, and hearing they not hear,

Mk. 4:10-25

[10] And when he was alone, those who were about him with the twelve asked him concerning the parables. [11] And he said to them, "To you has been given the secret of the kingdom of God, but for those outside every thing is in parables; [12] so that they may indeed see but not perceive, and may indeed hear but not understand; lest they should turn again, and be forgiven." [13] And he said to them, "Do you not understand this parable? How then will

Lk. 8:9-18

[9] And when his disciples asked him what this parable meant, [10] he said, "To you it has been given to know the secrets of the kingdom of God; but for others they are in parables, so that seeing they may not see, and hearing they may not understand. [11] Now the parable is this: The seed is the word of God. [12] The ones along the path are those who have heard; then the devil comes and takes away the word from their hearts, that they may not be-

John

[a] Some ancient authorities add here and in verse 43 *to hear.*

Mt. 13:10-23

nor do they understand.
14 With them indeed is
fulfilled the prophecy
of Isaiah which says:

'You shall indeed
hear but never
understand,
and you shall in-
deed see but
never perceive.
15 For this people's
heart has grown
dull,
and their ears are
heavy of hear-
ing,
and their eyes
they have
closed,
lest they should per-
ceive with their
eyes,
and hear with
their ears,
and understand with
their heart,
and turn for me
to heal them.'

16 But blessed are your
eyes, for they see, and
your ears, for they hear.
17 Truly, I say to you,
many prophets and
righteous men longed
to see what you see,
and did not see it, and
to hear what you hear,
and did not hear it.

18 "Hear then the
parable of the sower.
19 When any one hears

Mk. 4:10-25

you understand all the
parables? 14 The sower
sows the word. 15 And
these are the ones along
the path, where the
word is sown; when
they hear, Satan im-
mediately comes and
takes away the word
which is sown in them.
16 And these in like
manner are the ones
sown upon rocky
ground, who, when
they hear the word, im-
mediately receive it
with joy; 17 and they
have no root in them-
selves, but endure for
a while; then, when
tribulation or persecu-
tion arises on account
of the word, immedi-
ately they fall away.[b]
18 And others are the
ones sown among
thorns; they are those
who hear the word,
19 but the cares of the
world, and the delight
in riches, and the de-
sire for other things,
enter in and choke the
word, and it proves un-
fruitful. 20 But those
that were sown upon
the good soil are the
ones who hear the
word and accept it and
bear fruit, thirtyfold
and sixtyfold and a

Lk. 8:9-18

lieve and be saved.
13 And the ones on the
rock are those who,
when they hear the
word, receive it with
joy; but these have no
root, they believe for a
while and in time of
temptation fall away.
14 And as for what fell
among the thorns, they
are those who hear,
but as they go on their
way they are choked by
the cares and riches
and pleasures of life,
and their fruit does not
mature. 15 And as for
that in the good soil,
they are those who,
hearing the word, hold
it fast in an honest and
good heart, and bring
forth fruit with pa-
tience.

16 "No one after
lighting a lamp covers
it with a vessel, or puts
it under a bed, but
puts it on a stand, that
those who enter may
see the light. 17 For
nothing is hid that
shall not be made mani-
fest, nor anything se-
cret that shall not be
known and come to
light. 18 Take heed
then how you hear; for
to him who has will
more be given, and

John

b Or *stumble.*

Mt. 13:10-23

the word of the kingdom and does not understand it, the evil one comes and snatches away what is sown in his heart; this is what was sown along the path. 20 As for what was sown on rocky ground, this is he who hears the word and immediately receives it with joy; 21 yet he has no root in himself, but endures for a while, and when tribulation or persecution arises on account of the word, immediately he falls away.[c] 22 As for what was sown among thorns, this is he who hears the word, but the cares of the world and the delight in riches choke the word, and it proves unfruitful. 23 As for what was sown on good soil, this is he who hears the word and understands it; he indeed bears fruit, and yields, in one case a hundredfold, in another sixty, and in another thirty."

Mk. 4:10-25

hundredfold."

21 And he said to them, "Is a lamp brought in to be put under a bushel, or under a bed, and not on a stand? 22 For there is nothing hid, except to be made manifest; nor is anything secret, except to come to light. 23 If any man has ears to hear, let him hear." 24 And he said to them, "Take heed what you hear; the measure you give will be the measure you get, and still more will be given you. 25 For to him who has will more be given; and from him who has not, even what he has will be taken away."

Lk. 8:9-18

from him who has not, even what he thinks that he has will be taken away."

John

c. The weeds, with explanation

Mt. 13:24-30, 36-43

24 Another parable he put before them, saying, "The kingdom of heaven may be compared to a man who sowed good seed in his field; 25 but while men were sleep-

[c] Or *stumbles.*

ing, his enemy came and sowed weeds among the wheat, and went away. 26 So when
the plants came up and bore grain, then the weeds appeared also. 27 And the
servants[a] of the householder came and said to him, 'Sir, did you not sow good seed
in your field? How then has it weeds?' 28 He said to them, 'An enemy has done this.'
The servants[a] said to him, 'Then do you want us to go and gather them?' 29 But he
said, 'No; lest in gathering the weeds you root up the wheat along with them. 30 Let
both grow together until the harvest; and at harvest time I will tell the reapers,
Gather the weeds first and bind them in bundles to be burned, but gather the wheat
into my barn.' "

36 Then he left the crowds and went into the house. And his disciples came to him,
saying, "Explain to us the parable of the weeds of the field." 37 He answered, "He
who sows the good seed is the Son of man; 38 the field is the world, and the good
seed means the sons of the kingdom; the weeds are the sons of the evil one, 39 and
the enemy who sowed them is the devil; the harvest is the close of the age, and the
reapers are angels. 40 Just as the weeds are gathered and burned with fire, so will it
be at the close of the age. 41 The Son of man will send his angels, and they will
gather out of his kingdom all causes of sin and all evil-doers, 42 and throw them into
the furnace of fire; there men will weep and gnash their teeth. 43 Then the righteous
will shine like the sun in the kingdom of their Father. He who has ears, let him
hear."

d. The virile seed and the fertile earth

Mk. 4:26-29

26 And he said, "The kingdom of God is as if a man should scatter seed upon the
ground, 27 and should sleep and rise night and day, and the seed should sprout and
grow, he knows not how. 28 The earth produces of itself, first the blade, then the
ear, then the full grain in the ear. 29 But when the grain is ripe, at once he puts in
the sickle, because the harvest has come."

e. The mustard seed; the leaven

Mt. 13:31-33

31 Another parable he put before them, saying, "The kingdom of heaven is like a grain of mustard seed which a man took
and sowed in his field; 32 it is
the smallest of all seeds, but when it has grown it is the greatest of shrubs and becomes a tree, so that the birds of the air come and make nests in its branches."

Mk. 4:30-32

30 And he said, "With what can we compare the kingdom of God, or what parable shall we
use for it? 31 It is like a grain
of mustard seed, which, when sown upon the ground, is the smallest of all the seeds on
earth; 32 yet when it is sown it
grows up and becomes the greatest of all shrubs, and puts forth large branches, so that the

Luke

John

[a] Or *slaves.*

Mt. 13:31-33	Mk. 4:30-32	Luke	John
[33] He told them another parable. "The kingdom of heaven is like leaven which a woman took and hid in three measures of meal, till it was all leavened."	birds of the air can make nests in its shade."		

(See also article 86)

f. Jesus' custom of using parables

Mt. 13:34,35	Mk. 4:33,34	Luke	John
[34] All this Jesus said to the crowds in parables; indeed he said nothing to them without a parable. [35] This was to fulfill what was spoken by the prophet:* "I will open my mouth in parables, I will utter what has been hidden since the foundation of the world."	[33] With many such parables he spoke the word to them, as they were able to hear it; [34] he did not speak to them without a parable, but privately to his own disciples he explained everything.		

g. The hidden treasure; the pearl of great value; the net; treasures old and new

Mt. 13:44-52

[44] "The kingdom of heaven is like treasure hidden in a field, which a man found and covered up; then in his joy he goes and sells all that he has and buys that field.

[45] "Again, the kingdom of heaven is like a merchant in search of fine pearls, [46] who, on finding one pearl of great value, went and sold all that he had and bought it.

[47] "Again, the kingdom of heaven is like a net which was thrown into the sea and gathered fish of every kind; [48] when it was full, men drew it ashore and sat down and sorted the good into vessels but threw away the bad. [49] So it will be at the close of the age. The angels will come out and separate the evil from the righteous, [50] and throw them into the furnace of fire; there men will weep and gnash their teeth.

[51] "Have you understood all this?" They said to him, "Yes." [52] And he said to them, "Therefore every scribe who has been trained for the kingdom of heaven is like a householder who brings out of his treasure what is new and what is old."

§ 47. Jesus calms the storm on the Sea of Galilee

Mt. 8:18, 23-27	Mk. 4:35-41	Lk. 8:22-25	John
[18] Now when Jesus saw great crowds	[35] On that day, when evening had come, he	[22] One day he got into a boat with his dis-	

* Some ancient authorities read *the prophet Isaiah.*

Mt. 8: 18,23-27

around him, he gave orders to go over to the other side.

[23] And when he got into the boat, his disciples followed him. [24] And behold, there arose a great storm on the sea, so that the boat was being swamped by the waves; but he was asleep. [25] And they went and woke him, saying, "Save, Lord; we are perishing." [26] And he said to them, "Why are you afraid, O men of little faith?" Then he rose and rebuked the winds and the sea; and there was a great calm. [27] And the men marveled, saying, "What sort of man is this, that even winds and sea obey him?"

Mk. 4:35-41

said to them, "Let us go across to the other side." [36] And leaving the crowd, they took him with them, just as he was, in the boat. And other boats were with him. [37] And a great storm of wind arose, and the waves beat into the boat, so that the boat was already filling. [38] But he was in the stern, asleep on the cushion; and they woke him and said to him, "Master, do you not care if we perish?" [39] And he awoke and rebuked the wind, and said to the sea, "Peace! Be still!" And the wind ceased, and there was a great calm. [40] He said to them, "Why are you afraid? Have you no faith?" [41] And they were filled with awe, and said to one another, "Who then is this, that even wind and sea obey him?"

Lk. 8:22-25

ciples, and he said to them, "Let us go across to the other side of the lake." So they set out, [23] and as they sailed he fell asleep. And a storm of wind came down on the lake, and they were filling with water, and were in danger. [24] And they went and woke him, saying, "Master, Master, we are perishing!" And he awoke and rebuked the wind and the raging waves; and they ceased, and there was a calm. [25] He said to them, "Where is your faith?" And they were afraid, and they wondered, saying to one another, "Who then is this, that he commands even wind and water, and they obey him?"

John

§ 48. Jesus heals and helps many

a. The Gerasene demoniac

Mt. 8:28-34

[28] And when he came to the other side, to the country of the Gadarenes,[f] two demoniacs

Mk. 5:1-20

[1] They came to the other side of the sea, to the country of the Gerasenes.[g] [2] And when he

Lk. 8:26-39

[26] Then they arrived at the country of the Gerasenes,[g] which is opposite Galilee. [27] And

John

[f] Many ancient authorities read *Gergesenes;* some, *Gerasenes.*
[g] Some ancient authorities read *Gergesenes,* some *Gadarenes.*

Mt. 8:28-34

met him, coming out of the tombs, so fierce that no one could pass that way. [29] And behold, they cried out, "What have you to do with us, O Son of God? Have you come here to torment us before the time?" [30] Now a herd of many swine was feeding at some distance from them. [31] And the demons begged him, "If you cast us out, send us away into the herd of swine." [32] And he said to them, "Go." So they came out and went into the swine; and behold, the whole herd rushed down the steep bank into the sea, and perished in the waters. [33] The swineherds fled, and going into the city they told everything, and what had happened to the demoniacs. [34] And behold, all the city came out to meet Jesus; and when they saw him, they begged him to leave their neighborhood.

Mk. 5:1-20

had come out of the boat, there met him out of the tombs a man with an unclean spirit, [3] who lived among the tombs; and no one could bind him any more, even with a chain; [4] for he had often been bound with fetters and chains, but the chains he wrenched apart, and the fetters he broke in pieces; and no one had the strength to subdue him. [5] Night and day among the tombs and the mountains he was always crying out, and bruising himself with stones. [6] And when he saw Jesus from afar, he ran and worshiped him; [7] and crying out with a loud voice, he said, "What have you to do with me, Jesus, Son of the Most High God? I adjure you by God, do not torment me." [8] For he had said to him, "Come out of the man, you unclean spirit!" [9] And Jesus[h] asked him, "What is your name?" He replied, "My name is Legion; for we are many." [10] And he begged him eagerly not to send

Lk. 8:26-39

as he stepped out on land, there met him a man from the city who had demons; for a long time he had worn no clothes, and he lived not in a house but in the tombs. [28] When he saw Jesus, he cried out and fell down before him, and said with a loud voice, "What have you to do with me, Jesus, Son of the Most High God? I beseech you, do not torment me." [29] For he had commanded the unclean spirit to come out of the man. (For many a time it had seized him; he was kept under guard, and bound with chains and fetters, but he broke the bonds and was driven by the demon into the desert.) [30] Jesus then asked him, "What is your name?" And he said, "Legion"; for many demons had entered him. [31] And they begged him not to command them to depart into the abyss. [32] Now a large herd of swine was feeding there on the hillside; and they begged him to let them enter these.

John

[h] Greek *he*.

Mt. 8	Mk. 5:1-20	Lk. 8:26-39	John

Mk. 5:1-20

them out of the coun-
try. [11] Now a great herd
of swine was feeding
there on the hillside;
[12] and they begged
him, "Send us to
the swine, let us enter
into them." [13] So he
gave them leave. And
the unclean spirits
came out, and entered
into the swine; and the
herd, numbering about
two thousand, rushed
down the steep bank
into the sea, and were
drowned in the sea.

[14] The swineherds
fled, and told it in the
city and in the country.
And people came to
see what it was that
had happened. [15] And
they came to Jesus, and
saw the demoniac sit-
ting there, clothed and
in his right mind, the
man who had had the
legion; and they were
afraid. [16] And those
who saw it told what
had happened to the
demoniac and to the
swine. [17] And they be-
gan to beg Jesus[i] to
depart from their
neighborhood. [18] And
as he was getting into
the boat, the man who
had been possessed with
demons begged him

Lk. 8:26-39

And he allowed them.
[33] Then the demons
came out of the man
and entered the swine,
and the herd rushed
down the steep bank
into the lake and were
drowned.

[34] When the herds-
men saw what had hap-
pened, they fled, and told
it in the city and in the
country. [35] Then people
went out to see what
had happened, and they
came to Jesus, and
found the man from
whom the demons had
gone, sitting at the feet
of Jesus, clothed and in
his right mind; and
they were afraid.
[36] And those who had
seen it told them how
he who had been pos-
sessed with demons
was healed. [37] Then all
the people of the sur-
rounding country of
the Gerasenes[g] asked
him to depart from
them; for they were
seized with great fear;
so he got into the boat
and returned. [38] The
man from whom the de-
mons had gone begged
that he might be
with him; but he sent
him away, saying,
[39] "Return to your

[g] Some ancient authorities read *Gadarenes, some Gergesenes.*
[i] Greek *him.*

Mt. 8

Mk. 5:1-20

that he might be with him. 19 But he refused, and said to him, "Go home to your friends, and tell them how much the Lord has done for you, and how he has had mercy on you." 20 And he went away and began to proclaim in the Decapolis how much Jesus had done for him; and all men marveled.

Lk. 8:26-39

home, and declare how much God has done for you." And he went away, proclaiming throughout the whole city how much Jesus had done for him.

John

b. Jairus' daughter and the woman with hemorrhage

Mt. 9:18-26

18 While he was thus speaking to them, behold, a ruler came in and knelt before him, saying, "My daughter has just died; but come and lay your hand on her, and she will live." 19 And Jesus rose and followed him, with his disciples. 20 And behold, a woman who had suffered from a hemorrhage for twelve years came up behind him and touched the fringe of his garment; 21 for she said to herself, "If I only touch his garment, I shall be made well." 22 Jesus turned, and seeing her he said, "Take heart, my daughter; your faith has

Mk. 5:21-43

21 And when Jesus had crossed again in the boat to the other side, a great crowd gathered about him; and he was beside the sea. 22 Then came one of the rulers of the synagogue, Jairus by name; and seeing him, he fell at his feet, 23 and besought him, saying, "My little daughter is at the point of death. Come and lay your hands on her, so that she may be made well, and live." 24 And he went with him.

And a great crowd followed him and thronged about him. 25 And there was a woman who had had a

Lk. 8:40-56

40 Now when Jesus returned, the crowd welcomed him, for they were all waiting for him. 41 And there came a man named Jairus, who was a ruler of the synagogue; and falling at Jesus' feet he besought him to come to his house, 42 for he had an only daughter, about twelve years of age, and she was dying.

As he went, the people pressed round him. 43 And a woman who had suffered from a flow of blood for twelve years[j] and could not be healed by any one, 44 came up behind him, and touched the fringe of his garment;

John

[j] Some ancient authorities add *and had spent all her living upon physicians.*

Mt. 9:18-26

made you well." And
instantly the woman
was made well. 23 And
when Jesus came to the
ruler's house, and saw
the flute players, and
the crowd making a
tumult, 24 he said, "De-
part; for the girl is not
dead but sleeping."
And they laughed at
him. 25 But when the
crowd had been put
outside, he went in and
took her by the hand,
and the girl arose.
26 And the report of
this went through all
that district.

Mk. 5:21-43

flow of blood for
twelve years, 26 and who
had suffered much un-
der many physicians,
and had spent all that
she had, and was no
better but rather grew
worse. 27 She had heard
the reports about Jesus,
and came up behind
him in the crowd and
touched his garment.
28 For she said, "If I
touch even his gar-
ments, I shall be made
well." 29 And immedi-
ately the hemorrhage
ceased; and she felt in
her body that she was
healed of her disease
30 And Jesus, perceiv-
ing in himself that
power had gone forth
from him, immediately
turned about in the
crowd, and said, "Who
touched my garments?"
31 And his disciples
said to him, "You see
the crowd pressing
around you, and yet
you say, 'Who touched
me?'" 32 And he
looked around to see
who had done it. 33 But
the woman, knowing
what had been done to
her, came in fear and
trembling and fell
down before him, and
told him the whole

Lk. 8:40-56

and immediately her
flow of blood ceased.
45 And Jesus said,
"Who was it that
touched me?" When
all denied it, Peter and
those who were with
him[k] said, "Master, the
multitudes surround
you and press upon
you!" 46 But Jesus said,
"Some one touched me;
for I perceive that
power has gone forth
from me." 47 And
when the woman saw
that she was not hid-
den, she came trem-
bling, and falling down
before him declared in
the presence of all the
people why she had
touched him, and how
she had been immedi-
ately healed. 48 And he
said to her, "Daughter,
your faith has made
you well; go in peace."
49 While he was still
speaking, a man from
the ruler's house came
and said, "Your daugh-
ter is dead; do not
trouble the Teacher any
more." 50 But Jesus on
hearing this answered
him, "Do not fear; only
believe, and she shall
be well." 51 And
when he came to the
house, he permitted no

John

k Some ancient authorities omit *and those who were with him.*

Mt. 9

Mk. 5:21-43

truth. [34] And he said
to her, "Daughter, your
faith has made you
well; go in peace, and
be healed of your dis-
ease."
[35] While he was still
speaking, there came
from the ruler's house
some who said, "Your
daughter is dead. Why
trouble the Teacher any
further?" [36] But ignor-
ing[l] what they said,
Jesus said to the ruler
of the synagogue, "Do
not fear, only believe."
[37] And he allowed no
one to follow him ex-
cept Peter and James
and John the brother
of James. [38] When
they came to the house
of the ruler of the syna-
gogue, he saw a tumult,
and people weeping
and wailing loudly.
[39] And when he had
entered, he said to
them, "Why do you
make a tumult and
weep? The child is not
dead but sleeping.
[40] And they laughed at
him. But he put them
all outside, and took
the child's father and
mother and those who
were with him, and
went in where the
child was. [41] Taking

Lk. 8:40-56

one to enter with him,
except Peter and John
and James, and the
father and mother of
the maiden. [52] And all
were weeping and be-
wailing her; but he
said, "Do not weep; for
she is not dead but
sleeping." [53] And they
laughed at him, know-
ing that she was dead.
[54] But taking her by
the hand he called, say-
ing, "Child, arise."
[55] And her spirit re-
turned, and she got up
at once; and he di-
rected that something
should be given her to
eat. [56] And her parents
were amazed; but he
charged them to tell no
one what had hap-
pened.

John

[l] Or *overhearing*. Many ancient authorities read *hearing*.

Mt. 9 | Mk. 5:21-43 | Lk. 8 | John

(Mk. 5:21-43)
her by the hand he said
to her, "Talitha cumi";
which means, "Little
girl, I say to you, arise."
42 And immediately the
girl got up and walked;
for she was twelve years
old. And immediately
they were overcome
with amazement.
43 And he strictly
charged them that no
one should know this,
and told them to give
her something to eat.

c. Two blind men, and a dumb demoniac

Mt. 9:27-34

27 And as Jesus passed on from there, two blind men followed him, crying aloud,
"Have mercy on us, Son of David." 28 When he entered the house, the blind men
came to him; and Jesus said to them, "Do you believe that I am able to do this?"
They said to him, "Yes, Lord." 29 Then he touched their eyes, saying, "According to
your faith be it done to you." 30 And their eyes were opened. And Jesus sternly
charged them, "See that no one knows it." 31 But they went away and spread his
fame through all that district.
32 As they were going away, behold, a dumb demoniac was brought to him. 33 And
when the demon had been cast out, the dumb man spoke; and the crowds marveled,
saying, "Never was anything like this seen in Israel." 34 But the Pharisees said, "He
casts out demons by the prince of demons."

§ 49. Jesus returns to Nazareth and is not honored

Mt. 13:53-58

53 And when Jesus had
finished these parables, he went
away from there, 54 and coming
to his own country he taught
them in their synagogue, so that
they were astonished, and said,
"Where did this man get this
wisdom and these mighty
works? 55 Is not this the carpen-

Mk. 6:1-6a

1 He went away from there
and came to his own country;
and his disciples followed him.
2 And on the sabbath he began
to teach in the synagogue; and
many who heard him were
astonished, saying, "Where did
this man get all this? What is
the wisdom given to him?

Luke

John

Mt. 13:53-58	Mk. 6:1-6a	Luke	John
er's son? Is not his mother called Mary? And are not his brothers James and Joseph and Simon and Judas? [56] And are not all his sisters with us? Where then did this man get all this?" [57] And they took offense at him. But Jesus said to them, "A prophet is not without honor except in his own country and in his own house." [58] And he did not do many mighty works there, because of their unbelief.	What mighty works are wrought by his hands! [3] Is not this the carpenter, the son of Mary and brother of James and Joses and Judas and Simon, and are not his sisters here with us?" And they took offense[m] at him. [4] And Jesus said to them, "A prophet is not without honor, except in his own country, and among his own kin, and in his own house." [5] And he could do no mighty work there, except that he laid his hands upon a few sick people and healed them. [6a] And he marveled because of their unbelief. (See also article 27)		

Section H. Christ's Sending Forth of the Twelve and His Journey into Phoenicia

§ 50. The twelve are instructed and sent out to minister

a. The plight of the people; the sending of the twelve

Mt. 9:35—10:4	Mk. 6:6b, 7	Lk. 9:1, 2	John
[35] And Jesus went about all the cities and villages, teaching in their synagogues and preaching the gospel of the kingdom, and healing every disease and every infirmity. [36] When he saw the crowds, he had compassion for them, because they were harassed and helpless, like sheep without a shepherd. [37] Then he said to his	[6b] And he went about among the villages teaching. [7] And he called to him the twelve, and began to send them out two by two, and gave them authority over the unclean spirits.	[1] And he called the twelve together and gave them power and authority over all demons and to cure diseases. [2] And he sent them out to preach the kingdom of God and to heal.	

[m] Or *stumbled.*

Mt. 9:35—10:4 | Mk. 6 | Lk. 9 | John

disciples, "The harvest is plentiful, but the laborers are few; [38] pray therefore the Lord of the harvest to send out laborers into his harvest."

[1] And he called to him his twelve disciples and gave them authority over unclean spirits, to cast them out, and to heal every disease and every infirmity. [2] The names of the twelve apostles are these: first, Simon, who is called Peter, and Andrew his brother; James the son of Zebedee, and John his brother; [3] Philip and Bartholomew, Thomas and Matthew the tax collector; James the son of Alphaeus, and Thaddaeus;[a] [4] Simon the Cananaean, and Judas Iscariot, who betrayed him.

b. Instructions for the journey

Mt. 10:5-15

[5] These twelve Jesus sent out, charging them, "Go nowhere among the Gentiles, and enter no town of the Samaritans, [6] but go rather to the lost sheep of the house of Israel. [7] And preach as you go, saying, 'The kingdom of heaven is at hand.' [8] Heal the sick, raise the dead, cleanse lepers, cast out demons. You received without pay, give without pay. [9] Take no gold, nor silver, nor copper in your purses,[b] [10] no bag for your journey, nor two tunics, nor sandals, nor a staff; for the laborer deserves his food. [11] And whatever town or village you en-

Mk. 6:8-11

[8] He charged them to take nothing for their journey except a staff; no bread, no bag, no money in their purses;[b] [9] but to wear sandals and not put on two tunics. [10] And he said to them, "Where you enter a house, stay there until you leave the place. [11] And if any place will not receive you and they refuse to hear you, when you leave, shake off the dust that is on your feet for a testimony against them."

Lk. 9:3-5

[3] And he said to them, "Take nothing for your journey, no staff, nor bag, nor bread, nor money; and do not have two tunics. [4] And whatever house you enter, stay there, and from there depart. [5] And wherever they do not receive you, when you leave that city shake off the dust from your feet as a testimony against them."

John

[a] Some ancient authorities read *Lebbaeus* or *Lebbaeus called Thaddaeus.*
[b] Greek *girdles.*

Mt. 10:5-15	Mk. 6	Lk. 9	John
ter, find out who is worthy in it, and stay with him until you depart. [12] As you enter the house, salute it. [13] And if the house is worthy, let your peace come upon it; but if it is not worthy, let your peace return to you. [14] And if any one will not receive you or listen to your words, shake off the dust from your feet as you leave that house or town. [15] Truly, I say to you, it shall be more tolerable on the day of judgment for the land of Sodom and Gomorrah than for that town."			

c. The persecution of the disciples and their fearless witness

Mt. 10:16-33

[16] "Lo, I send you out as sheep in the midst of wolves; so be wise as serpents and innocent as doves. [17] Beware of men; for they will deliver you up to councils, and flog you in their synagogues, [18] and you will be dragged before governors and kings for my sake, to bear testimony before them and the Gentiles. [19] When they deliver you up, do not be anxious how you are to speak or what you are to say; for what you are to say will be given to you in that hour; [20] for it is not you who speak, but the Spirit of your Father speaking through you. [21] Brother will deliver up brother to death, and the father his child, and children will rise against parents and have them put to death; [22] and you will be hated by all for my name's sake. But he who endures to the end will be saved. [23] When they persecute you in one town, flee to the next; for truly, I say to you, you will not have gone through all the towns of Israel, before the Son of man comes.

[24] "A disciple is not above his teacher, nor a servant[c] above his master; [25] it is enough for the disciple to be like his teacher, and the servant[c] like his master If they have called the master of the house Beelzebub,[d] how much more will they malign those of his household.

[26] "So have no fear of them; for nothing is covered that will not be revealed, or hidden that will not be known. [27] What I tell you in the dark, utter in the light; and what you hear whispered, proclaim upon the housetops. [28] And do not fear those who kill the body but cannot kill the soul; rather fear him who can destroy both soul and body in hell.[e] [29] Are not two sparrows sold for a penny? And not one of them will fall to the ground without your Father's will. [30] But even the hairs of your head are all numbered. [31] Fear not, therefore; you are of more value than many sparrows. [32] So every one who acknowledges me before men, I also will acknowledge before my Father who is in heaven; [33] but whoever denies me before men, I also will deny before my Father who is in heaven."

c Or *slave*.
d Greek *Beelzebul*.
e Greek *Gehenna*.

d. The cost and rewards of discipleship and service

Mt. 10:34—11:1

34 "Do not think that
I have come to bring
peace on earth; I have
not come to bring
peace, but a sword.
35 For I have come to
set a man against his
father, and a daughter
against her mother, and
a daughter - in - law
against her mother-in-
law; 36 and a man's foes
will be those of his
own household. 37 He
who loves father or
mother more than me
is not worthy of me;
and he who loves son
or daughter more than
me is not worthy of
me; 38 and he who does
not take his cross and
follow me is not
worthy of me. 39 He
who finds his life will
lose it, and he who
loses his life for my
sake will find it.

40 "He who receives
you receives me, and he
who receives me re-
ceives him who sent
me. 41 He who receives
a prophet because he is
a prophet shall receive
a prophet's reward, and
he who receives a
righteous man because
he is a righteous man
shall receive a right-

Mk. 6:12, 13

12 So they went out
and preached that men
should repent. 13 And
they cast out many
demons, and anointed
with oil many that
were sick and healed
them.

Lk. 9:6

6 And they departed
and went through the
villages, preaching the
gospel and healing
everywhere.

John

Mt. 10:34—11:1 | Mk. 6 | Lk. 9 | John

eous man's reward. 42 And whoever gives to one of these little ones even a cup of cold water because he is a disciple, truly, I say to you, he shall not lose his reward."
1 And when Jesus had finished instructing his twelve disciples, he went on from there to teach and preach in their cities.

(See also article 77)

§ 51. John the Baptist is martyred by Herod and Herodias

Mt. 14:1-12

1 At that time Herod the tetrarch heard about the fame of Jesus; 2 and he said to his servants, "This is John the Baptist, he has been raised from the dead; that is why these powers are at work in him." 3 For Herod had seized John and bound him and put him in prison, for the sake of Herodias, his brother Philip's wife;[g] because John said to him, 4 "It is not lawful for you to have her." 5 And though he wanted to put him to death, he feared the people, because they held him to be a prophet. 6 But when Herod's birthday came, the daughter of Herodias danced before the company, and pleased Herod, 7 so that he promised with an oath to give her whatever she might ask.

Mk. 6:14-29

14 King Herod heard of it; for Jesus' name had become known. Some[f] said, "John the baptizer has been raised from the dead; that is why these powers are at work in him." 15 But others said, "It is Elijah." And others said, "It is a prophet, like one of the prophets of old." 16 But when Herod heard of it he said, "John, whom I beheaded, has been raised." 17 For Herod had sent and seized John, and bound him in prison for the sake of Herodias, his brother Philip's wife; because he had married her. 18 For John had said to Herod, "It is not lawful for you to have your brother's wife." 19 And Herodias had a grudge against him, and wanted to kill him. But she could not,

Lk. 9:7-9

7 Now Herod the tetrarch heard of all that was done, and he was perplexed, because it was said by some that John had been raised from the dead, 8 by some that Elijah had appeared, and by others that one of the old prophets had risen. 9 Herod said, "John I beheaded; but who is this about whom I hear such things?" And he sought to see him.

John

[f] Some ancient authorities read *he*.
[g] A few ancient authorities read *his brother's wife*.

Mt. 14:1-12

8 Prompted by her
mother, she said, "Give
me the head of John
the Baptist here on a
platter." 9 And the king
was sorry; but because
of his oaths and his
guests he commanded
it to be given; 10 he
sent and had John be-
headed in the prison,
11 and his head was
brought on a platter
and given to the girl,
and she brought it to
her mother. 12 And his
disciples came and took
the body and buried it;
and they went and told
Jesus.

Mk. 6:14-29

20 for Herod feared
John, knowing that he
was a righteous and
holy man, and kept
him safe. When he
heard him, he was
much perplexed; and
yet he heard him
gladly. 21 But an op-
portunity came when
Herod on his birthday
gave a banquet for his
courtiers and officers
and the leading men of
Galilee. 22 For when
Herodias' daughter
came in and danced,
she pleased Herod and
his guests; and the king
said to the girl, "Ask
me for whatever you
wish, and I will grant
it." 23 And he vowed
to her, "Whatever you
ask me, I will give you,
even half of my king-
dom." 24 And she went
out, and said to her
mother, "What shall I
ask?" And she said,
"The head of John the
baptizer." 25 And she
came in immediately
with haste to the king,
and asked, saying, "I
want you to give me at
once the head of John
the Baptist on a plat-
ter." 26 And the king
was exceedingly sorry;
but because of his oaths
and his guests he did

Lk. 9

John

Mt. 14 | Mk. 6:14-29 | Lk. 9 | John

Mk. 6:14-29

not want to break his word to her. [27] And immediately the king sent a soldier of the guard and gave orders to bring his head. He went and beheaded him in the prison, [28] and brought his head on a platter, and gave it to the girl; and the girl gave it to her mother. [29] When the disciples heard of it, they came and took his body, and laid it in a tomb.

§ 52. Five thousand are fed after the twelve return to Jesus

Mt. 14:13-21

[13] Now when Jesus heard this, he withdrew from there in a boat to a lonely place apart. But when the crowds heard it they followed him on foot from the towns. [14] As he went ashore he saw a great throng; and he had compassion on them, and healed their sick. [15] When it was evening, the disciples came to him and said, "This is a lonely place, and the day is now over; send

Mk. 6:30-44

[30] The apostles returned to Jesus, and told him all that they had done and taught. [31] And he said to them, "Come away by yourselves to a lonely place, and rest a while." For many were coming and going, and they had no leisure even to eat. [32] And they went away in the boat to a lonely place by themselves. [33] Now many saw them going, and knew them, and they ran there on foot from

Lk. 9:10-17

[10] On their return the apostles told him what they had done. And he took them and withdrew apart to a city called Bethsaida. [11] When the crowds learned it, they followed him; and he welcomed them and spoke to them of the kingdom of God, and cured those who had need of healing. [12] Now the day began to wear away; and the twelve came and said to him, "Send the crowd away, to

Jn. 6:1-14

[1] After this Jesus went to the other side of the sea of Galilee, which is the sea of Tiberias. [2] And a multitude followed him, because they saw the signs which he did on those who were diseased. [3] Jesus went up into the hills, and there sat down with his disciples. [4] Now the Passover, the feast of the Jews, was at hand. [5] Lifting up his eyes, then, and seeing that a multitude was

Mt. 14:13-21

the crowds away to
go into the villages
and buy food for
themselves.''
16 Jesus said, "They
need not go away;
you give them
something to eat."
17 They said to
him, "We have
only five loaves
here and two fish."
18 And he said,
"Bring them here
to me." 19 Then
he ordered the
crowds to sit down
on the grass; and
taking the five
loaves and the two
fish he looked up
to heaven, and
blessed, and broke
and gave the loaves
to the disciples,
and the disciples
gave them to the
crowds. 20 And
they all ate and
were satisfied. And
they took up
twelve baskets full
of the broken
pieces left over.
21 And those who
ate were about five
thousand men, be-
sides women and
children.

Mk. 6:30-44

all the towns, and
got there ahead of
them. 34 As he
landed he saw a
great throng, and
he had compassion
on them, because
they were like
sheep without a
shepherd; and he
began to teach
them many things.
35 And when it
grew late, his dis-
ciples came to him
and said, "This is
a lonely place, and
the hour is now
late; 36 send them
away, to go into
the country and
villages round
about and buy
themselves some-
thing to eat."
37 But he answered
them, "You give
them something to
eat." And they
said to him, "Shall
we go and buy two
hundred denarii[a]
worth of bread,
and give it to them
to eat?" 38 And he
said to them,
"How many loaves
have you? Go and
see." And when
they had found
out, they said,

Lk. 9:10-17

go into the villages
and country round
about, to lodge and
get provisions; for
we are here in a
lonely place."
13 But he said to
them, "You give
them something to
eat." They said,
"We have no more
than five loaves
and two fish—un-
less we are to go
and buy food for
all these people."
14 For there were
about five thou-
sand men. And he
said to his dis-
ciples, "Make them
sit down in com-
panies, about fifty
each." 15 And they
did so, and made
them all sit down.
16 And taking the
five loaves and the
two fish he looked
up to heaven, and
blessed and broke
them, and gave
them to the dis-
ciples to set be-
fore the crowd.
17 And all ate and
were satisfied. And
they took up what
was left over,
twelve baskets of
broken pieces.

Jn. 6:1-14

coming to him,
Jesus said to
Philip, "How are
we to buy bread,
so that these
people may eat?"
6 This he said to
test him, for he
himself knew what
he would do.
7 Philip answered
him, "Two hun-
dred denarii[a]
would not buy
enough bread for
each of them to
get a little."
8 One of his dis-
ciples, Andrew,
Simon Peter's
brother, said to
him, 9 "There is a
lad here who has
five barley loaves
and two fish; but
what are they
among so many?"
10 Jesus said,
"Make the people
sit down." Now
there was much
grass in the place;
so the men sat
down, in number
about five thou-
sand. 11 Jesus
then took the
loaves, and when
he had given
thanks, he dis-
tributed them to

[a] See note on Matt. 18:28.

Mt. 14	Mk. 6:30-44	Lk. 9	Jn. 6:1-14
	"Five, and two fish." [39] Then he commanded them all to sit down by companies upon the green grass. [40] So they sat down in groups, by hundreds and by fifties. [41] And taking the five loaves and the two fish he looked up to heaven, and blessed, and broke the loaves, and gave them to the disciples to set before the people; and he divided the two fish among them all. [42] And they all ate, and were satisfied. [43] And they took up twelve baskets full of broken pieces and of the fish. [44] And those who ate the loaves were five thousand men.		those who were seated; so also the fish, as much as they wanted. [12] And when they had eaten their fill, he told his disciples, "Gather up the fragments left over, that nothing may be lost." [13] So they gathered them up and filled twelve baskets with fragments from the five barley loaves, left by those who had eaten. [14] When the people saw the sign which he had done, they said, "This is indeed the prophet who is to come into the world!"

(See also article 58)

§ 53. Jesus refuses a crown; prays; walks on the sea; returns to Gennesaret

Mt. 14:22-36	Mk. 6:45-56	Luke	Jn. 6:15-24
[22] Then he made the disciples get into the boat and go before him to the other side, while he dismissed the	[45] Immediately he made his disciples get into the boat and go before him to the other side, to Bethsaida,		[15] Perceiving then that they were about to come and take him by force to make him king, Jesus withdrew

Mt. 14:22-36

crowds. 23 And after he had dismissed the crowds, he went up into the hills by himself to pray. When evening came, he was there alone, 24 but the boat by this time was out on the sea,[i] beaten by the waves; for the wind was against them. 25 And in the fourth watch of the night he came to them, walking on the sea. 26 But when the disciples saw him walking on the sea, they were terrified, saying "It is a ghost!" And they cried out for fear. 27 But immediately he spoke to them, saying, "Take heart, it is I: have no fear."

28 And Peter answered him, "Lord, if it is you, bid me come to you on the water." 29 He said, "Come." So Peter got out of the boat and walked on the water and came to Jesus; 30 but when he saw the wind,[k] he was afraid, and beginning to sink he cried out, "Lord, save me." 31 Jesus immediately reached out his hand and caught him, saying to

Mk. 6:45-56

while he dismissed the crowd. 46 And after he had taken leave of them, he went into the hills to pray. 47 And when evening came, the boat was out on the sea, and he was alone on the land. 48 And he saw that they were distressed in rowing, for the wind was against them. And about the fourth watch of the night he came to them, walking on the sea. He meant to pass by them, 49 but when they saw him walking on the sea they thought it was a ghost, and cried out; 50 for they all saw him, and were terrified. But immediately he spoke to them and said, "Take heart, it is I; have no fear." 51 And he got into the boat with them and the wind ceased. And they were utterly astounded, 52 for they did not understand about the loaves, but their hearts were hardened.

53 And when they had crossed over, they came to land at Gennesaret, and moored to the shore. 54 And when

Luke

Jn. 6:15-24

again to the hills by himself.

16 When evening came, his disciples went down to the sea, 17 got into a boat, and started across the sea to Capernaum. It was now dark, and Jesus had not yet come to them. 18 The sea rose because a strong wind was blowing. 19 When they had rowed about three or four miles,[j] they saw Jesus walking on the sea and drawing near to the boat. They were frightened, 20 but he said to them, "It is I; do not be afraid." 21 Then they were glad to take him into the boat, and immediately the boat was at the land to which they were going.

22 On the next day the people who remained on the other side of the sea saw that there had been only one boat there, and that Jesus had not entered the boat with his disciples, but that his disciples had gone away alone. 23 However, boats from Tiberias came near the

[i] Some ancient authorities read *was many furlongs distant from the land.*
[j] Greek *twenty-five or thirty stadia.*
[k] Many ancient authorities read *strong wind.*

Mt. 14:22-36

him, "O man of little
faith, why did you
doubt?" 32 And when
they got into the boat,
the wind ceased. 33 And
those in the boat wor-
shiped him, saying,
"Truly you are the Son
of God."
34 And when they
had crossed over, they
landed at Gennesaret.
35 And when the men
of that place recognized
him, they sent round to
all that region and
brought to him all that
were sick, 36 and be-
sought him that they
might only touch the
fringe of his garment;
and as many as touched
it were made well.

Mk. 6:45-56

they got out of the
boat, immediately the
people recognized him,
55 and ran about the
whole neighborhood
and began to bring sick
people on their pallets
to any place where they
heard he was. 56 And
wherever he came, in
villages, cities, or country, they laid the sick in
the market places, and
besought him that they
might touch even the
fringe of his garment;
and as many as touched
it were made well.

Luke

Jn. 6:15-24

place where they ate
the bread after the
Lord had given thanks.
24 So when the people
saw that Jesus was not
there, nor his disciples,
they themselves got
into the boats and
went to Capernaum,
seeking Jesus.

§ 54. Jesus discourses on the Bread of Life; the Jews debate; many disciples fall away

Jn. 6:25-71

25 When they found him on the other side of the sea, they said to him, "Rabbi,
when did you come here?" 26 Jesus answered them, "Truly, truly, I say to you, you
seek me, not because you saw signs, but because you ate your fill of the loaves.
27 Do not labor for the food which perishes, but for the food which endures to
eternal life, which the Son of man will give to you; for on him has God the Father
set his seal." 28 Then they said to him, "What must we do, to be doing the work
of God?" 29 Jesus answered them, "This is the work of God, that you believe in
him whom he has sent." 30 So they said to him, "Then what sign do you do, that
we may see, and believe you? What work do you perform? 31 Our fathers ate
the manna in the wilderness; as it is written, 'He gave them bread from heaven to
eat.' " 32 Jesus then said to them, "Truly, truly, I say to you, it was not Moses who
gave you the bread from heaven; my Father gives you the true bread from heaven.
33 For the bread of God is that which comes down from heaven, and gives life to
the world." 34 They said to him, "Lord, give us this bread always."
35 Jesus said to them, "I am the bread of life; he who comes to me shall not

hunger, and he who believes in me shall never thirst. 36 But I said to you that you
have seen me and yet do not believe. 37 All that the Father gives me will come to
me; and him who comes to me I will not cast out. 38 For I have come down from
heaven, not to do my own will, but the will of him who sent me; 39 and this is the
will of him who sent me, that I should lose nothing of all that he has given me, but
raise it up at the last day. 40 For this is the will of my Father, that every one who
sees the Son and believes in him should have eternal life; and I will raise him up at
the last day."

41 The Jews then murmured at him, because he said, "I am the bread which came
down from heaven." 42 They said, "Is not this Jesus, the son of Joseph, whose
father and mother we know? How does he now say, 'I have come down from
heaven'?" 43 Jesus answered them, "Do not murmur among yourselves. 44 No one
can come to me unless the Father who sent me draws him; and I will raise him up
at the last day. 45 It is written in the prophets, 'And they shall all be taught by
God.' Every one who has heard and learned from the Father comes to me. 46 Not
that any one has seen the Father except him who is from God; he has seen the
Father. 47 Truly, truly, I say to you, he who believes has eternal life. 48 I am the
bread of life. 49 Your fathers ate the manna in the wilderness, and they died.

50 "This is the bread which comes down from heaven, that a man may eat of it
and not die. 51 I am the living bread which came down from heaven; if any one
eats of this bread, he will live for ever; and the bread which I shall give for the
life of the world is my flesh."

52 The Jews then disputed among themselves, saying, "How can this man give
us his flesh to eat?" 53 So Jesus said to them, "Truly, truly, I say to you, unless you
eat the flesh of the Son of man and drink his blood, you have no life in you; 54 he
who eats my flesh and drinks my blood has eternal life, and I will raise him up at
the last day. 55 For my flesh is food indeed, and my blood is drink indeed. 56 He
who eats my flesh and drinks my blood abides in me, and I in him. 57 As the living
Father sent me, and I live because of the Father, so he who eats me will live
because of me. 58 This is the bread which came down from heaven, not such as the
fathers ate and died; he who eats this bread will live forever." 59 This he said in the
synagogue, as he taught at Capernaum.

60 Many of his disciples, when they heard it, said, "This is a hard saying; who
can listen to it?" 61 But Jesus, knowing in himself that his disciples mumured at
it, said to them, "Do you take offense at this? 62 Then what if you were to see the
Son of man ascending where he was before? 63 It is the spirit that gives life, the
flesh is of no avail; the words that I have spoken to you are spirit and life. 64 But
there are some of you that do not believe." For Jesus knew from the first who
those were that did not believe, and who it was that should betray him. 65 And
he said, "This is why I told you that no one can come to me unless it is granted
him by the Father."

66 After this many of his disciples drew back and no longer went about with him.
67 Jesus said to the twelve, "Will you also go away?" 68 Simon Peter answered

him, "Lord, to whom shall we go? You have the words of eternal life; 69 and we
have believed, and have come to know, that you are the Holy One of God."
70 Jesus answered them, "Did I not choose you, the twelve, and one of you is a
devil?" 71 He spoke of Judas the son of Simon Iscariot, for he, one of the twelve,
was to betray him.

§ 55. Jesus condemns the traditionalism of the elders; declares that the source of evil is within

Mt. 15:1-20

1 Then Pharisees and scribes
came to Jesus from Jerusalem
and said, 2 "Why do your disciples transgress the tradition of
the elders? For they do not
wash their hands when they eat."
3 He answered them, "And why
do you transgress the commandment of God for the sake of
your tradition? 4 For God commanded, 'Honor your father and
your mother,' and, 'He who
speaks evil of father or mother,
let him surely die.' 5 But you
say, 'If any one tells his father
or his mother, What you would
have gained from me is given to
God,[n] he need not honor his
father.' 6 So, for the sake of
your tradition, you have made
void the law[p] of God. 7 You
hypocrites! Well did Isaiah
prophesy of you when he said:

8 'This people honors me with their lips,
but their heart is far from me;
9 in vain do they worship me,
teaching as doctrines the precepts of men.' "

10 And he called the people to

Mk. 7:1-23

1 Now when the Pharisees
gathered together to him, with
some of the scribes, who had
come from Jerusalem, 2 they
saw that some of his disciples
ate with hands defiled, that is,
unwashed. 3 (For the Pharisees,
and all the Jews, do not eat unless they wash their hands,
observing the tradition of the
elders; 4 and when they come
from the market place, they do
not eat unless they purify[l] themselves; and there are many other
traditions which they observe,
the washing of cups and pots
and vessels of bronze.[m]) 5 And
the Pharisees and the scribes
asked him, "Why do your disciples not live[o] according to the
tradition of the elders, but eat
with hands defiled?" 6 And he
said to them, "Well did Isaiah
prophesy of you hypocrites, as
it is written,

'This people honors me with their lips,
but their heart is far from me;
7 in vain do they worship me,
teaching as doctrines the precepts of men.'

Luke

John

[l] Some ancient authorities read *baptize*.
[m] Some ancient authorities add *and beds*.
[n] Or *an offering*.
[o] Greek *walk*.
[p] Many ancient authorities read *word*.

Mt. 15:1-20 | Mk. 7:1-23 | Luke | John

Mt. 15:1-20

him and said to them, "Hear
and understand: 11 not what
goes into the mouth defiles a
man, but what comes out of the
mouth, this defiles a man."
12 Then the disciples came and
said to him, "Do you know that
the Pharisees were offended
when they heard this saying?"
13 He answered, "Every plant
which my heavenly Father has
not planted will be rooted up.
14 Let them alone; they are
blind guides. And if a blind
man leads a blind man, both will
fall into a pit." 15 But Peter
said to him, "Explain the parable to us." 16 And he said, "Are
you also still without understanding? 17 Do you not see
that whatever goes into the
mouth passes into the stomach,
and so passes on?[r] 18 But what
comes out of the mouth proceeds from the heart, and this
defiles a man. 19 For out of the
heart come evil thoughts, murder, adultery, fornication, theft,
false witness, slander. 20 These
are what defile a man; but to eat
with unwashed hands does not
defile a man."

Mk. 7:1-23

8 You leave the commandment
of God, and hold fast the tradition of men."

9 And he said to them, "You
have a fine way of rejecting the
commandment of God, in order
to keep your tradition! 10 For
Moses said, 'Honor your father
and your mother'; and, 'He who
speaks evil of father or mother,
let him surely die'; 11 but you
say, 'If a man tells his father
or his mother, What you would
have gained from me is Corban'
(that is, given to God)[q]—
12 then you no longer permit
him to do anything for his
father or mother, 13 thus making
void the word of God through
your tradition which you hand
on. And many such things you
do."

14 And he called the people to
him again, and said to them,
"Hear me, all of you, and understand: 15 there is nothing outside a man which by going into
him can defile him; but the
things which come out of a man
are what defile him."[s] 17 And
when he had entered the house,
and left the people, his disciples
asked him about the parable.
18 And he said to them, "Then
are you also without understanding? Do you not see that whatever goes into a man from outside cannot defile him, 19 since
it enters, not his heart but his
stomach, and so passes on?"[t]

[q] Or *an offering.*
[r] Or *is evacuated.*
[s] Many ancient authorities add verse 16, *"If any man has ears to hear, let him hear."*
[t] Or *is evacuated.*

Mt. 15 | Mk. 7:1-23 | Luke | John

(Thus he declared all foods clean.) 20 And he said, "What comes out of a man is what defiles a man. 21 For from within, out of the heart of man, come evil thoughts, fornication, theft, murder, adultery, 22 coveting, wickedness, deceit, licentiousness, an evil eye, slander, pride, foolishness. 23 All these evil things come from within, and they defile a man."

§ 56. Jesus journeys toward Tyre and Sidon; a Syrophoenician woman's daughter is healed

Mt. 15:21-28 | Mk. 7:24-30 | Luke | John

Mt. 15:21-28

21 And Jesus went away from there and withdrew to the district of Tyre and Sidon. 22 And behold, a Canaanite woman from that region came out and cried, "Have mercy on me, O Lord, Son of David; my daughter is severely possessed by a demon." 23 But he did not answer her a word. And his disciples came and begged him, saying, "Send her away, for she is crying after us." 24 He answered, "I was sent only to the lost sheep of the house of Israel." 25 But she came and knelt before him, saying, "Lord, help me." 26 And he answered, "It is not fair to take the children's bread and throw it to the dogs." 27 She said, "Yes, Lord, yet even the dogs eat the crumbs that fall from their masters' table." 28 Then Jesus answered her, "O woman, great is your

Mk. 7:24-30

24 And from there he arose and went away to the region of Tyre and Sidon.[a] And he entered a house, and would not have any one know it; yet he could not be hid. 25 But immediately a woman, whose little daughter was possessed by an unclean spirit, heard of him, and came and fell down at his feet. 26 Now the woman was a Greek, a Syrophoenician by race. And she begged him to cast the demon out of her daughter. 27 And he said to her, "Let the children first be fed, for it is not right to take the children's bread and throw it to the dogs." 28 But she answered him, "Yes, Lord; yet even the dogs under the table eat the children's crumbs." 29 And he said to her, "For this saying you may go your way; the demon has left your daughter." 30 And she went home, and

[a] Some ancient authorities omit *and Sidon.*

Mt. 15:21-28

faith! Be it done for you as you desire." And her daughter was healed instantly.

Mk. 7:24-30

found the child lying in bed, and the demon gone.

Luke John

§ 57. Jesus returns through the region of the Decapolis; heals a deaf mute

Mt. 15:29-31

29 And Jesus went on from there and passed along the sea of Galilee. And he went up into the hills, and sat down there. 30 And great crowds came to him, bringing with them the lame, the maimed, the blind, the dumb, and many others, and they put them at his feet, and he healed them, 31 so that the throng wondered, when they saw the dumb speaking, the maimed whole, the lame walking and the blind seeing; and they glorified the God of Israel.

Mk. 7:31-37

31 Soon after this he returned from the region of Tyre, and went through Sidon to the sea of Galilee, through the region of the Decapolis. 32 And they brought to him a man who was deaf and had an impediment in his speech; and they besought him to lay his hand upon him. 33 And taking him aside from the multitude privately, he put his fingers into his ears, and he spat and touched his tongue; 34 and looking up to heaven, he sighed, and said to him, "Ephphatha," that is, "Be opened." 35 And his ears were opened, his tongue was released, and he spoke plainly. 36 And he charged them to tell no one; but the more he charged them, the more zealously they proclaimed it. 37 And they were astonished beyond measure, saying, "He has done all things well; he even makes the deaf hear and the dumb speak."

Luke John

§ 58. Four thousand are fed; Christ departs to the region of Magadan

Mt. 15:32-39

32 Then Jesus called his disciples to him and said, "I have compassion on the crowd, because they have been with me now three days, and have nothing to eat; and I am unwilling to send them away hungry, lest

Mk. 8:1-10

1 In those days, when again a great crowd had gathered, and they had nothing to eat, he called his disciples to him, and said to them, 2 "I have compassion on the crowd, because they have been with me now three

Luke John

Mt. 15:32-39	Mk. 8:1-10	Luke	John

Mt. 15:32-39

they faint on the way." 33 And the disciples said to him, "Where are we to get bread enough in the desert to feed so great a crowd?" 34 And Jesus said to them, "How many loaves have you?" They said, "Seven, and a few small fish." 35 And commanding the crowd to sit down on the ground, 36 he took the seven loaves and the fish, and having given thanks he broke them and gave them to the disciples, and the disciples gave them to the crowds. 37 And they all ate and were satisfied; and they took up seven baskets full of the broken pieces left over. 38 Those who ate were four thousand men, besides women and children. 39 And sending away the crowds, he got into the boat and went to the region of Magadan.

Mk. 8:1-10

days, and have nothing to eat; 3 and if I send them away hungry to their homes, they will faint on the way; and some of them have come a long way." 4 And his disciples answered him, "How can one feed these men with bread here in the desert?" 5 And he asked them, "How many loaves have you?" They said, "Seven." 6 And he commanded the crowd to sit down on the ground; and he took the seven loaves, and having given thanks he broke them and gave them to his disciples to set before the people; and they set them before the crowd. 7 And they had a few small fish; and having blessed them, he commanded that these also should be set before them. 8 And they ate, and were satisfied; and they took up the broken pieces left over, seven baskets full. 9 And there were about four thousand people. 10 And he sent them away; and immediately he got into the boat with his disciples, and went to the district of Dalmanutha.[v]

(See also article 52)

§ 59. Pharisees and Sadducees ask for a sign; Jesus warns the disciples to beware of their spirit

Mt. 16:1-12	Mk. 8:11-21	Luke	John

Mt. 16:1-12

1 And the Pharisees and Sadducees came, and to test him they asked him to show them a sign from heaven. 2 He answered them,[w] "When it is eve-

Mk. 8:11-21

11 The Pharisees came and began to argue with him, seeking from him a sign from heaven, to test him. 12 And he sighed deeply in his spirit, and said,

[v] Some ancient authorities read *Magadan* or *Magdala*.
[w] Many ancient authorities omit the following words to the end of verse 3.

Mt. 16:1-12

ning, you say, 'It will be fair weather; for the sky is red.' 3 And in the morning, 'It will be stormy today, for the sky is red and threatening. You know how to interpret the face of the heaven, but you cannot interpret the signs of the times. 4 An evil and adulterous generation seeks for a sign, but no sign shall be given to it except the sign of Jonah." So he left them and departed.

5 When the disciples reached the other side, they had forgotten to bring any bread. 6 Jesus said to them, "Take heed and beware of the leaven of the Pharisees and Sadducees." 7 And they discussed it among themselves, saying, "We brought no bread." 8 But Jesus, aware of this, said, "O men of little faith, why do you discuss among yourselves the fact that you have no bread? 9 Do you not yet perceive? Do you not remember the five loaves of the five thousand, and how many baskets you gathered? 10 Nor the seven loaves of the four thousand, and how many baskets you gathered? 11 How is it that you fail to perceive that I did not speak about bread? Beware of the leaven of the Pharisees and Sadducees." 12 Then they understood that he did not tell them to beware of the leaven of bread, but of the teaching of the Pharisees and Sadducees.

Mk. 8:11-21

"Why does this generation seek for a sign? Truly, I say to you, no sign shall be given to this generation." 13 And he left them, and getting into the boat again he departed to the other side.

14 Now they had forgotten to bring bread; and they had only one loaf with them in the boat. 15 And he cautioned them, saying, "Take heed, beware of the leaven of the Pharisees and the leaven of Herod."[a] 16 And they discussed it with one another, saying, "We have no bread." 17 And being aware of it, Jesus said to them, "Why do you discuss the fact that you have no bread? Do you not yet perceive or understand? Are your hearts hardened? 18 Having eyes do you not see, and having ears do you not hear? And do you not remember? 19 When I broke the five loaves for the five thousand, how many baskets full of broken pieces did you take up?" They said to him, "Twelve." 20 "And the seven for the four thousand, how many baskets full of broken pieces did you take up?" And they said to him, "Seven." 21 And he said to them, "Do you not yet understand?"

Luke

John

[a] Some ancient authorities read *the Herodians.*

§ 60. A blind man is healed near Bethsaida

Mk. 8:22-26

22 And they came to Bethsaida. And some people brought to him a blind man,
and begged him to touch him. 23 And he took the blind man by the hand, and led
him out of the village; and when he had spit on his eyes and laid his hands upon
him, he asked him, "Do you see anything?" 24 And he looked up and said, "I see
men; but they look like trees, walking." 25 Then again he laid his hands upon his
eyes; and he looked intently and was restored, and saw everything clearly. 26 And
he sent him away to his home, saying, "Do not even enter the village."

Section I. Christ's Journey to Caesarea Philippi and His Transfiguration

§ 61. Peter confesses Jesus' Messiahship

Mt. 16:13-20

13 Now when Jesus
came into the district
of Caesarea Philippi,
he asked his disciples,
"Who do men say that
the Son of man is?"
14 And they said, "Some
say John the Baptist,
others say Elijah, and
others Jeremiah or one
of the prophets." 15 He
said to them, "But who
do you say that I am?"
16 Simon Peter replied,
"You are the Christ,
the Son of the living
God." 17 And Jesus answered him, "Blessed
are you, Simon Bar-Jona! For flesh and
blood has not revealed
this to you, but my
Father who is in
heaven. 18 And I tell
you, you are Peter,[a] and
on this rock[b] I will

Mk. 8:27-30

27 And Jesus went
on with his disciples, to
the villages of Caesarea Philippi; and on
the way he asked his
disciples, "Who do men
say that I am?" 28 And
they told him, "John
the Baptist"; and others,
"Elijah"; and others,
"One of the prophets."
29 And he asked them,
"But who do you say
that I am?" Peter answered him, "You are
the Christ." 30 And he
charged them to tell no
one about him.

Lk. 9:18-20

18 Now it happened
that as he was praying
alone the disciples
were with him; and he
asked them, "Who do
the people say that I
am?" 19 And they answered, "John the
Baptist; but others say,
Elijah; and others, that
one of the old prophets
has risen." 20 And he
said to them, "But who
do you say that I am?"
And Peter answered,
"The Christ of God."

John

[a] Greek *Petros*.
[b] Greek *petra*.

Mt. 16:13-20 | Mk. 8 | Lk. 9 | John

Mt. 16:13-20

build my church, and the powers of death[c] shall not prevail against it. [19] I will give you the keys of the kingdom of heaven, and whatever you bind on earth shall be bound in heaven, and whatever you loose on earth shall be loosed in heaven." [20] Then he strictly charged the disciples to tell no one that he was the Christ.

§ 62. Jesus foretells his suffering, death, and resurrection; rebukes Peter's remonstrance

Mt. 16:21-23 | Mk. 8:31-33 | Lk. 9:21, 22 | John

Mt. 16:21-23

[21] From that time Jesus began to show his disciples that he must go to Jerusalem and suffer many things from the elders and chief priests and scribes, and be killed, and on the third day be raised. [22] And Peter took him and began to rebuke him saying, "God forbid, Lord! This shall never happen to you." [23] But he turned and said to Peter, "Get behind me, Satan! You are a hindrance[d] to me; for you are not on the side of God, but of men."

Mk. 8:31-33

[31] And he began to teach them that the Son of man must suffer many things, and be rejected by the elders and the chief priests and the scribes, and be killed, and after three days rise again. [32] And he said this plainly. And Peter took him, and began to rebuke him. [33] But turning and seeing his disciples, he rebuked Peter, and said, "Get behind me, Satan! For you are not on the side of God, but of men."

Lk. 9:21, 22

[21] But he charged and commanded them to tell this to no one, [22] saying, "The Son of man must suffer many things, and be rejected by the elders and chief priests and scribes, and be killed, and on the third day be raised."

[c] Greek *the gates of Hades.*
[d] Greek *stumbling-block.*

§ 63. Jesus speaks of cross-bearing and finding one's life

Mt. 16:24-28

[24] Then Jesus told his disciples, "If any man would come after me, let him deny himself and take up his cross and follow me. [25] For whoever would save his life will lose it, and whoever loses his life for my sake will find it. [26] For what will it profit a man, if he gains the whole world and forfeits his life? Or what shall a man give in return for his life? [27] For the Son of man is to come with his angels in the glory of his Father, and then he will repay every man for what he has done. [28] Truly, I say to you, there are some standing here who will not taste death before they see the Son of man coming in his kingdom."

Mk. 8:34—9:1

[34] And he called to him the multitude with his disciples, and said to them, "If any man would come after me, let him deny himself and take up his cross and follow me. [35] For whoever would save his life will lose it; and whoever loses his life for my sake and the gospel's will save it. [36] For what does it profit a man, to gain the whole world and forfeit his life? [37] For what can a man give in return for his life? [38] For whoever is ashamed of me and of my words in this adulterous and sinful generation, of him will the Son of man also be ashamed, when he comes in the glory of his Father with the holy angels." [1] And he said to them, "Truly, I say to you, there are some standing here who will not taste death before they see the kingdom of God come with power."

Lk. 9:23-27

[23] And he said to all, "If any man would come after me, let him deny himself and take up his cross daily and follow me. [24] For whoever would save his life will lose it; but whoever loses his life for my sake, he will save it. [25] For what does it profit a man if he gains the whole world and loses or forfeits himself? [26] For whoever is ashamed of me and of my words, of him will the Son of man be ashamed when he comes in his glory and the glory of the Father and of the holy angels. [27] But I tell you truly, there are some standing here who will not taste of death before they see the kingdom of God."

John

§ 64. The transfiguration takes place; Elijah's second coming is discussed

Mt. 17:1-13

[1] And after six days Jesus took with him

Mk. 9:2-13

[2] And after six days Jesus took with him

Lk. 9:28-36

[28] Now about eight days after these sayings

John

Mt. 17:1-13

Peter and James and John his brother, and led them up a high mountain apart. 2 And he was transfigured before them, and his face shone like the sun, and his garments became white as light. 3 And behold, there appeared to them Moses and Elijah, talking with him. 4 And Peter said to Jesus, "Lord, it is well that we are here; if you wish, I will make three booths here, one for you and one for Moses and one for Elijah." 5 He was still speaking, when lo, a bright cloud overshadowed them, and a voice from the cloud said, "This is my beloved Son,[f] with whom I am well pleased; listen to him." 6 When the disciples heard this, they fell on their faces, and were filled with awe. 7 But Jesus came and touched them, saying, "Rise, and have no fears." 8 And when they lifted up their eyes, they saw no one but Jesus only.

9 And as they were coming down the

Mk. 9:2-13

Peter and James and John, and led them up a high mountain apart by themselves; and he was transfigured before them, 3 and his garments became glistening, intensely white, as no fuller on earth could bleach them. 4 And there appeared to them Elijah with Moses; and they were talking to Jesus. 5 And Peter said to Jesus, "Master,[e] it is well that we are here: let us make three booths, one for you and one for Moses and one for Elijah." 6 For he did not know what to say, for they were exceedingly afraid. 7 And a cloud overshadowed them, and a voice came out of the cloud, "This is my beloved Son;[g] listen to him." 8 And suddenly looking around they no longer saw any one with them but Jesus only.

9 And as they were coming down the mountain, he charged them to tell no one what they had seen, until the Son of man should have risen from

Lk. 9:28-36

he took with him Peter and John and James, and went up on the mountain to pray. 29 And as he was praying, the appearance of his countenance was altered, and his raiment became dazzling white. 30 And behold, two men talked with him, Moses and Elijah, 31 who appeared in glory and spoke of his departure, which he was to accomplish at Jerusalem. 32 Now Peter and those who were with him were heavy with sleep but kept awake, and they saw his glory and the two men who stood with him. 33 And as the men were parting from him, Peter said to Jesus, "Master, it is well that we are here; let us make three booths, one for you and one for Moses and one for Elijah"—not knowing what he said. 34 As he said this, a cloud came and overshadowed them; and they were afraid as they entered the cloud. 35 And a voice came out of the cloud, say-

John

[e] Or *Rabbi.*
[f] Or *my Son, my* (or *the*) *Beloved.*
[g] Or *my Son, my* (or *the*) *Beloved.*

Mt. 17:1-13

mountain, Jesus com-
manded them, "Tell no
one the vision, until the
Son of man is raised
from the dead." 10 And
the disciples asked him,
"Then why do the
scribes say that first
Elijah must come?"
11 He replied, "Elijah
does come, and he is
to restore all things;
12 but I tell you that
Elijah has already come,
and they did not know
him, but did to him
whatever they pleased.
So also the Son of man
will suffer at their
hands." 13 Then the
disciples understood
that he was speaking to
them of John the Bap-
tist.

Mk. 9:2-13

the dead. 10 So they
kept the matter to
themselves, questioning
what the rising from
the dead meant. 11 And
they asked him, "Why
do the scribes say that
first Elijah must come?"
12 And he said to
them, "Elijah does
come first to restore all
things; and how is it
written of the Son of
man, that he should
suffer many things and
be treated with con-
tempt? 13 But I tell
you that Elijah has
come, and they did to
him whatever they
pleased, as it is written
of him."

Lk. 9:28-36

ing, "This is my Son,
my Chosen;[h] listen to
him!" 36 And when
the voice had spoken,
Jesus was found alone.
And they kept silence
and told no one in
those days anything of
what they had seen.

John

§ 65. The epileptic boy is healed

Mt. 17:14-21

14 And when they
came to the crowd, a
man came up to him
and kneeling before him
said, 15 "Lord, have mercy
on my son, for he is an
epileptic and he suffers
terribly; for often he
falls into the fire, and
often into the water.
16 And I brought him
to your disciples, and
they could not heal
him." 17 And Jesus an-

Mk. 9:14-29

14 And when they
came to the disciples,
they saw a great crowd
about them, and scribes
arguing with them.
15 And immediately all
the crowd, when they
saw him, were greatly
amazed, and ran up to
him and greeted him.
16 And he asked them,
"What are you discuss-
ing with them?"
17 And one of the

Lk. 9:37-43a

37 On the next day,
when they had come
down from the moun-
tain, a great crowd met
him. 38 And behold, a
man from the crowd
cried, "Master, I beg
you to look upon my
son, for he is my only
child; 39 and behold, a
spirit seizes him, and
he suddenly cries out;
it convulses him till he
foams, and shatters

John

[h] Many ancient authorities read *my Beloved.*

Mt. 17:14-21	Mk. 9:14-29	Lk. 9:37-43a	John
swered, "O faithless and perverse generation, how long am I to be with you? How long am I to bear with you? Bring him here to me." 18 And Jesus rebuked him, and the demon came out of him, and the boy was cured instantly. 19 Then the disciples came to Jesus privately and said, "Why could we not cast it out?" 20 He said to them, "Because of your little faith. For truly, I say to you, if you have faith as a grain of mustard seed, you will say to this mountain, 'Move hence to yonder place,' and it will move; and nothing will be impossible to you."[i]	crowd answered him, "Teacher, I brought my son to you, for he has a dumb spirit; 18 and wherever it seizes him, it dashes him down; and he foams and grinds his teeth and becomes rigid; and I asked your disciples to cast it out, and they were not able." 19 And he answered them, "O faithless generation, how long am I to be with you? How long am I to bear with you? Bring him to me." 20 And they brought the boy to him; and when the spirit saw him, immediately it convulsed the boy, and he fell on the ground and rolled about, foaming at the mouth. 21 And Jesus[j] asked his father, "How long has he had this?" And he said, "From childhood. 22 And it has often cast him into the fire and into the water, to destroy him; but if you can do anything, have pity on us and help us." 23 And Jesus said to him, "If you can! All things are possible to him who believes." 24 Immediately the	him, and will hardly leave him. 40 And I begged your disciples to cast it out, but they could not." 41 Jesus answered, "O faithless and perverse generation, how long am I to be with you and bear with you? Bring your son here." 42 While he was coming, the demon tore him and convulsed him. But Jesus rebuked the unclean spirit, and healed the boy, and gave him back to his father. 43a And all were astonished at the majesty of God.	

[i] Some ancient authorities insert verse 21, *"But this kind never comes out except by prayer and fasting."*
[j] Greek *he.*

Mt. 17 | Mk. 9:14-29 | Lk. 9 | John

father of the child cried out[k] and said, "I believe;
help my unbelief!" [25] And when Jesus saw that a
crowd came running together, he rebuked the unclean spirit, saying to it, "You dumb and deaf spirit,
I command you, come out of him, and never enter
him again." [26] And after crying out and convulsing
him terribly, it came out, and the boy was like a
corpse; so that most of them said, "He is dead."
[27] But Jesus took him by the hand and lifted him
up, and he arose. [28] And when he had gone home,
his disciples asked him privately, "Why could we
not cast it out?" [29] And he said to them, "This kind
cannot be driven out by anything but prayer."[l]

§ 66. Jesus foretells his death and resurrection a second time

Mt. 17:22, 23

[22] As they were gathering[m] in Galilee, Jesus said to them, "The Son of man is to be delivered into the hands of men, [23] and they will kill him, and he will be raised on the third day." And they were greatly distressed.

Mk. 9:30-32

[30] They went on from there and passed through Galilee. And he would not have any one know it; [31] for he was teaching his disciples, saying to them, "The Son of man will be delivered into the hands of men, and they will kill him; and when he is killed, after three days he will rise." [32] But they did not understand the saying, and they were afraid to ask him.

Lk. 9:43b-45

[43b] But while they were all marveling at everything he did, he said to his disciples, [44] "Let these words sink into your ears; for the Son of man is to be delivered into the hands of men." [45] But they did not understand this saying, and it was concealed from them, that they should not perceive it; and they were afraid to ask him about this saying.

John

§ 67. The half-shekel tax is found in the mouth of a fish

Mt. 17:24-27

[24] When they came to Capernaum, the collectors of the half-shekel tax went up
to Peter and said, "Does not your teacher pay the tax?" [25] He said, "Yes." And
when he came home, Jesus spoke to him first, saying, "What do you think, Simon?

[k] Many ancient authorities add *with tears.*
[l] Many ancient authorities add *and fasting.*
[m] Some ancient authorities read *abode.*

From whom do kings of the earth take toll or tribute? From their sons or from others?" [26] And when he said, "From others," Jesus said to him, "Then the sons are free. [27] However, not to give offense to them, go to the sea and cast a hook, and take the first fish that comes up, and when you open its mouth you will find a shekel; take that and give it to them for me and for yourself."

§ 68. The disciples dispute about rank; Jesus teaches childlike humility, self-denial, and concern for the young and the lowly

Mt. 18:1-14

[1] At that time the disciples came to Jesus, saying, "Who is the greatest in the kingdom of heaven?" [2] And calling to him a child, he put him in the midst of them, [3] and said, "Truly, I say to you, unless you turn and become like children, you will never enter the kingdom of heaven. [4] Whoever humbles himself like this child, he is the greatest in the kingdom of heaven.

[5] "Whoever receives one such child in my name receives me; [6] but whoever causes one of these little ones who believe in me to sin,[n] it would be better for him to have a great millstone fastened round his neck and to be drowned in the depth of the sea.

[7] "Woe to the world for temptations to sin![p]

Mk. 9:33-50

[33] And they came to Capernaum; and when he was in the house he asked them, "What were you discussing on the way?" [34] But they were silent; for on the way they had discussed with one another who was the greatest. [35] And he sat down and called the twelve; and he said to them, "If any one would be first, he must be last of all and servant of all." [36] And he took a child, and put him in the midst of them; and taking him in his arms, he said to them, [37] "Whoever receives one such child in my name receives me; and whoever receives me, receives not me but him who sent me."

[38] John said to him, "Teacher, we saw a man casting out demons in your name;[o] and we forbade him,

Lk. 9:46-50

[46] And an argument arose among them as to which of them was the greatest. [47] But when Jesus perceived the thought of their hearts, he took a child and put him by his side, [48] and said to them, "Whoever receives this child in my name receives me, and whoever receives me receives him who sent me; for he who is least among you all is the one who is great."

[49] John answered, "Master, we saw a man casting out demons in your name, and we forbade him, because he does not follow with us." [50] But Jesus said to him, "Do not forbid him; for he that is not against you is for you."

John

[n] Greek *causes . . . to stumble.*
[o] Some ancient authorities add *who does not follow us.*
[p] Greek *stumbling-blocks.*

Mt. 18:1-14

For it is necessary that temptations come, but woe to the man by whom the temptation comes! 8 And if your hand or your foot causes you to sin, cut it off and throw it from you; it is better for you to enter life maimed or lame than with two hands or two feet to be thrown into the eternal fire. 9 And if your eye causes you to sin, pluck it out and throw it from you; it is better for you to enter life with one eye than with two eyes to be thrown into the hell[r] of fire.

10 "See that you do not despise one of these little ones; for I tell you that in heaven their angels always behold the face of my Father who is in heaven.[s] 12 What do you think? If a man has a hundred sheep, and one of them has gone astray, does he not leave the ninety-nine on the hills and go in search of the one that went astray? 13 And if he finds it truly, I say to you, he rejoices over it more than over the

Mk. 9:33-50

because he was not following us." 39 But Jesus said, "Do not forbid him; for no one who does a mighty work in my name will be able soon after to speak evil of me. 40 For he that is not against us is for us. 41 For truly, I say to you, whoever gives you a cup of water to drink because you bear the name of Christ, will by no means lose his reward.

42 "Whoever causes one of these little ones who believe in me to sin,[q] it would be better for him if a great millstone were hung round his neck and he were thrown into the sea. 43 And if your hand causes you to sin,[q] cut it off; it is better for you to enter life maimed than with two hands to go to hell,[r] to the unquenchable fire.[t] 45 And if your foot causes you to sin,[q] cut it off; it is better for you to enter life lame than with two feet to be thrown into hell.[r, t] 47 And if your eye causes you to sin,[q] pluck it out; it is bet-

Lk. 9

John

[q] Or *stumble.*
[r] Greek *Gehenna.*
[s] Some ancient authorities add verse 11, *For the Son of man came to save that which was lost.*
[t] Verses 44 and 46 (which are identical with verse 48) are omitted by the best ancient authorities.

Mt. 18:1-14	Mk. 9:33-50	Lk. 9	John
ninety-nine that never went astray. [14] So it is not the will of my[u] Father who is in heaven that one of these little ones should perish."	ter for you to enter the kingdom of God with one eye than with two eyes to be thrown into hell,[r] [48] where their worm does not die, and the fire is not quenched. [49] For every one will be salted with fire.[v] [50] Salt is good; but if the salt has lost its saltness, how will you season it? Have salt in yourselves, and be at peace with one another."		

(See also article 91a)

§ 69. Jesus deals with reconciliation and forgiveness; gives the parable of the unforgiving servant

Mt. 18:15-35

[15] "If your brother sins against you, go and tell him his fault, between you and him alone. If he listens to you, you have gained your brother. [16] But if he does not listen, take one or two others along with you, that every word may be confirmed by the evidence of two or three witnesses. [17] If he refuses to listen to them, tell it to the church; and if he refuses to listen even to the church, let him be to you as a Gentile and a tax collector. [18] Truly, I say to you, whatever you bind on earth will be bound in heaven, and whatever you loose on earth will be loosed in heaven. [19] Again I say to you, if two of you agree on earth about anything they ask, it will be done for them by my Father in heaven. [20] For where two or three are gathered in my name, there am I in the midst of them."

[21] Then Peter came up and said to him, "Lord, how often shall my brother sin against me, and I forgive him? As many as seven times?" [22] Jesus said to him, "I do not say to you seven times, but seventy times seven.[w]

[23] "Therefore the kingdom of heaven may be compared to a king who wished to settle accounts with his servants. [24] When he began the reckoning, one was brought to him who owed him ten thousand talents;[x] [25] and as he could not pay, his lord ordered him to be sold, with his wife and children and all that he had, and payment to be made. [26] So the servant fell on his knees, imploring him, 'Lord, have patience with me, and I will pay you everything.' [27] And out of pity for him the lord of that

[r] Greek *Gehenna.*
[u] Some ancient authorities read *your.*
[v] Many ancient authorities add *and every sacrifice will be salted with salt.*
[w] Or *seventy-seven times.*
[x] This talent was probably worth about a thousand dollars.

servant released him and forgave him the debt. 28 But that same servant, as he went
out, came upon one of his fellow servants who owed him a hundred denarii;[y] and
seizing him by the throat he said, 'Pay what you owe.' 29 So his fellow servant fell
down and besought him, 'Have patience with me, and I will pay you.' 30 He refused
and went and put him in prison till he should pay the debt. 31 When his fellow
servants saw what had taken place, they were greatly distressed, and they went and
reported to their lord all that had taken place. 32 Then his lord summoned him and
said to him, 'You wicked servant! I forgave you all that debt because you besought
me; 33 and should not you have had mercy on your fellow servant, as I had mercy
on you?' 34 And in anger his lord delivered him to the jailers,[z] till he should pay all
his debt. 35 So also my heavenly Father will do to every one of you, if you do not
forgive your brother from your heart."

[y] The denarius was worth about twenty cents.
[z] Greek *torturers.*

Section J. Christ's Attendance at the Feasts of Tabernacles and Dedication

§ 70. Jesus attends the feast of Tabernacles; meets hostility

a. Goes privately to the feast

Jn. 7:1-15

1 After this Jesus went about in Galilee; he would not go about in Judea,
because the Jews[a] sought to kill him. 2 Now the Jews' feast of Tabernacles was at
hand. 3 So his brothers said to him, "Leave here and go to Judea, that your
disciples may see the works you are doing. 4 For no man works in secret if he seeks
to be known openly. If you do these things, show yourself to the world." 5 For
even his brothers did not believe in him. 6 Jesus said to them, "My time has not
yet come, but your time is always here. 7 The world cannot hate you, but it hates
me because I testify of it that its works are evil. 8 Go to the feast yourselves; I am
not[b] going up to the feast, for my time has not yet fully come." 9 So saying, he
remained in Galilee.

10 But after his brothers had gone up to the feast, then he also went up, not
publicly but in private. 11 The Jews were looking for him at the feast, and saying,
"Where is he?" 12 And there was much muttering about him among the people.
While some said, "He is a good man," others said, "No, he is leading the people
astray." 13 Yet for fear of the Jews no one spoke openly of him.

14 About the middle of the feast Jesus went up into the temple and taught.
15 The Jews marveled at it, saying, "How is it that this man has learning,[c] when
he has never studied?"

[a] Or *Judeans.*
[b] Many ancient authorities add *yet.*
[c] Or *this man knows his letters.*

b. Faces enemies

Jn. 7:16-24

16 So Jesus answered them, "My teaching is not mine, but his who sent me;
17 if any man's will is to do his will, he shall know whether the teaching is from God
or whether I am speaking on my own authority. 18 He who speaks on his own
authority seeks his own glory; but he who seeks the glory of him who sent him is
true, and in him there is no falsehood. 19 Did not Moses give you the law? Yet
none of you keeps the law. Why do you seek to kill me?" 20 The people answered,
"You have a demon! Who is seeking to kill you?" 21 Jesus answered them, "I did
one deed, and you all marvel at it. 22 Moses gave you circumcision (not that it is
from Moses, but from the fathers), and you circumcise a man upon the sabbath.
23 If on the sabbath a man receives circumcision, so that the law of Moses may
not be broken, are you angry with me because on the sabbath I made a man's
whole body well? 24 Do not judge by appearances, but judge with right judgment."

c. Is considered and denied as the Christ

Jn. 7:25-52

25 Some of the people of Jerusalem therefore said, "Is not this the man whom
they seek to kill? 26 And here he is, speaking openly, and they say nothing to him!
Can it be that the authorities really know that this is the Christ? 27 Yet we know
where this man comes from; and when the Christ appears, no one will know where
he comes from." 28 So Jesus proclaimed, as he taught in the temple, "You know
me, and you know where I come from? But I have not come of my own accord;
he who sent me is true, and him you do not know. 29 I know him, for I come from
him, and he sent me." 30 So they sought to arrest him; but no one laid hands on
him, because his hour had not yet come. 31 Yet many of the people believed in
him; they said, "When the Christ appears, will he do more signs than this man has
done?"

32 The Pharisees heard the crowd thus muttering about him, and the chief priests
and Pharisees sent officers to arrest him. 33 Jesus then said, "I shall be with you
a little longer, and then I go to him who sent me; 34 you will seek me and you will
not find me; where I am you cannot come." 35 The Jews said to one another,
"Where does this man intend to go that we shall not find him? Does he intend to
go to the Dispersion among the Greeks and teach the Greeks? 36 What does he
mean by saying, 'You will seek me and you will not find me,' and, 'Where I am
you cannot come'?"

37 On the last day of the feast, the great day, Jesus stood up and proclaimed,
"If any one thirst, let him come to me and drink. 38 He who believes in me, as[d]
the scripture has said, 'Out of his heart shall flow rivers of living water.'" 39 Now
this he said about the Spirit, which those who believed in him were to receive; for
as yet the Spirit had not been given, because Jesus was not yet glorified.

[d] Or *let him come to me, and let him who believes in me drink. As.*

40 When they heard these words, some of the people said, "This is really the
prophet." 41 Others said, "This is the Christ." But some said, "Is the Christ to
come from Galilee? 42 Has not the scripture said that the Christ is descended from
David, and comes from Bethlehem, the village where David was?" 43 So there was
a division among the people over him. 44 Some of them wanted to arrest him, but
no one laid hands on him.
45 The officers then went back to the chief priests and Pharisees, who said to
them, "Why did you not bring him?" 46 The officers answered, "No man ever spoke
like this man!" 47 The Pharisees answered them, "Are you led astray, you also?
48 Have any of the authorities or of the Pharisees believed in him? 49 But this
crowd, who do not know the law, are accursed." 50 Nicodemus, who had gone to
him before, and who was one of them, said to them, 51 "Does our law judge a man
without first giving him a hearing and learning what he does?" 52 They replied,
"Are you from Galilee too? Search and you will see that no prophet is to rise
from Galilee."[e]

§ 71. Jesus debates with Jews in the temple

a. On the Son as light of the world

Jn. 8:12-30

12 Again Jesus spoke to them, saying, "I am the light of the world; he who
follows me will not walk in darkness, but will have the light of life." 13 The Pharisees
then said to him, "You are bearing witness to yourself; your testimony is not true."
14 Jesus answered, "Even if I do bear witness to myself, my testimony is true, for
I know whence I have come and whither I am going, but you do not know whence I
come or whither I am going. 15 You judge according to the flesh, I judge no one.
16 Yet even if I do judge, my judgment is true, for it is not I alone that judge, but
I and he[f] who sent me. 17 In your law it is written that the testimony of two men
is true; 18 I bear witness to myself, and the Father who sent me bears witness to me."
19 They said to him therefore, "Where is your Father?" Jesus answered, "You
know neither me nor my Father; if you knew me, you would know my Father also."
20 These words he spoke in the treasury, as he taught in the temple; but no one
arrested him, because his hour had not yet come.
21 Again he said to them, "I go away, and you will seek me and die in your sin;
where I am going, you cannot come." 22 Then said the Jews, "Will he kill himself,
since he says, 'Where I am going, you cannot come'?" 23 He said to them, "You
are from below, I am from above; you are of this world, I am not of this world.

[e] Most of the ancient authorities either omit 7:53 - 8:11, or insert it, with variations of the text, here or at the end of this gospel or after Luke 21:38:
53 *They went each to his own house.* 1 *but Jesus went to the Mount of Olives.* 2 *Early in the morning he came again to the temple; all the people came to him, and he sat down and taught them.* 3 *The scribes and the Pharisees brought a woman who had been caught in adultery, and placing her in the midst* 4 *they said to him, "Teacher, this woman has been caught in the act of adultery.* 5 *Now in the law Moses commanded us to stone such. What do you say about her?"* 6 *This they said to test him, that they might have some charge to bring against him. Jesus bent down and wrote with his finger on the ground.* 7 *And as they continued to ask him, he stood up and said to them, "Let him who is without sin among you be the first to throw a stone at her."* 8 *And once more he bent down and wrote with his finger on the ground.* 9 *But when they heard it, they went away, one by one, beginning with the eldest, and Jesus was left alone with the woman standing before him.* 10 *Jesus looked up and said to her, "Woman, where are they? Has no one condemned you?"* 11 *She said, "No one, Lord." And Jesus said, "Neither do I condemn you; go, and do not sin again."*

[f] Many ancient authorities read *the Father*.

24 I told you that you would die in your sins, for you will die in your sins unless you
believe that I am he." 25 They said to him, "Who are you?" Jesus said to them,
"Even what I have told you from the beginning.[g] 26 I have much to say about you
and much to judge; but he who sent me is true, and I declare to the world what I
have heard from him." 27 They did not understand that he spoke to them of the
Father. 28 So Jesus said, "When you have lifted up the Son of man, then you will
know that I am he, and that I do nothing on my own authority but speak thus as the
Father taught me. 29 And he who sent me is with me; he has not left me alone,
for I always do what is pleasing to him." 30 As he spoke thus, many believed in him.

b. On spiritual freedom

Jn. 8:31-38

31 Jesus said to the Jews who had believed in him, "If you continue in my word,
you are my disciples, 32 and you will know the truth, and the truth will make you
free." 33 They answered him, "We are descendants of Abraham, and have never
been in bondage to any one. How is it that you say, 'You will be made free'?"
34 Jesus answered them, "Truly, truly, I say to you, every one who commits sin
is a slave to sin. 35 The slave does not continue in the house forever; the son
continues forever. 36 So if the Son makes you free, you will be free indeed. 37 I
know that you are descendants of Abraham; yet you seek to kill me, because my
word finds no place in you. 38 I speak of what I have seen with my Father, and
you do what you have heard from your father."

c. On sons of Abraham and the Son of God

Jn. 8:39-59

39 They answered him, "Abraham is our father." Jesus said to them, "If you
were Abraham's children, you would do what Abraham did, 40 but now you seek to
kill me, a man who has told you the truth which I heard from God; this is not what
Abraham did. 41 You do what your father did." They said to him, "We were
not born of fornication; we have one Father, even God." 42 Jesus said to them,
"If God were your Father, you would love me, for I proceeded and came forth
from God; I came not of my own accord, but he sent me. 43 Why do you not
understand what I say? It is because you cannot bear to hear my word. 44 You are
of your father the devil, and your will is to do your father's desires. He was a
murderer from the beginning, and has nothing to do with the truth, because there
is no truth in him. When he lies, he speaks according to his own nature, for he is a
liar and the father of lies. 45 But, because I tell the truth, you do not believe me.
46 Which of you convicts me of sin? If I tell the truth, why do you not believe me?
47 He who is of God hears the words of God; the reason why you do not hear them
is that you are not of God."
48 The Jews answered him, "Are we not right in saying that you are a Samaritan
and have a demon?" 49 Jesus answered, "I have not a demon; I honor my Father,

[g] Or *Why do I talk to you at all?*

and you dishonor me. [50] Yet I do not seek my own glory; there is One who seeks
it and he will be the judge. [51] Truly, truly, I say to you, if any one keeps my
word, he will never see death." [52] The Jews said to him, "Now we know that you
have a demon. Abraham died, as did the prophets; and you say, 'If any one
keeps my word, he will never taste death.' [53] Are you greater than our father
Abraham, who died? And the prophets died! Whom do you make yourself to
be?" [54] Jesus answered, "If I glorify myself, my glory is nothing; it is my Father
who glorifies me, of whom you say that he is your God. [55] But you have not known
him; I know him. If I said, I do not know him, I should be a liar like you; but I
do know him and I keep his word. [56] Your father Abraham rejoiced that he was
to see my day; he saw it and was glad." [57] The Jews then said to him, "You are
not yet fifty years old, and have you seen Abraham?"[h] [58] Jesus said to them,
"Truly, truly, I say to you, before Abraham was, I am." [59] So they took up stones
to throw at him; but Jesus hid himself, and went out of the temple.

§ 72. Jesus heals the man born blind

Jn. 9:1-41

[1] As he passed by, he saw a man blind from his birth. [2] And his disciples asked
him, "Rabbi, who sinned, this man or his parents, that he was born blind?" [3] Jesus
answered, "It was not that this man sinned, or his parents, but that the works of
God might be made manifest in him. [4] We must work the works of him who sent
me, while it is day; night comes, when no one can work. [5] As long as I am in the
world, I am the light of the world." [6] As he said this, he spat on the ground and
made clay of the spittle and anointed the man's eyes with the clay, [7] saying to him,
"Go, wash in the pool of Siloam" (which means Sent). So he went and washed
and came back seeing. [8] The neighbors and those who had seen him before as a
beggar, said, "Is not this the man who used to sit and beg?" [9] Some said, "It
is he"; others said, "No, but he is like him." He said, "I am the man." [10] They
said to him, "Then how were your eyes opened?" [11] He answered, "The man
called Jesus made clay and anointed my eyes and said to me, 'Go to Siloam and
wash'; so I went and washed and received my sight." [12] They said to him, "Where
is he?" He said, "I do not know."

[13] They brought to the Pharisees the man who had formerly been blind. [14] Now
it was a sabbath day when Jesus made the clay and opened his eyes. [15] The
Pharisees again asked him how he had received his sight. And he said to them,
"He put clay on my eyes, and I washed, and I see." [16] Some of the Pharisees said,
"This man is not from God, for he does not keep the sabbath." But others said,
"How can a man who is a sinner do such signs?" There was a division among
them. [17] So they again said to the blind man, "What do you say about him, since
he has opened your eyes?" He said, "He is a prophet."

[18] The Jews did not believe that he had been blind and had received his sight,

[h] Some ancient authorities read *has Abraham seen you?*

until they called the parents of the man who had received his sight, 19 and asked
them, "Is this your son, who you say was born blind? How then does he now see?"
20 His parents answered, "We know that this is our son, and that he was born
blind; 21 but how he now sees we do not know, nor do we know who opened his
eyes. Ask him; he is of age, he will speak for himself." 22 His parents said this
because they feared the Jews, for the Jews had already agreed that if any one
should confess him to be Christ, he was to be put out of the synagogue. 23 Therefore his parents said, "He is of age, ask him."

24 So for the second time they called the man who had been blind, and said to
him, "Give God the praise; we know that this man is a sinner." 25 He answered,
"Whether he is a sinner, I do not know; one thing I know, that though I was blind,
now I see." 26 They said to him, "What did he do to you? How did he open your
eyes?" 27 He answered them, "I have told you already, and you would not listen.
Why do you want to hear it again? Do you too want to become his disciples?"
28 And they reviled him, saying, "You are his disciple, but we are disciples of
Moses. 29 We know that God has spoken to Moses, but for this man, we do not
know where he comes from." 30 The man answered, "Why, this is a marvel! You
do not know where he comes from, and yet he opened my eyes. 31 We know that
God does not listen to sinners, but if any one is a worshiper of God and does his
will, God listens to him. 32 Never since the world began has it been heard that any
one opened the eyes of a man born blind. 33 If this man were not from God, he
could do nothing." 34 They answered him, "You were born in utter sin, and would
you teach us?" And they cast him out.

35 Jesus heard that they had cast him out, and having found him he said, "Do
you believe in the Son of man?"[i] 36 He answered, "And who is he, sir, that I may
believe in him?" 37 Jesus said to him, "You have seen him, and it is he who speaks
to you." 38 He said, "Lord, I believe"; and he worshiped him. 39 Jesus said, "For
judgment I came into this world, that those who do not see may see, and that those
who see may become blind." 40 Some of the Pharisees near him heard this, and
they said to him, "Are we also blind?" 41 Jesus said to them, "If you were blind,
you would have no guilt; but now that you say, 'We see,' your guilt remains.

§ 73. The good shepherd is portrayed in an allegory

Jn. 10:1-21

1 "Truly, truly, I say to you, he who does not enter the sheepfold by the door but
climbs in by another way, that man is a thief and a robber; 2 but he who enters by
the door is the shepherd of the sheep. 3 To him the gatekeeper opens; the sheep
hear his voice, and he calls his own sheep by name and leads them out. 4 When he
has brought out all his own, he goes before them, and the sheep follow him, for
they know his voice. 5 A stranger they will not follow, but they will flee from him,
for they do not know the voice of strangers." 6 This figure Jesus used with them,
but they did not understand what he was saying to them.

[i] Many ancient authorities read *the Son of God*.

7 So Jesus again said to them, "Truly, truly, I say to you, I am the door of the
sheep. 8 All who came before me are thieves and robbers; but the sheep did not
heed them. 9 I am the door; if any one enters by me, he will be saved, and will
go in and out and find pasture. 10 The thief comes only to steal and kill and
destroy; I came that they may have life, and have it abundantly. 11 I am the good
shepherd. The good shepherd lays down his life for the sheep. 12 He who is a
hireling and not a shepherd, whose own the sheep are not, sees the wolf coming
and leaves the sheep and flees; and the wolf snatches them and scatters them.
13 He flees because he is a hireling and cares nothing for the sheep. 14 I am the
good shepherd; I know my own and my own know me, 15 as the Father knows me
and I know the Father; and I lay down my life for the sheep. 16 And I have other
sheep, that are not of this fold; I must bring them also, and they will heed my
voice. So there shall be one flock, one shepherd. 17 For this reason the Father loves
me, because I lay down my life, that I may take it again. 18 No one takes it from
me, but I lay it down of my own accord. I have power to lay it down, and I have
power to take it again; this charge I have received from my Father."

19 There was again a division among the Jews because of these words. 20 Many
of them said, "He has a demon, and he is mad; why listen to him?" 21 Others
said, "These are not the sayings of one who has a demon. Can a demon open the
eyes of the blind?"

§ 74. Jesus attends the feast of Dedication in Jerusalem; returns beyond Jordan

Jn. 10:22-42

22 It was the feast of the Dedication at Jerusalem; 23 it was winter, and Jesus
was walking in the temple, in the portico of Solomon. 24 So the Jews gathered
round him and said to him, "How long will you keep us in suspense? If you are
the Christ, tell us plainly." 25 Jesus answered them, "I told you, and you do not
believe. The works that I do in my Father's name, they bear witness to me; 26 but
you do not believe, because you do not belong to my sheep. 27 My sheep hear my
voice, and I know them, and they follow me; 28 and I give them eternal life, and
they shall never perish, and no one shall snatch them out of my hand. 29 My
Father, who has given them to me,[f] is greater than all, and no one is able to
snatch them out of the Father's hand. 30 I and the Father are one."

31 The Jews took up stones again to stone him. 32 Jesus answered them, "I
have shown you many good works from the Father; for which of these do you stone
me?" 33 The Jews answered him, "We stone you for no good work but for
blasphemy; because you, being a man, make yourself God." 34 Jesus answered
them, "Is it not written in your law, 'I said, you are gods'? 35 If he called them
gods to whom the word of God came (and scripture cannot be broken), 36 do you
say of him whom the Father consecrated and sent into the world, 'You are
blaspheming,' because I said, 'I am the Son of God'? 37 If I am not doing the

[f] Some ancient authorities read *What my Father has given to me.*

works of my Father, then do not believe me; [38] but if I do them, even though you do not believe me, believe the works, that you may know and understand that the Father is in me and I am in the Father." [39] Again they tried to arrest him, but he escaped from their hands.

[40] He went away again across the Jordan to the place where John at first baptized, and there he remained. [41] And many came to him; and they said, "John did no sign, but everything that John said about this man was true." [42] And many believed in him there.

Section K. Christ's Further Work As Reported Largely by Luke Alone*

§ 75. Jesus departs from Galilee through Samaria to Judea beyond the Jordan

Mt. 19:1, 2

[1] Now when Jesus had finished these sayings, he went away from Galilee and entered the region of Judea beyond the Jordan; [2] and large crowds followed him, and he healed them there.

Mk. 10:1

[1] And he left there and went to the region of Judea and beyond the Jordan, and crowds gathered to him again; and again, as his custom was, he taught them.

Lk. 9:51-56

[51] When the days drew near for him to be received up, he set his face to go to Jerusalem. And he sent messengers ahead of him, [52] who went and entered a village of the Samaritans, to make ready for him; [53] but the people would not receive him, because his face was set toward Jerusalem. [54] And when his disciples James and John saw it, they said, "Lord, do you want us to bid fire come down from heaven and consume them?"[a] [55] But he turned and rebuked them.[b] [56] And they went on to another village.

John

[a] Some ancient authorities add *as Elijah did.*
[b] Some ancient authorities add *and he said, "You do not know what manner of spirit you are of; for the Son of man came not to destroy men's lives but to save them."*

* Sections K and L include the materials which pertain to what is often called *Christ's Perean Ministry.*

§ 76. Jesus sets tests for three hesitant disciples

Mt. 8:19-22	Mark	Lk. 9:57-62	John
19 And a scribe came up and said to him, "Master, I will follow you wherever you go." 20 And Jesus said to him, "Foxes have holes, and birds of the air have nests; but the Son of man has nowhere to lay his head." 21 Another of the disciples said to him, "Lord, let me first go and bury my father." 22 But Jesus said to him, "Follow me, and leave the dead to bury their own dead."		57 As they were going along the road, a man said to him, "I will follow you wherever you go." 58 And Jesus said to him, "Foxes have holes, and birds of the air have nests; but the Son of man has nowhere to lay his head." 59 To another he said, "Follow me." But he said, "Lord, let me first go and bury my father." 60 But he said to him, "Leave the dead to bury their own dead; but as for you, go and proclaim the kingdom of God." 61 Another said, "I will follow you, Lord; but let me first say farewell to those at my home." 62 Jesus said to him, "No one who puts his hand to the plow and looks back is fit for the kingdom of God."	

§ 77. Seventy, instructed and sent out to minister, return

Lk. 10:1-24

1 After this the Lord appointed seventy[c] others, and sent them on ahead of him,
two by two, into every town and place where he himself was about to come. 2 And
he said to them, "The harvest is plentiful, but the laborers are few; pray therefore the
Lord of the harvest to send out laborers into his harvest. 3 Go your way; behold, I
send you out as lambs in the midst of wolves. 4 Carry no purse, no bag, no sandals;
and salute no one on the road. 5 Whatever house you enter, first say, 'Peace be to this
house!' 6 And if a son of peace is there, your peace shall rest upon him; but if not,
it shall return to you. 7 And remain in the same house, eating and drinking what
they provide, for the laborer deserves his wages; do not go from house to house.
8 Whenever you enter a town and they receive you, eat what is set before you; 9 heal
the sick in it and say to them, 'The kingdom of God has come near to you.' 10 But
whenever you enter a town and they do not receive you, go into its streets and say,
11 'Even the dust of your town that clings to our feet, we wipe off against you;
nevertheless know this, that the kingdom of God has come near.' 12 I tell you, it shall
be more tolerable on that day for Sodom than for that town.

[c] Many ancient authorities read *seventy-two.*

[13] "Woe to you, Chorazin! woe to you, Bethsaida! For if the mighty works done in you had been done in Tyre and Sidon, they would have repented long ago, sitting in sackcloth and ashes. [14] But it shall be more tolerable in the judgment for Tyre and Sidon than for you. [15] And you, Capernaum, will you be exalted to heaven? You shall be brought down to Hades.

[16] "He who hears you hears me, and he who rejects you rejects me, and he who rejects me, rejects him who sent me."

[17] The seventy[c] returned with joy, saying, "Lord, even the demons are subject to us in your name!" [18] And he said to them, "I saw Satan fall like lightning from heaven. [19] Behold, I have given you authority to tread upon serpents and scorpions, and over all the power of the enemy; and nothing shall hurt you. [20] Nevertheless do not rejoice in this, that the spirits are subject to you; but rejoice that your names are written in heaven."

[21] In the same hour he rejoiced in the Holy Spirit and said, "I thank thee, Father, Lord of heaven and earth, that thou hast hidden these things from the wise and understanding and revealed them to babes; yea, Father, for such was thy gracious will.[d] [22] All things have been delivered to me by my Father; and no one knows who the Son is except the Father, or who the Father is except the Son and any one to whom the Son chooses to reveal him."

[23] Then turning to the disciples he said privately, "Blessed are the eyes which see what you see! [24] For I tell you that many prophets and kings desired to see what you see, and did not see it, and to hear what you hear, and did not hear it."

(See also articles 42c, d and 50)

§ 78. Jesus tells the parable of the good Samaritan

Lk. 10:25-37

[25] And behold, a lawyer stood up to put him to the test, saying, "Teacher, what shall I do to inherit eternal life?" [26] He said to him, "What is written in the law? How do you read?" [27] And he answered, "You shall love the Lord your God with all your heart, and with all your soul, and with all your strength, and with all your mind; and your neighbor as yourself." [28] And he said to him, "You have answered right; do this, and you will live."

[29] But he, desiring to justify himself, said to Jesus, "And who is my neighbor?" [30] Jesus replied, "A man was going down from Jerusalem to Jericho, and he fell among robbers, who stripped him and beat him, and departed, leaving him half-dead. [31] Now by chance a priest was going down that road; and when he saw him he passed by on the other side. [32] So likewise a Levite, when he came to the place and saw him, passed by on the other side. [33] But a Samaritan, as he journeyed, came to where he was; and when he saw him, he had compassion, [34] and went to him and bound up his wounds, pouring on oil and wine; then he set him on his own beast and brought him to an inn, and took care of him. [35] And the next day he took out two

[c] Many ancient authorities read *seventy-two.*
[d] Or *so it was well-pleasing before thee.*

denarii[e] and gave them to the innkeeper, saying, 'Take care of him; and whatever
more you spend, I will repay you when I come back.' 36 Which of these three, do
you think, proved neighbor to the man who fell among the robbers?" 37 He said,
"The one who showed mercy on him." And Jesus said to him, "Go and do likewise."

§ 79. Jesus visits the home of Martha and Mary in Bethany

Lk. 10:38-42

38 Now as they went on their way, he entered a village; and a woman named
Martha received him into her house. 39 And she had a sister called Mary, who sat
at the Lord's feet and listened to his teaching. 40 But Martha was distracted with
much serving; and she went to him and said, "Lord, do you not care that my sister
has left me to serve alone? Tell her then to help me." 41 But the Lord answered her,
"Martha, Martha, you are anxious and troubled about many things; 42 one thing is
needful.[f] Mary has chosen the good portion, which shall not be taken away from her."

§ 80. Jesus teaches his disciples how to prevail in prayer; speaks parable of the friend calling at midnight. The Lord's Prayer

Lk. 11:1-13

1 He was praying in a certain place, and when he ceased, one of his disciples said
to him, "Lord, teach us to pray, as John taught his disciples." 2 And he said to them,
"When you pray, say:

"Father, hallowed be thy name. Thy kingdom come. 3 Give us each day our daily
bread;[g] 4 and forgive us our sins, for we ourselves forgive every one who is indebted
to us; and lead us not into temptation."

5 And he said to them, "Which of you who has a friend will go to him at midnight
and say to him, 'Friend, lend me three loaves; 6 for a friend of mine has arrived on a
journey, and I have nothing to set before him'; 7 and he will answer from within, 'Do
not bother me; the door is now shut, and my children are with me in bed; I cannot
get up and give you anything'? 8 I tell you, though he will not get up and give him
anything because he is his friend, yet because of his importunity he will rise and
give him whatever he needs. 9 And I tell you, Ask, and it will be given you; seek,
and you will find; knock, and it will be opened to you. 10 For every one who asks
receives, and he who seeks finds, and to him who knocks it will be opened. 11 What
father among you, if his son asks for[h] a fish, will instead of a fish give him a serpent;
12 or if he asks for an egg, will give him a scorpion? 13 If you then, who are evil,
know how to give good gifts to your children, how much more will the heavenly
Father give the Holy Spirit to those who ask him?"

(See also Matt. 6:9-15, article 39e)

[e] See note on Matt. 18:28.
[f] Many ancient authorities read *few things are needful, or only one.*
[g] Or *our bread for the morrow.*
[h] Some ancient authorities insert *a loaf, will give him a stone: or if he asks for.*

§ 81. Jesus discusses casting out demons by Beelzebub, the sign of Jonah, and inner light

Lk. 11:14-36

[14] Now he was casting out a demon that was dumb; when the demon had gone
out, the dumb man spoke, and the people marveled. [15] But some of them said, "He
casts out demons by Beelzebub,[t] the prince of demons"; [16] while others, to try him,
sought from him a sign from heaven. [17] But he, knowing their thoughts, said to
them, "Every kingdom divided against itself is laid waste, and house falls upon
house. [18] And if Satan also is divided against himself, how will his kingdom stand?
For you say that I cast out demons by Beelzebub. [19] And if I cast out demons by
Beelzebub, by whom do your sons cast them out? Therefore they shall be your
judges. [20] But if it is by the finger of God that I cast out demons, then the kingdom
of God has come upon you. [21] When a strong man, fully armed, guards his own
palace, his goods are in peace; [22] but when one stronger than he assails him and
overcomes him, he takes away his armor in which he trusted, and divides his spoil.
[23] He who is not with me is against me; and he who does not gather with me scatters.

[24] "When the unclean spirit has gone out of a man, he passes through waterless
places seeking rest; and finding none he says, 'I will return to my house from which
I came.' [25] And when he comes he finds it swept and put in order. [26] Then he goes
and brings seven other spirits more evil than himself, and they enter and dwell there;
and the last state of that man becomes worse than the first."

[27] As he said this, a woman in the crowd raised her voice and said to him, "Blessed
is the womb that bore you, and the breasts that you sucked!" [28] But he said, "Blessed
rather are those who hear the word of God and keep it!"

[29] When the crowds were increasing, he began to say, "This generation is an evil
generation; it seeks a sign, but no sign shall be given to it except the sign of Jonah.
[30] For as Jonah became a sign to the men of Nineveh, so will the Son of man be to
this generation. [31] The queen of the South will arise at the judgment with the men
of this generation and condemn them; for she came from the ends of the earth to
hear the wisdom of Solomon, and behold, something greater than Solomon is here.
[32] The men of Nineveh will arise at the judgment with this generation and condemn
it; for they repented at the preaching of Jonah, and behold, something greater than
Jonah is here.

[33] "No one after lighting a lamp puts it in a cellar or under a bushel, but on a
stand, that those who enter may see the light. [34] Your eye is the lamp of your body;
when your eye is sound, your whole body is full of light; but when it is not sound,
your body is full of darkness. [35] Therefore be careful lest the light in you be darkness.
[36] If then your whole body is full of light, having no part dark, it will be wholly
bright, as when a lamp with its rays gives you light."

(See also article 45)

[t] Greek *Beelzebul.*

§ 82. At a Pharisee's table Jesus pronounces woes upon Pharisees and lawyers

Lk. 11:37-54

37 While he was speaking, a Pharisee asked him to dine with him; so he went in
and sat at table. 38 The Pharisee was astonished to see that he did not first wash
before dinner. 39 And the Lord said to him, "Now you Pharisees cleanse the outside
of the cup and of the dish, but inside you are full of extortion and wickedness. 40 You
fools! Did not he who made the outside make the inside also? 41 But give for alms
those things which are within; and behold, everything is clean for you.

42 "But woe to you Pharisees! For you tithe mint and rue and every herb, and
neglect justice and the love of God; these you ought to have done without neglecting
the others. 43 Woe to you Pharisees! For you love the best seats in synagogues and
salutations in the market places. 44 Woe to you! For you are like graves which are
not seen, and men walk over them without knowing it."

45 One of the lawyers answered him, "Teacher, in saying this you reproach us
also." 46 And he said, "Woe to you lawyers also! For you load men with burdens
hard to bear, and you yourselves do not touch the burdens with one of your fingers.
47 Woe to you! For you build the tombs of the prophets whom your fathers killed.
48 So you are witnesses and consent to the deeds of your fathers; for they killed them,
and you build their tombs. 49 Therefore also the Wisdom of God said, 'I will send
them prophets and apostles, some of whom they will kill and persecute,' 50 that the
blood of all the prophets, shed from the foundation of the world, may be required
of this generation, 51 from the blood of Abel to the blood of Zechariah, who perished
between the altar and the sanctuary. Yes, I tell you, it shall be required of this
generation. 52 Woe to you lawyers! For you have taken away the key of knowledge;
you did not enter yourselves, and you hindered those who were entering."

53 As he went away from there, the scribes and the Pharisees began to press
him hard, and to provoke him to speak of many things, 54 lying in wait for him, to
catch at something he might say.

(See also article 113)

§ 83. Jesus talks to the disciples on trust and watchfulness

a. God's care of the confessor

Lk. 12:1-12

1 In the meantime, when so many thousands of the multitude had gathered together
that they trod upon one another, he began to say to his disciples first, "Beware of the
leaven of the Pharisees, which is hypocrisy. 2 Nothing is covered up that will not be
revealed, or hidden that will not be known. 3 Whatever you have said in the dark
shall be heard in the light, and what you have whispered in private rooms shall be
proclaimed upon the housetops.

4 "I tell you, my friends, do not fear those who kill the body, and after that have
no more that they can do. 5 But I will warn you whom to fear: fear him who, after
he has killed, has power to cast into hell;[j] yes, I tell you, fear him! 6 Are not five

[j] Greek *Gehenna.*

sparrows sold for two pennies? And not one of them is forgotten before God. 7 Why, even the hairs of your head are all numbered. Fear not; you are of more value than many sparrows.

8 "And I tell you, every one who acknowledges me before men, the Son of man also will acknowledge before the angels of God; 9 but he who denies me before men will be denied before the angels of God. 10 And every one who speaks a word against the Son of man will be forgiven; but he who blasphemes against the Holy Spirit will not be forgiven. 11 And when they bring you before the synagogues and the rulers and the authorities, do not be anxious how or what you are to answer or what you are to say; 12 for the Holy Spirit will teach you in that very hour what you ought to say."

b. The parable of the foolish rich man

Lk. 12:13-21

13 One of the multitude said to him, "Teacher, bid my brother divide the inheritance with me." 14 But he said to him, "Man, who made me a judge or divider over you?" 15 And he said to them, "Take heed, and beware of all covetousness; for a man's life does not consist in the abundance of his possessions." 16 And he told them a parable, saying, "The land of a rich man brought forth plentifully; 17 and he thought to himself, 'What shall I do, for I have nowhere to store my crops?' 18 And he said, 'I will do this: I will pull down my barns, and build larger ones; and there I will store all my grain and my goods. 19 And I will say to my soul, Soul, you have ample goods laid up for many years; take your ease, eat, drink, be merry.' 20 But God said to him, 'Fool! This night your soul is required of you; and the things you have prepared, whose will they be?' 21 So is he who lays up treasure for himself, and is not rich toward God."

c. Trust in God's providence

Lk. 12:22-34

22 And he said to his disciples, "Therefore I tell you, do not be anxious about your life, what you shall eat, nor about your body, what you shall put on. 23 For life is more than food, and the body more than clothing. 24 Consider the ravens: they neither sow nor reap, they have neither storehouse nor barn, and yet God feeds them. Of how much more value are you than the birds! 25 And which of you by being anxious can add a cubit to his span of life?[k] 26 If then you are not able to do as small a thing as that, why are you anxious about the rest? 27 Consider the lilies, how they grow; they neither toil nor spin;[l] yet I tell you, even Solomon in all his glory was not arrayed like one of these. 28 But if God so clothes the grass which is alive in the field today and tomorrow is thrown into the oven, how much more will he clothe you, O men of little faith? 29 And do not seek what you are to eat and what you are to drink, nor be of anxious mind. 30 For all the nations of

[k] Or *to his stature.*
[l] A few ancient authorities read *Consider the lilies; they neither spin nor weave.*

the world seek these things; and your Father knows that you need them. 31 Instead,
seek his[m] kingdom, and these things shall be yours as well.

32 "Fear not, little flock, for it is your Father's good pleasure to give you the kingdom. 33 Sell your possessions, and give alms; provide yourselves with purses that do
not grow old, with a treasure in the heavens that does not fail, where no thief
approaches and no moth destroys. 34 For where your treasure is, there will your heart
be also."

(See also article 39f)

d. The parable of the watchful servants

Lk. 12:35-48

35 "Let your loins be girded and your lamps burning, 36 and be like men who are
waiting for their master to come home from the marriage feast, so that they may
open to him at once when he comes and knocks. 37 Blessed are those servants whom
the master finds awake when he comes; truly, I say to you, he will gird himself and
have them sit at table and come and serve them. 38 If he comes in the second watch,
or in the third, and finds them so, blessed are those servants! 39 But know this, that
if the householder had known at what hour the thief was coming, he would have
been awake and[n] would not have left this house to be broken into. 40 You also
must be ready; for the Son of man is coming at an hour you do not expect."

41 Peter said, "Lord, are you telling this parable for us or for all?" 42 And the
Lord said, "Who then is the faithful and wise steward, whom his master will set
over his household, to give them their portion of food at the proper time? 43 Blessed
is that servant whom his master finds so doing when he comes. 44 Truly I tell you,
he will set him over all his possessions. 45 But if that servant says in his heart, 'My
master is delayed in coming,' and begins to beat the menservants and the maid-
servants, and to eat and drink and get drunk, 46 the master of that servant will come
on a day when he does not expect him and at an hour he does not know, and will
punish[o] him, and put him with the unfaithful. 47 And that servant who knew his
master's will, but did not make ready or act according to his will, shall receive a
severe beating. 48 But he who did not know, and did what deserved a beating, shall
receive a light beating. Every one to whom much is given, of him will much be
required; and of him to whom men commit much they will demand the more.

e. Interpreting the signs of the times

Lk. 12:49-59

49 "I came to cast fire upon the earth; and would that it were already kindled!
50 I have a baptism to be baptized with; and how I am constrained until it is
accomplished! 51 Do you think that I have come to give peace on earth? No, I tell
you, but rather division; 52 for henceforth in one house there will be five divided,
three against two and two against three; 53 they will be divided, father against son

[m] Some ancient authorities read *God's*.
[n] Some ancient authorities omit *would have been awake and.*
[o] Or *cut him in pieces.*

and son against father, mother against daughter and daughter against her mother,
mother-in-law against her daughter-in-law and daughter-in-law against her mother-
in-law."
54 He also said to the multitudes, "When you see a cloud rising in the west, you
say at once, 'A shower is coming'; and so it happens. 55 And when you see the south
wind blowing, you say, 'There will be scorching heat'; and it happens. 56 You
hypocrites! You know how to interpret the appearance of earth and sky; but why
do you not know how to interpret the present time?
57 "And why do you not judge for yourselves what is right? 58 As you go with
your accuser before the magistrate, make an effort to settle with him on the way, lest
he drag you to the judge, and the judge hand you over to the officer, and the officer
put you in prison. 59 I tell you, you will never get out till you have paid the very
last copper!"

§ 84. Disasters of Galileans teach urgency of repentance; Jesus speaks the parable of the unfruitful fig tree

Lk. 13:1-9

1 There were some present at that very time who told him of the Galileans whose
blood Pilate had mingled with their sacrifices. 2 And he answered them, "Do you
think that these Galileans were worse sinners than all the other Galileans, because
they suffered thus? 3 I tell you, No; but unless you repent you will all likewise
perish. 4 Or those eighteen upon whom the tower in Siloam fell and killed them, do
you think that they were worse offenders than all the others who dwelt in Jerusalem?
5 I tell you, No; but unless you repent you will all likewise perish."
6 And he told this parable: "A man had a fig tree planted in his vineyard; and
he came seeking fruit on it and found none. 7 And he said to the vinedresser, 'Lo,
these three years I have come seeking fruit on this fig tree, and I find none. Cut
it down; why should it use up the ground?' 8 And he answered him, 'Let it alone,
sir, this year also, till I dig about it and put on manure. 9 And if it bears fruit next
year, well and good; but if not, you can cut it down.' "

§ 85. Jesus heals a stooped woman on the sabbath; meets criticism

Lk. 13:10-17

10 Now he was teaching in one of the synagogues on the sabbath. 11 And there
was a woman who had had a spirit of infirmity for eighteen years; she was bent
over and could not fully straighten herself. 12 And when Jesus saw her, he called
her and said to her, "Woman, you are freed from your infirmity." 13 And he laid his
hands upon her, and immediately she was made straight, and she praised God. 14 But
the ruler of the synagogue, indignant because Jesus had healed on the sabbath, said
to the people, "There are six days on which work ought to be done; come on those
days and be healed, and not on the sabbath day." 15 Then the Lord answered him,
"You hypocrites! Does not each of you on the sabbath untie his ox or his ass from

the manger, and lead it away to water it? 16 And ought not this woman, a daughter
of Abraham whom Satan bound for eighteen years, be loosed from this bond on the
sabbath day?" 17 As he said this, all his adversaries were put to shame; and all the
people rejoiced at all the glorious things that were done by him.

§ 86. Jesus likens the kingdom to mustard seed and leaven

Lk. 13:18-21

18 He said therefore, "What is the kingdom of God like? And to what shall I
compare it? 19 It is like a grain of mustard seed which a man took and sowed in
his garden; and it grew and became a tree, and the birds of the air made nests in its
branches."
20 And again he said, "To what shall I compare the kingdom of God? 21 It is like
leaven which a woman took and hid in three measures of meal, till it was all
leavened."

(See also article 46e)

§ 87. Jesus discusses the question whether but few are saved

Lk. 13:22-30

22 He went on his way through towns and villages, teaching, and journeying toward
Jerusalem. 23 And some one said to him, "Lord, will those who are saved be few?"
And he said to them, 24 "Strive to enter by the narrow door; for many, I tell you,
will seek to enter and will not be able. 25 When once the householder has risen up
and shut the door, you will begin to stand outside and to knock at the door, saying,
'Lord, open to us.' He will answer you, 'I do not know where you come from.'
26 Then you will begin to say, 'We ate and drank in your presence, and you taught
in our streets.' 27 But he will say, 'I tell you, I do not know where you come from;
depart from me, all you workers of iniquity!' 28 There you will weep and gnash
your teeth, when you see Abraham and Isaac and Jacob and all the prophets in the
kingdom of God and you yourselves thrust out. 29 And men will come from east
and west, and from north and south, and sit at table in the kingdom of God. 30 And
behold, some are last who will be first, and some are first who will be last."

§ 88. Jesus replies to the warning that Herod will kill him; laments over Jerusalem

Lk. 13:31-35

31 At that very hour some Pharisees came, and said to him, "Get away from here,
for Herod wants to kill you." 32 And he said to them, "Go and tell that fox, 'Behold,
I cast out demons and perform cures today and tomorrow, and the third day I finish
my course. 33 Nevertheless I must go on my way today and tomorrow and the day
following; for it cannot be that a prophet should perish away from Jerusalem.' 34 O
Jerusalem, Jerusalem, killing the prophets and stoning those who are sent to you!
How often would I have gathered your children together as a hen gathers her
brood under her wings, and you would not! 35 Behold, your house is forsaken! And

(See also Matt. 23:37-39, article 113)

I tell you, you will not see me until you say, 'Blessed be he who comes in the name of
the Lord!' "

§ 89. Jesus dines with a chief Pharisee; heals a dropsical man; teaches humility; gives a parable of the great banquet

Lk. 14:1-24

1 One sabbath when he went to dine at the house of a ruler who belonged to the
Pharisees, they were watching him. 2 And behold, there was a man before him who
had dropsy. 3 And Jesus spoke to the lawyers and Pharisees, saying, "Is it lawful to
heal on the sabbath, or not?" 4 But they were silent. Then he took him and healed
him, and let him go. 5 And he said to them, "Which of you, having an ass[p] or an
ox that has fallen into a well, will not immediately pull him out on a sabbath day?"
6 And they could not reply to this.

7 Now he told a parable to those who were invited, when he marked how they
chose the places of honor, saying to them, 8 "When you are invited by any one
to a marriage feast, do not sit down in a place of honor, lest a more eminent man
than you be invited by him; 9 and he who invited you both will come and say to
you, 'Give place to this man,' and then you will begin with shame to take the lowest
place. 10 But when you are invited, go and sit in the lowest place, so that when
your host comes he may say to you, 'Friend, go up higher'; then you will be honored
in the presence of all who sit at table with you. 11 "For every one who exalts himself
will be humbled, and he who humbles himself will be exalted."

12 He said also to the man who had invited him, "When you give a dinner or a
banquet, do not invite your friends or your brothers or your kinsmen or rich neighbors,
lest they also invite you in return, and you be repaid. 13 But when you give a feast,
invite the poor, the maimed, the lame, the blind, 14 and you will be blessed, because
they cannot repay you. You will be repaid at the resurrection of the just."

15 When one of those who sat at table with him heard this, he said to him,
"Blessed is he who shall eat bread in the kingdom of God!" 16 But he said to him,
"A man once gave a great banquet, and invited many; 17 and at the time for the
banquet he sent his servant to say to those who had been invited, 'Come; for all is now
ready.' 18 But they all alike began to make excuses. The first said to him, 'I have
bought a field, and I must go out and see it; I pray you, have me excused.' 19 And
another said, 'I have bought five yoke of oxen, and I go to examine them; I pray
you, have me excused. 20 And another said, 'I have married a wife, and therefore I
cannot come.' 21 So the servant came and reported this to his master. Then the
householder in anger said to his servant, 'Go out quickly to the streets and lanes of
the city, and bring in the poor and maimed and blind and lame.' 22 And the
servant said, 'Sir, what you commanded has been done, and still there is room.'
23 And the master said to the servant, 'Go out to the highways and hedges, and
compel people to come in, that my house may be filled. 24 For I tell you, none of
those men who were invited shall taste my banquet.' "

(See also article 111c)

[p] Many ancient authorities read *a son*.

§ 90. Jesus discusses the cost of discipleship

Lk. 14:25-35

[25] Now great multitudes accompanied him; and he turned and said to them, [26] "If
any one comes to me and does not hate his own father and mother and wife and
children and brothers and sisters, yes, and even his own life, he cannot be my disciple.
[27] Whoever does not bear his own cross and come after me, cannot be my disciple.
[28] For which of you, desiring to build a tower, does not first sit down and count the
cost, whether he has enough to complete it? [29] Otherwise, when he has laid a
foundation, and is not able to finish, all who see it begin to mock him, [30] saying,
'This man began to build, and was not able to finish.' [31] Or what king, going to
encounter another king in war, will not sit down first and take counsel whether
he is able with ten thousand to meet him who comes against him with twenty
thousand? [32] And if not, while the other is yet a great way off, he sends an embassy
and asks terms of peace. [33] So therefore, whoever of you does not renounce all that
he has cannot be my disciple.

[34] "Salt is good; but if salt has lost its taste, how shall its saltness be restored?
[35] It is fit neither for the land nor for the dunghill; men throw it away. He who
has ears to hear, let him hear."

§ 91. Three parables on grace and two parables on wealth are given

a. The lost sheep

Lk. 15:1-7

[1] Now the tax collectors and sinners were all drawing near to hear him. [2] And
the Pharisees and the scribes murmured, saying, "This man receives sinners and
eats with them."

[3] So he told them this parable: [4] "What man of you, having a hundred sheep,
if he has lost one of them, does not leave the ninety-nine in the wilderness, and go
after the one which is lost, until he finds it? [5] And when he has found it, he lays it on
his shoulders, rejoicing. [6] And when he comes home, he calls together his friends
and his neighbors, saying to them, 'Rejoice with me, for I have found my sheep which
was lost.' [7] Even so, I tell you, there will be more joy in heaven over one sinner who
repents than over ninety-nine righteous persons who need no repentance."

(See also Matt. 18:10-14, article 68)

b. The lost coin

Lk. 15:8-10

[8] "Or what woman, having ten silver coins,[q] if she loses one coin, does not light
a lamp and sweep the house and seek diligently until she finds it? [9] And when she
has found it, she calls together her friends and neighbors, saying, 'Rejoice with me,
for I have found the coin which I had lost.' [10] Even so, I tell you, there is joy
before the angels of God over one sinner who repents."

[q] The drachma, rendered here by *silver coin,* was about sixteen cents.

c. The lost son

Lk. 15:11-32

[11] And he said, "There was a man who had two sons; [12] and the younger of them
said to his father, 'Father, give me the share of property that falls to me.' And he
divided his living between them. [13] Not many days later, the younger son gathered
all he had and took his journey into a far country, and there he squandered his
property in loose living. [14] And when he had spent everything, a great famine arose
in that country, and he began to be in want. [15] So he went and joined himself to
one of the citizens of that country, who sent him into his fields to feed swine. [16] And
he would gladly have fed on[r] the pods that the swine ate; and no one gave him
anything. [17] But when he came to himself he said, 'How many of my father's hired
servants have bread enough and to spare, but I perish here with hunger! [18] I will
arise and go to my father, and I will say to him, Father, I have sinned against heaven
and before you; [19] I am no longer worthy to be called your son; treat me as one of
your hired servants.' [20] And he arose and came to his father. But while he was yet at
a distance, his father saw him and had compassion, and ran and embraced him and
kissed him. [21] And the son said to him, 'Father, I have sinned against heaven and
before you; I am no longer worthy to be called your son.'[s] [22] But the father said to
his servants, 'Bring quickly the best robe, and put it on him; and put a ring on his
hand, and shoes on his feet; [23] and bring the fatted calf and kill it, and let us eat
and make merry; [24] for this my son was dead, and is alive again; he was lost, and
is found.' And they began to make merry.

[25] "Now his elder son was in the field; and as he came and drew near to the house,
he heard music and dancing. [26] And he called one of the servants and asked what
this meant. [27] And he said to him, 'Your brother has come, and your father has
killed the fatted calf, because he has received him safe and sound.' [28] But he was
angry and refused to go in. His father came out and entreated him, [29] but he
answered his father, 'Lo, these many years I have served you, and I never disobeyed
your command; yet you never gave me a kid, that I might make merry with my
friends. [30] But when this son of yours came, who has devoured your living with
harlots, you killed for him the fatted calf!' [31] And he said to him, 'Son, you are
always with me, and all that is mine is yours. [32] It was fitting to make merry and be
glad, for this your brother was dead, and is alive; he was lost, and is found.' "

d. The dishonest steward

Lk. 16:1-18

[1] He also said to the disciples, "There was a rich man who had a steward, and
charges were brought to him that this man was wasting his goods. [2] And he called
him and said to him, 'What is this that I hear about you? Turn in the account of
your stewardship, for you can no longer be steward.' [3] And the steward said to
himself, 'What shall I do, since my master is taking the stewardship away from

[r] Many ancient authorities read *filled his belly with.*
[s] Some ancient authorities add *treat me as one of your hired servants.*

me? I am not strong enough to dig, and I am ashamed to beg. 4 I have decided
what to do, so that people may receive me into their houses when I am put out of
the stewardship.' 5 So, summoning his master's debtors one by one, he said to the
first, 'How much do you owe my master?' 6 He said, 'A hundred measures of oil.'
And he said to him, 'Take your bill, and sit down quickly and write fifty.' 7 Then
he said to another, 'And how much do you owe?' He said, 'A hundred measures
of wheat.' He said to him, 'Take your bill, and write eighty.' 8 The master com-
mended the dishonest steward for his prudence; for the sons of this world[f] are
wiser in their own generation than the sons of light. 9 And I tell you, make friends
for yourselves by means of unrighteous mammon, so that when it fails they may
receive you into the eternal habitations.

10 "He who is faithful in a very little is faithful also in much; and he who is
dishonest in a very little is dishonest also in much. 11 If then you have not been
faithful in the unrighteous mammon, who will entrust to you the true riches? 12 And
if you have not been faithful in that which is another's, who will give you that which
is your own? 13 No servant can serve two masters; for either he will hate the one
and love the other, or he will be devoted to the one and despise the other. You
cannot serve God and mammon."

14 The Pharisees, who were lovers of money, heard all this, and they scoffed at
him. 15 But he said to them, "You are those who justify yourselves before men, but
God knows your hearts; for what is exalted among men is an abomination in the
sight of God.

16 "The law and the prophets were until John; since then the good news of the
kingdom of God is preached, and every one enters it violently. 17 But it is easier for
heaven and earth to pass away, than for one dot of the law to become void.

18 "Every one who divorces his wife and marries another commits adultery, and
he who marries a woman divorced from her husband commits adultery.

e. The rich man and Lazarus

Lk. 16:19-31

19 "There was a rich man, who was clothed in purple and fine linen and who
feasted sumptuously every day. 20 And at his gate lay a poor man named Lazarus,
full of sores, 21 who desired to be fed with what fell from the rich man's table;
moreover the dogs came and licked his sores. 22 The poor man died and was carried
by the angels to Abraham's bosom. The rich man also died and was buried; 23 and
in Hades, being in torment, he lifted up his eyes, and saw Abraham far off and
Lazarus in his bosom. 24 And he called out, 'Father Abraham, have mercy upon me,
and send Lazarus to dip the end of his finger in water and cool my tongue; for I am
in anguish in this flame.' 25 But Abraham said, 'Son, remember that you in your
lifetime received your good things, and Lazarus in like manner evil things; but
now he is comforted here, and you are in anguish. 26 And besides all this, between
us and you a great chasm has been fixed, in order that those who would pass from

[f] Greek *age*.

here to you may not be able, and none may cross from there to us.' [27] And he said,
'Then I beg you, father, to send him to my father's house, [28] for I have five brothers,
so that he may warn them, lest they also come into this place of torment.' [29] But
Abraham said, 'They have Moses and the prophets; let them hear them.' [30] And
he said, 'No, father Abraham; but if some one goes to them from the dead, they
will repent.' [31] He said to him, 'If they do not hear Moses and the prophets, neither
will they be convinced if some one should rise from the dead.' "

§ 92. Jesus discusses forgiveness, faith, and service

Lk. 17:1-10

[1] And he said to his disciples, "Temptations to sin[u] are sure to come; but woe to
him by whom they come! [2] It would be better for him if a millstone were hung
round his neck and he were cast into the sea, than that he should cause one of these
little ones to sin.[v] [3] Take heed to yourselves; if your brother sins, rebuke him, and
if he repents, forgive him; [4] and if he sins against you seven times in the day, and
turns to you seven times, and says, 'I repent,' you must forgive him."

[5] The apostles said to the Lord, "Increase our faith!" [6] And the Lord said, "If
you had faith as a grain of mustard seed, you could say to this sycamine tree, 'Be
rooted up, and be planted in the sea,' and it would obey you.

[7] "Will any one of you, who has a servant plowing or keeping sheep, say to him
when he has come in from the field, 'Come at once and sit down at table'? [8] Will
he not rather say to him, 'Prepare supper for me, and gird yourself and serve me, till
I eat and drink; and afterward you shall eat and drink'? [9] Does he thank the
servant because he did what was commanded? [10] So you also, when you have done
all that is commanded you, say, 'We are unworthy servants; we have only done what
was our duty.' "

§ 93. Ten lepers are healed; one returns to thank Jesus

Lk. 17:11-19

[11] On the way to Jerusalem he was passing along between Samaria and Galilee.
[12] And as he entered a village, he was met by ten lepers, who stood at a distance
[13] and lifted up their voices and said, "Jesus, Master, have mercy on us." [14] When
he saw them he said to them, "Go and show yourselves to the priests." And as they
went they were cleansed. [15] Then one of them, when he saw that he was healed,
turned back, praising God with a loud voice; [16] and he fell on his face at Jesus'
feet, giving him thanks. Now he was a Samaritan. [17] Then said Jesus, "Were not
ten cleansed? Where are the nine? [18] Was no one found to return and give praise
to God except this foreigner?" [19] And he said to him, "Rise and go your way; your
faith has made you well."

[u] Or *stumbling-blocks.*
[v] Or *stumble.*

§ 94. Jesus discusses the nature of the kingdom's coming

Lk. 17:20-37

20 Being asked by the Pharisees when the kingdom of God was coming, he
answered them, "The kingdom of God is not coming with signs to be observed;
21 nor will they say, 'Lo, here it is!' or 'There!' for behold, the kingdom of God is
in the midst of[w] you."
22 And he said to the disciples, "The days are coming when you will desire to
see one of the days of the Son of man, and you will not see it. 23 And they will
say to you, 'Lo, there!' or 'Lo, here!' Do not go, do not follow them. 24 For as the
lightning flashes and lights up the sky from one side to the other, so will the Son
of man be in his day.[x] 25 But first he must suffer many things and be rejected by
this generation. 26 As it was in the days of Noah, so will it be in the days of the
Son of man. 27 They ate, they drank, they married, they were given in marriage,
until the day when Noah entered the ark, and the flood came and destroyed them
all. 28 Likewise as it was in the days of Lot—they ate, they drank, they bought, they
sold, they planted, they built, 29 but on the day when Lot went out from Sodom
fire and brimstone rained from heaven and destroyed them all—30 so will it be on
the day when the Son of man is revealed. 31 On that day, let him who is on the
housetop, with his goods in the house, not come down to take them away; and
likewise let him who is in the field not turn back. 32 Remember Lot's wife. 33 Whoever seeks to gain his life will lose it, but whoever loses his life will preserve it.
34 I tell you, in that night there will be two men in one bed; one will be taken and
the other left. 35 There will be two women grinding together; one will be taken
and the other left."[y] 37 And they said to him, "Where, Lord?" He said to them,
"Where the body is, there the eagles[z] will be gathered together."

(See also article 116a)

§ 95. Jesus gives parables of the widow and the judge and of the Pharisee and the tax collector

Lk. 18:1-14

1 And he told them a parable, to the effect that they ought always to pray and
not lose heart. 2 He said, "In a certain city there was a judge who neither feared
God nor regarded man; 3 and there was a widow in that city who kept coming to
him and saying, 'Vindicate me against my adversary.' 4 For a while he refused; but
afterward he said to himself, 'Though I neither fear God nor regard man, 5 yet
because this widow bothers me, I will vindicate her, or she will wear me out by
her continual coming.' " 6 And the Lord said, "Hear what the unrighteous judge says.
7 And will not God vindicate his elect, who cry to him day and night? Will he
delay long over them? 8 I tell you he will vindicate them speedily. Nevertheless,
when the Son of man comes, will he find faith on earth?"

[w] Or *within.*
[x] Some ancient authorities omit *in his day.*
[y] Some ancient authorities add verse 36, *"Two men will be in the field; one will be taken and the other left."*
[z] Or *vultures.*

[9] He also told this parable to some who trusted in themselves that they were righteous and despised others: [10] "Two men went up into the temple to pray, one a Pharisee and the other a tax collector. [11] The Pharisee stood and prayed thus with himself, 'God, I thank thee that I am not like other men, extortioners, unjust, adulterers, or even like this tax collector. [12] I fast twice a week, I give tithes of all that I get.' [13] But the tax collector, standing far off, would not even lift up his eyes to heaven, but beat his breast, saying, 'God, be merciful to me a sinner!' [14] I tell you, this man went down to his house justified rather than the other; for every one who exalts himself will be humbled, but he who humbles himself will be exalted."

Section L. Christ's Final Approach to Jerusalem*

§ 96. Jesus speaks concerning marriage and divorce

Mt. 19:3-12

[3] And Pharisees came up to him and tested him by asking, "Is it lawful to divorce one's wife for any cause?" [4] He answered, "Have you not read that he who made them from the beginning made them male and female, [5] and said, 'For this reason a man shall leave his father and mother and be joined to his wife, and the two shall become one'?[a] [6] So they are no longer two but one.[a] What therefore God has joined together, let not man put asunder." [7] They said to him, "Why then did Moses command one to give a certificate of divorce, and to put her away?" [8] He said to them, "For your hardness of heart Moses allowed you to divorce your wives, but from the beginning it was not so. [9] And I say to you: whoever divorces his wife, except for unchastity,[c] and marries

Mk. 10:2-12

[2] And Pharisees came up and in order to test him asked, "Is it lawful for a man to divorce his wife?" [3] He answered them, "What did Moses command you?" [4] They said, "Moses permitted a man to write a certificate of divorce, and to put her away." [5] But Jesus said to them, "For your hardness of heart he wrote you this commandment. [6] But from the beginning of creation, 'God made them male and female.' [7] 'For this reason a man shall leave his father and mother and be joined to his wife,[b] [8] and the two shall become one.'[a] So they are no longer two but one.[a] [9] What therefore God has joined together, let not man put asunder."

[10] And in the house the disciples asked him again about this matter. [11] And he said to them, "Whoever divorces his

Luke

John

[a] Greek *one flesh*.
[b] Some ancient authorities omit *and be joined to his wife*.
[c] Some ancient authorities, after *unchastity*, read *makes her commit adultery*.

* Section L includes the materials which pertain to what is sometimes designated *Christ's Later Judean Ministry*.

Mt. 19:3-12

another, commits adultery."[d]

[10] The disciples said to him, "If such is the case of a man with his wife, it is not expedient to marry." [11] But he said to them, "Not all men can receive this precept, but only those to whom it is given. [12] For there are eunuchs who have been so from birth, and there are eunuchs who have been made eunuchs by men, and there are eunuchs who have made themselves eunuchs for the sake of the kingdom of heaven. He who is able to receive this, let him receive it."

Mk. 10:2-12

wife and marries another, commits adultery against her; [12] and if she divorces her husband and marries another, she commits adultery."

Luke

John

§ 97. Jesus blesses little children

Mt. 19:13-15

[13] Then children were brought to him that he might lay his hands on them and pray. The disciples rebuked the people; [14] but Jesus said, "Let the children come to me, and do not hinder them; for to such belongs the kingdom of heaven." [15] And he laid his hands on them and went away.

Mk. 10:13-16

[13] And they were bringing children to him, that he might touch them; and the disciples rebuked them. [14] But when Jesus saw it he was indignant, and said to them, "Let the children come to me, do not hinder them; for to such belongs the kingdom of God. [15] Truly, I say to you, whoever does not receive the kingdom of God like a child shall not enter it." [16] And he took them in his arms and blessed them, laying his hands upon them.

Lk. 18:15-17

[15] Now they were bringing even infants to him that he might touch them; and when the disciples saw it, they rebuked them. [16] But Jesus called them to him, saying, "Let the children come to me, and do not hinder them; for to such belongs the kingdom of God. [17] Truly, I say to you, whoever does not receive the kingdom of God like a child shall not enter it."

John

[d] Some ancient authorities insert *and he who marries a divorced woman commits adultery.*

§ 98. A rich young ruler refuses discipleship; Jesus cites dangers of wealth

Mt. 19:16-30

16 And behold, one
came up to him, say-
ing, "Teacher, what
good deed must I do, to
have eternal life?"
17 And he said to him,
"Why do you ask me
about what is good?
One there is who is
good. If you would en-
ter life, keep the com-
mandments." 18 He
said to him, "Which?"
And Jesus said, "You
shall not kill, You shall
not commit adultery,
You shall not steal,
You shall not bear false
witness, 19 Honor your
father and your mother,
and, You shall love
your neighbor as your-
self." 20 The young
man said to him, "All
these I have observed;
what do I still lack?"
21 Jesus said to him,
"If you would be per-
fect, go, sell what you
possess and give it to
the poor, and you will
have treasure in
heaven; and come, fol-
low me." 22 When the
young man heard this
he went away sorrow-
ful; for he had great
possessions.

23 And Jesus said to
his disciples, "Truly, I
say to you, it will be

Mk. 10:17-31

17 And as he was set-
ting out on his journey,
a man ran up and knelt
before him, and asked
him, "Good teacher,
what must I do to in-
herit eternal life?"
18 And Jesus said to
him, "Why do you call
me good? No one is
good but God alone.
19 You know the com-
mandments: 'Do not
kill, Do not commit
adultery, Do not steal,
Do not bear false wit-
ness, Do not defraud,
Honor your father and
mother.'" 20 And he
said to him, "Teacher,
all these I have ob-
served from my youth."
21 And Jesus looking
upon him loved him,
and said to him, "You
lack one thing; go, sell
all that you have, and
give it to the poor, and
you will have treasure
in heaven; and come,
follow me." 22 At that
saying his countenance
fell, and he went away
sorrowful; for he had
great possessions.

23 And Jesus looked
around and said to his
disciples, "How hard it
will be for those who
have riches to enter the
kingdom of God!"

Lk. 18:18-30

18 And a ruler asked
him, "Good Teacher,
what shall I do to in-
herit eternal life?"
19 And Jesus said to
him, "Why do you call
me good? No one is
good but God alone.
20 You know the com-
mandments; Do not
commit adultery, Do not
kill, Do not steal, Do
not bear false witness,
Honor your father and
mother." 21 And he said,
"All these I have kept
from my youth."
22 And when Jesus
heard it, he said to
him, "One thing you
still lack. Sell all that
you have and distribute
to the poor, and you
will have treasure in
heaven; and come, fol-
low me." 23 But when
he heard this he be-
came sad, for he was
very rich. 24 Jesus
looking at him said,
"How hard it is for
those who have riches
to enter the kingdom
of God! 25 For it is
easier for a camel to go
through the eye of a
needle than for a rich
man to enter the king-
dom of God." 26 Those
who heard it said,
"Who then can be

John

Mt. 19:16-30

hard for a rich man to enter the kingdom of heaven. [24] Again I tell you, it is easier for a camel to go through the eye of a needle than for a rich man to enter the kingdom of God." [25] When the disciples heard this, they were greatly astonished, saying, "Who then can be saved?" [26] But Jesus looked at them and said to them, "With men this is impossible, but with God all things are possible." [27] Then Peter said in reply, "Lo, we have left everything and followed you. What then shall we have?" [28] Jesus said to them, "Truly, I say to you, in the new world, when the Son of man shall sit on his glorious throne, you who have followed me will also sit on twelve thrones, judging the twelve tribes of Israel. [29] And every one who has left houses or brothers or sisters or father or mother or children or lands, for my name's sake, will receive a hundredfold,[g] and in-

Mk. 10:17-31

[24] And the disciples were amazed at his words. But Jesus said to them again, "Children, how hard it is[e] to enter the kingdom of God! [25] It is easier for a camel to go through the eye of a needle than for a rich man to enter the kingdom of God." [26] And they were exceedingly astonished, and said to him,[f] "Then who can be saved?" [27] Jesus looked at them and said, "With men it is impossible, but not with God; for all things are possible with God." [28] Peter began to say to him, "Lo, we have left everything, and followed you." [29] Jesus said, "Truly, I say to you, there is no one who has left house or brothers or sisters or mother or father or children or lands, for my sake and for the gospel, [30] who will not receive a hundredfold now in this time, houses and brothers and sisters and mothers and children and lands, with persecutions, and in the age to come

Lk. 18:18-30

saved?" [27] But he said, "What is impossible with men is possible with God." [28] And Peter said, "Lo, we have left our homes and followed you." [29] And he said to them, "Truly, I say to you, there is no man who has left house or wife or brothers or parents or children, for the sake of the kingdom of God, [30] who will not receive manifold more in this time, and in the age to come eternal life."

John

[e] Some ancient authorities add *for those who trust in riches.*
[f] Many ancient authorities read *to one another.*
[g] Some ancient authorities read *manifold.*

Mt. 19:16-30

herit eternal life. 30 But many that are first will be last, and the last first."

Mk. 10:17-31

eternal life. 31 But many that are first will be last, and the last first."

Lk. 18

John

§ 99. Jesus gives a parable about the payment of laborers in a vineyard

Mt. 20:1-16

1 "For the kingdom of heaven is like a householder who went out early in the
morning to hire laborers for his vineyard. 2 After agreeing with the laborers for a
denarius[h] a day, he sent them into his vineyard. 3 And going out about the third
hour he saw others standing idle in the market place; 4 and to them he said, 'You
go into the vineyard too, and whatever is right I will give you.' So they went.
5 Going out again about the sixth hour and the ninth hour, he did the same.
6 And about the eleventh hour he went out and found others standing; and he
said to them, 'Why do you stand here idle all day?' 7 They said to him, 'Because
no one has hired us.' He said to them, 'You go into the vineyard too.' 8 And
when evening came, the owner of the vineyard said to his steward, 'Call the
laborers and pay them their wages, beginning with the last, up to the first.' 9 And
when those hired about the eleventh hour came, each of them received a denarius.
10 Now when the first came, they thought they would receive more; but each of them
also received a denarius. 11 And on receiving it they grumbled at the householder,
12 saying, 'These last worked only one hour, and you have made them equal to us
who have borne the burden of the day and the scorching heat.' 13 But he replied
to one of them, 'Friend, I am doing you no wrong; did you not agree with me for
a denarius? 14 Take what belongs to you, and go; I choose to give to this last as I
give to you. 15 Am I not allowed to do what I choose with what belongs to me?
Or do you begrudge my generosity[i]?' 16 So the last will be first, and the first last."

§ 100. Jesus foretells his death and resurrection the third time

Mt. 20:17-19

17 And as Jesus was going up to Jerusalem, he took the twelve disciples aside, and on the way he said to them, 18 "Behold, we are going up to Jerusalem; and the Son of man will be delivered to the chief priests and

Mk. 10:32-34

32 And they were on the road, going up to Jerusalem, and Jesus was walking ahead of them; and they were amazed, and those who followed were afraid. And he took the twelve again, and began to tell them what was to hap-

Lk. 18:31-34

31 And taking the twelve aside, he said to them, "Behold, we are going up to Jerusalem, and everything that is written of the Son of man by the prophets will be accomplished. 32 For he will be delivered to the Gentiles,

John

[h] See note on Matt. 18:28.
[i] Or *is your eye evil because I am good?*

Mt. 20:17-19

scribes, and they will condemn him to death, 19 and deliver him to the Gentiles to be mocked and scourged and crucified, and he will be raised on the third day."

Mk. 10:32-34

pen to him, 33 saying, "Behold, we are going up to Jerusalem; and the Son of man will be delivered to the chief priests and the scribes, and they will condemn him to death, and deliver him to the Gentiles; 34 and they will mock him, and spit upon him, and scourge him, and kill him; and after three days he will rise."

Lk. 18:31-34

and will be mocked and shamefully treated and spit upon; 33 they will scourge him and kill him, and on the third day he will rise." 34 But they understood none of these things; this saying was hid from them, and they did not grasp what was said.

John

§ 101. The ambition of James, John, and their mother is corrected

Mt. 20:20-28

20 Then the mother of the sons of Zebedee came up to him, with her sons, and kneeling before him she asked him for something. 21 And he said to her, "What do you want?" She said to him, "Command that these two sons of mine may sit, one at your right hand and one at your left, in your kingdom." 22 But Jesus answered, "You do not know what you are asking. Are you able to drink the cup that I am to drink?" They said to him, "We are able." 23 He said to them, "You will drink my cup, but to sit at my right hand and at my left is not mine to grant, but it is for those for whom it has been prepared by my Father." 24 And when the ten heard it, they were indignant at the two brothers. 25 But Jesus called them to him and said,

Mk. 10:35-45

35 And James and John, the sons of Zebedee, came forward to him, and said to him, "Teacher, we want you to do for us whatever we ask of you." 36 And he said to them, "What do you want me to do for you?" 37 And they said to him, "Grant us to sit, one at your right hand and one at your left, in your glory." 38 But Jesus said to them, "You do not know what you are asking. Are you able to drink the cup that I drink, or to be baptized with the baptism with which I am baptized?" 39 And they said to him, "We are able." And Jesus said to them, "The cup that I drink you will drink; and with the baptism with which I am baptized, you will be baptized; 40 but to sit at my right hand or at my left is not mine to grant; but it is for

Luke

John

Mt. 20:20-28

"You know that the rulers of the Gentiles lord it over them, and their great men exercise authority over them. 26 Not so shall it be among you; but whoever would be great among you must be your servant, 27 and whoever would be first among you must be your slave; 28 even as the Son of man came not to be served but to serve, and to give his life as a ransom for many."

Mk. 10:35-45

those for whom it has been prepared." 41 And when the ten heard it, they began to be indignant at James and John. 42 And Jesus called them to him and said to them, "You know that those who are supposed to rule over the Gentiles lord it over them, and their great men exercise authority over them. 43 But it shall not be so among you; but whoever would be great among you must be your servant, 44 and whoever would be first among you must be slave of all. 45 For the Son of man also came not to be served but to serve, and to give his life as a ransom for many."

Luke

John

§ 102. Blind Bartimaeus is healed near Jericho

Mt. 20:29-34

29 And as they went out of Jericho, a great crowd followed him. 30 And behold, two blind men sitting by the roadside, when they heard that Jesus was passing by, cried out,[f] "Have mercy on us, Son of David!" 31 The crowd rebuked them, telling them to hold their peace; but they cried out the more, "Lord, have mercy on us, Son of David!" 32 And Jesus stopped and called them, saying, "What do you

Mk. 10:46-52

46 And they came to Jericho; and as he was leaving Jericho with his disciples and a great multitude, Bartimaeus, a blind beggar, the son of Timaeus, was sitting by the roadside. 47 And when he heard that it was Jesus of Nazareth, he began to cry out and say, "Jesus, Son of David, have mercy on me!" 48 And many rebuked him, telling him to be silent; but he cried out all the more, "Son of David, have mercy on me!" 49 And

Lk. 18:35-43

35 As he drew near to Jericho, a blind man was sitting by the roadside begging; 36 and hearing a multitude going by, he inquired what this meant. 37 They told him, "Jesus of Nazareth is passing by." 38 And he cried, "Jesus, Son of David, have mercy on me!" 39 And those who were in front rebuked him, telling him to be silent; but he cried out all the more, "Son of David, have mercy on me!" 40 And Jesus stopped,

John

[f] Many ancient authorities insert *Lord*.

Mt. 20:29-34

want me to do for
you?" 33 They said to
him, "Lord, let our
eyes be opened."
34 And Jesus in pity
touched their eyes, and
immediately they re-
ceived their sight and
followed him.

Mk. 10:46-52

Jesus stopped and said,
"Call him." And they
called the blind man,
saying to him, "Take
heart; rise, he is calling
you." 50 And throwing
off his mantle he
sprang up and came to
Jesus. 51 And Jesus
said to him, "What do
you want me to do for
you?" And the blind
man said to him, "Mas-
ter,[k] let me receive my
sight." 52 And Jesus
said to him, "Go your
way; your faith has
made you well." And
immediately he re-
ceived his sight and
followed him on the
way.

Lk. 18:35-43

and commanded him to
be brought to him; and
when he came near, he
asked him, 41 "What do
you want me to do for
you?" He said, "Lord,
let me receive my
sight." 42 And Jesus
said to him, "Receive
your sight; your faith
has made you well."
43 And immediately he
received his sight and
followed him, glorify-
ing God; and all the
people, when they saw
it, gave praise to God.

John

§ 103. Zacchaeus, a tax collector in Jericho, receives Jesus

Lk. 19:1-10

1 He entered Jericho and was passing through. 2 And there was a man named
Zacchaeus; he was a chief tax collector, and rich. 3 And he sought to see who Jesus
was, but could not, on account of the crowd, because he was small of stature. 4 So
he ran on ahead and climbed up into a sycamore tree to see him, for he was to pass
that way. 5 And when Jesus came to the place, he looked up and said to him,
"Zacchaeus, make haste and come down; for I must stay at your house today." 6 So
he made haste and came down, and received him joyfully. 7 And when they saw it
they all murmured, "He has gone in to be the guest of a man who is a sinner."
8 And Zacchaeus stood and said to the Lord, "Behold, Lord, the half of my goods I
give to the poor; and if I have defrauded any one of anything, I restore it fourfold."
9 And Jesus said to him, "Today salvation has come to this house, since he also is a
son of Abraham. 10 For the Son of man came to seek and to save that which was
lost."

§ 104. Jesus gives the parable of the pounds; draws near to Jerusalem

Lk. 19:11-28

11 As they heard these things, he proceeded to tell a parable, because he was near

[k] Or *Rabbi*.

to Jerusalem, and because they supposed that the kingdom of God was to appear
immediately. 12 He said therefore, "A nobleman went into a far country to receive
kingly power[l] and then return. 13 Calling ten of his servants, he gave them ten
pounds,[m] and said to them, 'Trade with these till I come.' 14 But his citizens hated
him and sent an embassy after him, saying, 'We do not want this man to reign over
us.' 15 When he returned, having received the kingly power,[l] he commanded these
servants, to whom he had given the money, to be called to him, that he might know
what they had gained by trading. 16 The first came before him, saying, 'Lord, your
pound has made ten pounds more.' 17 And he said to him, 'Well done, good servant!
Because you have been faithful in a very little, you shall have authority over ten
cities.' 18 And the second came, saying, 'Lord, your pound has made five pounds.'
19 And he said to him, 'And you are to be over five cities.' 20 Then another came,
saying, 'Lord, here is your pound, which I kept laid away in a napkin; 21 for I was
afraid of you, because you are a severe man; you take up what you did not lay down,
and reap what you did not sow.' 22 He said to him, 'I will condemn you out of your
own mouth, you wicked servant! You knew that I was a severe man, taking up
what I did not lay down and reaping what I did not sow? 23 Why then did you not
put my money into the bank, and at my coming I should have collected it with
interest?' 24 And he said to those who stood by, 'Take the pound from him, and
give it to him who has the ten pounds.' 25 (And they said to him, 'Lord, he has ten
pounds!') 26 'I tell you, that to every one who has will more be given; but from
him who has not, even what he has will be taken away. 27 But as for these enemies
of mine, who did not want me to reign over them, bring them here and slay them
before me.' "

28 And when he had said this, he went on ahead, going up to Jerusalem.

§ 105. Lazarus is raised at Bethany

Jn. 11:1-44

1 Now a certain man was ill, Lazarus of Bethany, the village of Mary and her
sister Martha. 2 It was Mary who anointed the Lord with ointment and wiped his
feet with her hair, whose brother Lazarus was ill. 3 So the sisters sent to him,
saying, "Lord, he whom you love is ill." 4 But when Jesus heard it he said, "This
illness is not unto death; it is for the glory of God, so that the Son of God may
be glorified by means of it."

5 Now Jesus loved Martha and her sister and Lazarus. 6 So when he heard that
he was ill, he stayed two days longer in the place where he was. 7 Then after this
he said to the disciples, "Let us go into Judea again." 8 The disciples said to
him, "Rabbi, the Jews were but now seeking to stone you, and are you going
there again?" 9 Jesus answered, "Are there not twelve hours in the day? If any
one walks in the day, he does not stumble, because he sees the light of this world.
10 But if any one walks in the night, he stumbles, because the light is not in him."

[l] Greek *a kingdom.*
[m] The mina, rendered here by *pound,* was equal to about twenty dollars.

11 Thus he spoke, and then he said to them, "Our friend Lazarus has fallen asleep,
but I go to awake him out of sleep." 12 The disciples said to him, "Lord, if he
has fallen asleep, he will recover." 13 Now Jesus had spoken of his death, but they
thought that he meant taking rest in sleep. 14 Then Jesus told them plainly,
"Lazarus is dead; 15 and for your sake I am glad that I was not there, so that you
may believe. But let us go to him." 16 Thomas, called the Twin, said to his fellow
disciples, "Let us also go, that we may die with him."

17 Now when Jesus came, he found that Lazarus[n] had already been in the tomb
four days. 18 Bethany was near Jerusalem, and about two miles[o] off, 19 and many of
the Jews had come to Martha and Mary to console them concerning their
brother. 20 When Martha heard that Jesus was coming, she went and met him,
while Mary sat in the house. 21 Martha said to Jesus, "Lord, if you had been here,
my brother would not have died. 22 And even now I know that whatever you
ask from God, God will give you." 23 Jesus said to her, "Your brother will rise
again." 24 Martha said to him, "I know that he will rise again in the resurrection
at the last day." 25 Jesus said to her, "I am the resurrection and the life;[p] he who
believes in me, though he die, yet shall he live, 26 and whoever lives and believes
in me shall never die. Do you believe this?" 27 She said to him, "Yes, Lord; I
believe that you are the Christ, the Son of God, he who is coming into the world."

28 When she had said this, she went and called her sister Mary, saying quietly,
"The Teacher is here and is calling for you." 29 And when she heard it, she rose
quickly and went to him. 30 Now Jesus had not yet come to the village, but was
still in the place where Martha had met him. 31 When the Jews who were with her
in the house, consoling her, saw Mary rise quickly and go out, they followed her,
supposing that she was going to the tomb to weep there. 32 Then Mary, when she
came where Jesus was and saw him, fell at his feet, saying to him, "Lord, if you
had been here, my brother would not have died." 33 When Jesus saw her weeping,
and the Jews who came with her also weeping, he was deeply moved in spirit and
troubled; and 34 he said, "Where have you laid him?" They said to him, "Lord,
come and see." 35 Jesus wept. 36 So the Jews said, "See how he loved him!"
37 But some of them said, "Could not he who opened the eyes of the blind man
have kept this man from dying?"

38 Then Jesus, deeply moved again, came to the tomb; it was a cave, and a
stone lay upon it. 39 Jesus said, "Take away the stone." Martha, the sister of the
dead man, said to him, "Lord, by this time there will be an odor, for he has been
dead four days." 40 Jesus said to her, "Did I not tell you that if you would believe
you would see the glory of God?" 41 So they took away the stone. And Jesus
lifted up his eyes and said, "Father, I thank thee that thou hast heard me. 42 I knew
that thou hearest me always, but I have said this on account of the people standing by, that they may believe that thou didst send me." 43 When he had said
this, he cried with a loud voice, "Lazarus, come out." 44 The dead man came out,

[n] Greek *he.*
[o] Greek *fifteen stadia.*
[p] A few ancient authorities omit ***and the life.***

his hand: and feet bound with bandages, and his face wrapped with a cloth.
Jesus said to them, "Unbind him, and let him go."

§ 106. Jesus is condemned by the council; withdraws into Ephraim

Jn. 11:45-57

45 Many of the Jews therefore, who had come with Mary and had seen what
he did, believed in him; 46 but some of them went to the Pharisees and told them
what Jesus had done. 47 So the chief priests and the Pharisees gathered the
council, and said, "What are we to do? For this man performs many signs. 48 If
we let him go on thus, every one will believe in him, and the Romans will come
and destroy both our holy place[q] and our nation." 49 But one of them, Caiaphas,
who was high priest that year, said to them, "You know nothing at all; 50 you do
not understand that it is expedient for you that one man should die for the people,
and not that the whole nation should perish." 51 He did not say this of his own
accord, but being high priest that year he prophesied that Jesus should die for
the nation, 52 and not for the nation only, but to gather into one the children
of God who are scattered abroad. 53 So from that day on they took counsel
how to put him to death.

54 Jesus therefore no longer went about openly among the Jews, but went
from there to the country near the wilderness, to a town called Ephraim; and there
he stayed with the disciples.

55 Now the Passover of the Jews was at hand, and many went up from the
country to Jerusalem before the Passover, to purify themselves. 56 They were
looking for Jesus and saying to one another as they stood in the temple, "What
do you think? That he will not come to the feast?" 57 Now the chief priests and
the Pharisees had given orders that if any one knew where he was, he should let
them know, so that they might arrest him.

[q] Greek *our place.*

PART THREE

RECORDS OF CHRIST'S PASSION AND RESURRECTION

Section M. Christ's Passion Week: His Triumphal Entry and Conflict in Jerusalem

§ 107. Jesus enters Jerusalem with acclaim

Mt. 21:1-11

1 And when they
drew near to Jeru-
salem and came to
Bethphage, to the
Mount of Olives,
then Jesus sent
two disciples,
2 saying to them,
"Go into the vil-
lage opposite you,
and immediately
you will find an ass
tied, and a colt
with her; untie
them and bring
them to me. 3 If
any one says any-
thing to you, you
shall say, 'The Lord
has need of them,'
and he will send
them immedi-
ately." 4 This took
place to fulfill
what was spoken
by the prophet,
saying,
5 "Tell the daugh-
ter of Zion,
Behold, your
king is com-
ing to you,
humble, and
mounted on
an ass,

Mk. 11:1-11

1 And when
they drew near to
Jerusalem, to Beth-
phage and Bethany,
at the Mount of
Olives, he sent two
of his disciples,
2 and said to them,
"Go into the vil-
lage opposite you,
and immediately as
you enter it you
will find a colt
tied, on which no
one has ever sat;
untie it and bring
it. 3 If any one
says to you, 'Why
are you doing
this?' say, 'The
Lord has need of it
and will send it
back here immedi-
ately.'" 4 And
they went away,
and found a colt
tied at the door
out in the open
street; and they
untied it. 5 And
those who stood
there said to them,
"What are you
doing, untying the
colt?" 6 And they

Lk. 19:29-44

29 When he
drew near to Beth-
phage and Bethany,
at the mount that
is called Olivet, he
sent two of the
disciples, 30 saying,
"Go into the vil-
lage opposite,
where on entering
you will find a
colt tied, on which
no one has ever yet
sat; untie it and
bring it here.
31 If any one asks
you, 'Why are you
untying it?' you
shall say this, 'The
Lord has need of
it.'" 32 So those
who were sent
went away and
found it as he had
told them. 33 And
as they were unty-
ing the colt, its
owners said to
them, "Why are
you untying the
colt?" 34 And they
said, "The Lord
has need of it."
35 And they
brought it to Jesus,

Jn. 12:12-19

12 The next day
a great crowd
who had come to
the feast heard
that Jesus was
coming to Jerusa-
lem. 13 So they
took branches of
palm trees and
went out to meet
him, crying, "Ho-
sanna! Blessed be
he who comes in
the name of the
Lord, even the
King of Israel!"
14 And Jesus
found a young ass
and sat upon it; as
it is written,
15 "Fear not,
daughter of
Zion;
behold thy
king is com-
ing,
sitting on an
ass's colt!"
16 His disciples
did not under-
stand this at first;
but when Jesus
was glorified, then
they remembered
that this had been

Mt. 21:1-11

and on a colt,
the foal of an
ass."

6 The disciples went and did as Jesus had directed them; 7 they brought the ass and the colt, and put their clothes on them, and he sat thereon. 8 Most of the crowd spread their clothes on the road, and others cut branches from the trees and spread them on the road. 9 And the crowds that went before him and that followed him shouted, "Hosanna to the Son of David! Blessed be he who comes in the name of the Lord! Hosanna in the highest!" 10 And when he entered Jerusalem, all the city was stirred, saying, "Who is this?" 11 And the crowds said, "This is the prophet Jesus from Nazareth of Galilee."

Mk. 11:1-11

told them what Jesus had said; and they let them go. 7 And they brought the colt to Jesus, and threw their clothes on it; and he sat upon it. 8 And many spread their clothes on the road, and others spread leafy branches which they had cut from the fields. 9 And those who went before and those who followed cried out, "Hosanna! Blessed be he who comes in the name of the Lord! 10 Blessed be the kingdom of our father David that is coming! Hosanna in the highest!"

11 And he entered Jerusalem, and went into the temple; and when he had looked round at everything, as it was already late, he went out to Bethany with the twelve.

Lk. 19:29-44

and throwing their garments on the colt they set Jesus upon it. 36 And as he rode along, they spread their garments on the road. 37 As he was drawing near, at the descent of the Mount of Olives, the whole multitude of the disciples began to rejoice and praise God with a loud voice for all the mighty works that they had seen, 38 saying,

"Blessed be the
King who
comes in the
name of the
Lord!
Peace in heaven
and glory in
the highest!"

39 And some of the Pharisees in the multitude said to him, "Teacher, rebuke your disciples." 40 He answered, "I tell you, if these were silent, the very stones would cry out."

41 And when he drew near and saw the city he wept

Jn. 12:12-19

written of him and had been done to him. 17 The crowd that had been with him when he called Lazarus out of the tomb and raised him from the dead bore witness. 18 The reason why the crowd went to meet him was that they heard he had done this sign. 19 The Pharisees then said to one another, "You see that you can do nothing; look, the world has gone after him."

Mt. 21	Mk. 11	Lk. 19:29-44	Jn. 12
		over it, [42] saying, "Would that even today you knew the things that make for peace! But now they are hid from your eyes. [43] For the days shall come upon you, when your enemies will cast up a bank about you and surround you, and hem you in on every side, [44] and dash you to the ground, you and your children within you, and they will not leave one stone upon another in you; because you did not know the time of your visitation."	

§ 108. Jesus puts a curse upon an unfruitful fig tree, which withers; he declares the power of faith

Mt. 21:18-22	Mk. 11:12-14, 20-25	Luke	John
[18] In the morning, as he was returning to the city, he was hungry. [19] And seeing a fig tree by the wayside he went to it, and found on it nothing but leaves. And he said to it, "May no fruit ever come from you again!" And the fig tree withered at once. [20] When the disciples saw it they marveled, saying, "How did the fig tree wither at once?" [21] And Jesus answered them, "Truly, I say to	[12] On the following day, when they came from Bethany, he was hungry. [13] And seeing in the distance a fig tree in leaf, he went to see if he could find anything on it. When he came to it, he found nothing but leaves, for it was not the season for figs. [14] And he said to it, "May no one ever eat fruit from you again." And his disciples heard it. [20] As they passed by in the		

Mt. 21:18-22	Mk. 11:12-14, 20-25	Luke	John
you, if you have faith and never doubt, you will not only do what has been done to the fig tree, but even if you say to this mountain, 'Be taken up and cast into the sea,' it will be done. [22] And whatever you ask in prayer, you will receive, if you have faith."	morning, they saw the fig tree withered away to its roots. [21] And Peter remembered and said to him, "Master,[a] look! The fig tree which you cursed has withered." [22] And Jesus answered them, "Have faith in God. [23] Truly, I say to you, whoever says to this mountain, Be taken up and cast into the sea, and does not doubt in his heart, but believes that what he says will come to pass, it will be done for him. [24] Therefore I tell you, whatever you ask in prayer, believe that you receive it, and you will. [25] And whenever you stand praying, forgive, if you have anything against any one; so that your Father also who is in heaven may forgive you your trespasses."[b]		

§ 109. Jesus cleanses the temple and heals there; children praise him

Mt. 21:12-17	Mk. 11:15-19	Lk. 19:45-48	John
[12] And Jesus entered the temple of God[c] and drove out all who sold and bought in the temple, and he overturned the tables of the money-changers and the seats of those who sold pigeons. [13] He said to them, "It is written, 'My house shall be called a house of prayer'; but you make it a den of robbers."	[15] And they came to Jerusalem. And he entered the temple and began to drive out those who sold and those who bought in the temple, and he overturned the tables of the money-changers and the seats of those who sold pigeons; [16] and he would not allow any one to carry anything through the temple. [17] And he	[45] And he entered the temple and began to drive out those who sold, [46] saying to them, "It is written, 'My house shall be a house of prayer'; but you have made it a den of robbers." [47] And he was teaching daily in the temple. The chief priests and the scribes and the principal men of the people sought to de-	

[a] Or *Rabbi.*
[b] Many ancient authorities add verse 26, *"But if you do not forgive, neither will your Father who is in heaven forgive your trespasses."*
[c] Some ancient authorities omit *of God.*

Mt. 21:12-17

[14] And the blind and the lame came to him in the temple, and he healed them. [15] But when the chief priests and the scribes saw the wonderful things that he did, and the children crying out in the temple, "Hosanna to the Son of David!" they were indignant; [16] and they said to him, "Do you hear what these are saying?" And Jesus said to them, "Yes; have you never read,

'Out of the mouth of babes and sucklings
thou hast brought perfect praise'?"

[17] And leaving them, he went out of the city to Bethany and lodged there.

Mk. 11:15-19

taught, and said to them, "Is it not written, 'My house shall be called a house of prayer for all the nations'? But you have made it a den of robbers." [18] And the chief priests and the scribes heard it and sought a way to destroy him; for they feared him, because all the multitude was astonished at his teaching. [19] And when evening came they[d] went out of the city.

Lk. 19:45-48

stroy him; [48] but they did not find anything they could do, for all the people hung upon his words.

John

(See also article 20)

§ 110. Chief priests, scribes, and elders question the authority of Jesus

Mt. 21:23-27

[23] And when he entered the temple, the chief priests and the elders of the people came up to him as he was teaching, and said, "By what authority are you doing these things, and who gave you this authority?" [24] Jesus an-

Mk. 11:27-33

[27] And they came again to Jerusalem. And as he was walking in the temple, the chief priests and the scribes and the elders came to him, [28] and they said to him, "By what authority are you doing these things, or who

Lk. 20:1-8

[1] One day, as he was teaching the people in the temple and preaching the gospel, the chief priests and the scribes with the elders came up [2] and said to him, "Tell us by what authority you do these things, or who it is

John

[d] Some ancient authorities read *he*.

Mt. 21:23-27

swered them, "I also will ask you a question; and if you tell me the answer, then I also will tell you by what authority I do these things. [25] The baptism of John, whence was it? From heaven or from men?" And they argued with one another, "If we say, 'From heaven,' he will say to us, 'Why then did you not believe him?' [26] But if we say, 'From men,' we are afraid of the multitude; for all hold that John was a prophet." [27] So they answered Jesus, "We do not know." And he said to them, "Neither will I tell you by what authority I do these things."

Mk. 11:27-33

gave you this authority to do them?" [29] Jesus said to them, "I will ask you a question; answer me, and I will tell you by what authority I do these things. [30] Was the baptism of John from heaven or from men? Answer me." [31] And they argued with one another, "If we say, 'From heaven,' he will say, 'Why then did you not believe him?' [32] But shall we say, 'From men'?" — they were afraid of the people, for all held that John was a real prophet. [33] So they answered Jesus, "We do not know." And Jesus said to them, "Neither will I tell you by what authority I do these things."

Lk. 20:1-8

that gave you this authority." [3] He answered them, "I also will ask you a question; now tell me, [4] Was the baptism of John from heaven or from men?" [5] And they discussed it with one another, saying, "If we say, 'From heaven,' he will say, 'Why did you not believe him?' [6] But if we say, 'From men,' all the people will stone us; for they are convinced that John was a prophet." [7] So they answered that they did not know whence it was. [8] And Jesus said to them, "Neither will I tell you by what authority I do these things."

John

§ 111. Three parables on Israel's unfruitfulness are given

a. Two sons

Mt. 21:28-32

[28] "What do you think? A man had two sons, and he went to the first and said, 'Son, go and work in the vineyard today.' [29] And he answered, 'I will not'; but afterward he repented and went. [30] And he went to the second and said the same; and he answered, 'I go, sir,' but did not go. [31] Which of the two did the will of his father?" They said, "The first." Jesus said to them, "Truly, I say to you, the tax collectors and the harlots go into the kingdom of God before you. [32] For John came to you in the way of righteousness, and you did not believe him, but the tax collectors and the harlots believed him; and even when you saw it, you did not afterward repent and believe him."

b. Wicked tenants

Mt. 21:33-46

[33] "Hear another parable. There was a householder who planted a vineyard, and set a hedge around it, and dug a wine press in it, and built a tower, and let it out to tenants, and went into another country. [34] When the season of fruit drew near, he sent his servants to the tenants, to get his fruit; [35] and the tenants took his servants and beat one, killed another, and stoned another. [36] Again he sent other servants, more than the first; and they did the same to them. [37] Afterward he sent his son to them, saying, 'They will respect my son.' [38] But when the tenants saw the son, they said to themselves, 'This is the heir; come, let us kill him and have his inheritance.' [39] And they took him and cast him out of the vineyard, and killed him. [40] When therefore the owner of the vineyard comes, what will he do to those tenants?" [41] They said to him, "He will put those wretches to a miserable

Mk. 12:1-12

[1] And he began to speak to them in parables. "A man planted a vineyard, and set a hedge around it, and dug a pit for the wine press, and built a tower, and let it out to tenants, and went into another country. [2] When the time came, he sent a servant to the tenants, to get from them some of the fruit of the vineyard. [3] And they took him and beat him, and sent him away empty-handed. [4] Again he sent to them another servant, and they wounded him in the head, and treated him shamefully. [5] And he sent another, and him they killed; and so with many others, some they beat and some they killed. [6] He had still one other, a beloved son; finally he sent him to them, saying, 'They will respect my son.' [7] But those tenants said to one another, 'This is the heir; come, let us kill him, and the inheritance will be ours.' [8] And they took him and killed him, and cast him out of the vineyard. [9] What

Lk. 20:9-19

[9] And he began to tell the people this parable: "A man planted a vineyard, and let it out to tenants, and went into another country for a long while. [10] When the time came, he sent a servant to the tenants, that they should give him some of the fruit of the vineyard; but the tenants beat him, and sent him away empty-handed. [11] And he sent another servant; him also they beat and treated shamefully, and sent him away empty-handed. [12] And he sent yet a third; this one they wounded and cast out. [13] Then the owner of the vineyard said, 'What shall I do? I will send my beloved son; it may be they will respect him.' [14] But when the tenants saw him, they said to themselves, 'This is the heir; let us kill him, that the inheritance may be ours.' [15] And they cast him out of the vineyard and killed him. What then will the owner of the vineyard do to them? [16] He will come and destroy those

John

Mt. 21:33-46	Mk. 12:1-12	Lk. 20:9-19	John
death, and let out the vineyard to other tenants who will give him the fruits in their seasons." [42] Jesus said to them, "Have you never read in the scriptures: 'The very stone which the builders rejected has become the head of the corner; this was the Lord's doing, and it is marvelous in our eyes'? [43] Therefore I tell you, the kingdom of God will be taken away from you and given to a nation producing the fruits of it."[e] [45] When the chief priests and the Pharisees heard his parables, they perceived that he was speaking about them. [46] But when they tried to arrest him, they feared the multitudes, because they held him to be a prophet.	will the owner of the vineyard do? He will come and destroy the tenants and give the vineyard to others. [10] Have you not read this scripture: 'The very stone which the builders rejected has become the head of the corner; [11] this was the Lord's doing, and it is marvelous in our eyes'?" [12] And they tried to arrest him, but feared the multitude, for they perceived that he had told the parable against them; so they left him and went away.	tenants, and give the vineyard to others." When they heard this, they said, "God forbid!" [17] But he looked at them and said, "What then is this that is written: 'The very stone which the builders rejected has become the head of the corner'? [18] Every one who falls on that stone will be broken to pieces; but when it falls on any one it will crush him." [19] The scribes and the chief priests tried to lay hands on him at that very hour, but they feared the people; for they perceived that he had told this parable against them.	

c. Guests at the wedding feast of the king's son

Mt. 22:1-14

[1] And again Jesus spoke to them in parables, saying, [2] "The kingdom of heaven may be compared to a king who gave a marriage feast for his son, [3] and sent his servants to call those who were invited to the marriage feast; but they would not come. [4] Again he sent other servants, saying, 'Tell those who are invited, Behold,

[e] Some ancient authorities add verse 44, *"And he who falls on this stone will be broken to pieces; but when it falls on anyone, it will crush him."*

I have made ready my dinner, my oxen and my fat calves are killed, and everything is ready; come to the marriage feast.' 5 But they made light of it and went off, one to his farm, another to his business, 6 while the rest seized his servants, treated them shamefully, and killed them. 7 The king was angry, and he sent his troops and destroyed those murderers and burned their city. 8 Then he said to his servants, 'The wedding is ready, but those invited were not worthy. 9 Go therefore to the thoroughfares, and invite to the marriage feast as many as you find.' 10 And those servants went out into the streets and gathered all whom they found, both bad and good; so the wedding hall was filled with guests.

11 "But when the king came in to look at the guests, he saw there a man who had no wedding garment; 12 and he said to him, 'Friend, how did you get in here without a wedding garment?' And he was speechless. 13 Then the king said to the attendants, 'Bind him hand and foot, and cast him into the outer darkness; there men will weep and gnash their teeth.' 14 For many are called, but few are chosen."

(See also Luke 14:15-24, article 89)

§ 112. Scheming leaders put three questions; Jesus asks one

a. The Pharisees and Herodians: about paying taxes to Caesar

Mt. 22:15-22

15 Then the Pharisees went and took counsel how to entangle him in his talk. 16 And they sent their disciples to him, along with the Herodians, saying, "Master, we know that you are true, and teach the way of God truthfully, and care for no man; for you do not regard the position of men. 17 Tell us, then, what you think. Is it lawful to pay taxes to Caesar, or not?" 18 But Jesus, aware of their malice, said, "Why put me to the test, you hypocrites? 19 Show me the money for the tax." And they brought him

Mk. 12:13-17

13 And they sent to him some of the Pharisees and some of the Herodians, to entrap him in his talk. 14 And they came and said to him, "Teacher, we know that you are true, and care for no man; for you do not regard the position of men, but truly teach the way of God. Is it lawful to pay taxes to Caesar, or not? 15 Should we pay them, or should we not?" But knowing their hypocrisy, he said to them, "Why put me to the test? Bring me a coin,[f] and let me look at it." 16 And they brought one. And he

Lk. 20:20-26

20 So they watched him, and sent spies, who pretended to be sincere, that they might take hold of what he said, so as to deliver him up to the authority and jurisdiction of the governor. 21 They asked him, "Teacher, we know that you speak and teach rightly, and show no partiality, but truly teach the way of God. 22 Is it lawful for us to give tribute to Caesar, or not?" 23 But he perceived their craftiness, and said to them, 24 "Show me a coin.[f] Whose likeness and inscription has it?" They said, "Caesar's." 25 He said to them, "Then

John

[f] Greek *a dinarius*.

Mt. 22:15-22

a coin.[f] 20 And Jesus said to them, "Whose likeness and inscription is this?" 21 They said, "Caesar's." Then he said to them, "Render therefore to Caesar the things that are Caesar's, and to God the things that are God's." 22 When they heard it, they marveled; and they left him and went away.

Mk. 12:13-17

said to them, "Whose likeness and inscription is this?" They said to him, "Caesar's." 17 Jesus said to them, "Render to Caesar the things that are Caesar's, and to God the things that are God's." And they were amazed at him.

Lk. 20:20-26

render to Caesar the things that are Caesar's, and to God the things that are God's." 26 And they were not able in the presence of the people to catch him by what he said; but marveling at his answer they were silent.

John

b. The Sadducees: about the resurrection

Mt. 22:23-33

23 The same day Sadducees came to him, who say that there is no resurrection; and they asked him a question, 24 saying, "Teacher, Moses said, 'If a man dies, having no children, his brother must marry the widow, and raise up children for his brother.' 25 Now there were seven brothers among us; the first married, and died, and having no children left his wife to his brother. 26 So too the second and third, down to the seventh. 27 After them all, the woman died. 28 In the resurrection, therefore, to which of the seven will

Mk. 12:18-27

18 And Sadducees came to him, who say that there is no resurrection; and they asked him a question, saying, 19 "Teacher, Moses wrote for us that if a man's brother dies and leaves a wife, but leaves no child, the man[g] must take the wife, and raise up children for his brother. 20 There were seven brothers; the first took a wife, and when he died left no children; 21 and the second took her, and died, leaving no children; and the third likewise; 22 and the seven left no children. Last of all the woman also died. 23 In

Lk. 20:27-38

27 There came to him some Sadducees, those who say that there is no resurrection, 28 and they asked him a question, saying, "Teacher, Moses wrote for us that if a man's brother dies, having a wife but no children, the man[g] must take the wife and raise up children for his brother. 29 Now there were seven brothers; the first took a wife, and died without children; 30 and the second 31 and the third took her, and likewise all seven left no children and died. 32 Afterward the woman also died. 33 In the resurrection, there-

John

[f] Greek *a dinarius.*
[g] Greek *his brother.*

Mt. 22:23-33

she be wife? For they all had her."

[29] But Jesus answered them, "You are wrong, because you know neither the scriptures nor the power of God. [30] For in the resurrection they neither marry nor are given in marriage, but are like angels[a] in heaven. [31] And as for the resurrection of the dead, have you not read what was said to you by God, [32] 'I am the God of Abraham, and the God of Isaac, and the God of Jacob'? He is not God of the dead, but of the living." [33] And when the crowd heard it, they were astonished at his teaching.

Mk. 12:18-27

the resurrection whose wife will she be? For the seven had her as wife."

[24] Jesus said to them, "Is not this why you are wrong, that you know neither the scriptures nor the power of God? [25] For when they rise from the dead, they neither marry nor are given in marriage, but are like angels in heaven. [26] And as for the dead being raised, have you not read in the book of Moses, in the passage about the bush, how God said to him, 'I am the God of Abraham, and the God of Isaac, and the God of Jacob'? [27] He is not God of the dead, but of the living; you are quite wrong."

Lk. 20:27-38

fore, whose wife will the woman be? For the seven had her as wife."

[34] And Jesus said to them, "The sons of this age marry and are given in marriage; [35] but those who are accounted worthy to attain to that age and to the resurrection from the dead neither marry nor are given in marriage, [36] for they cannot die any more, because they are equal to angels and are sons of God, being sons of the resurrection. [37] But that the dead are raised, even Moses showed, in the passage about the bush, where he calls the Lord the God of Abraham and the God of Isaac and the God of Jacob. [38] Now he is not God of the dead, but of the living, for all live to him."

John

c. The scribes: about the great commandment

Mt. 22:34-40

[34] But when the Pharisees heard that he had silenced the Sadducees, they came together. [35] And one of them, a lawyer, asked

Mk. 12:28-34

[28] And one of the scribes came up and heard them disputing with one another, and seeing that he answered them well,

Lk. 20:39, 40

[39] And some of the scribes answered, "Teacher, you have spoken well." [40] For they no longer dared to ask him anything.

John

[a] Many ancient authorities add *of God.*

Mt. 22:34-40	Mk. 12:28-34	Lk. 20	John
him a question, to test him. [36] "Teacher, which is the great commandment in the law?" [37] And he said to him, "You shall love the Lord your God with all your heart, and with all your soul, and with all your mind. [38] This is the great and first commandment. [39] And a second is like it, You shall love your neighbor as yourself. [40] On these two commandments depend all the law and the prophets."	asked him, "Which commandment is the first of all?" [29] Jesus answered, "The first is, 'Hear, O Israel: The Lord our God, the Lord is one; [30] and you shall love the Lord your God with all your heart, and with all your soul, and with all your mind, and with all your strength.' [31] The second is this, 'You shall love your neighbor as yourself.' There is no other commandment greater than these." [32] And the scribe said to him, "You are right, Teacher; you have truly said that he is one, and there is no other but he; [33] and to love him with all the heart, and with all the understanding, and with all the strength, and to love one's neighbor as oneself, is much more than all whole burnt offerings and sacrifices." [34] And when Jesus saw that he answered wisely, he said to him, "You are not far from the kingdom of God." And after that no one dared to ask him any question.		

d. Jesus: about the Messiah's ancestry

Mt. 22:41-46

[41] Now while the Pharisees were gathered together, Jesus asked them a question, [42] saying, "What do you think of the Christ? Whose son is he?" They said to him, "The son of David." [43] He said to them, "How is it then that David, inspired by the Spirit,[j] calls him Lord, saying,

[44] 'The Lord said to my Lord,
Sit at my right hand,
till I put thy enemies under thy feet'?

[45] If David thus calls him Lord, how is he his son?" [46] And no one was able to answer him a word, nor from that day did any one dare to ask him any more questions.

Mk. 12:35-37

[35] And as Jesus taught in the temple, he said, "How can the scribes say that the Christ is the son of David? [36] David himself, inspired by[i] the Holy Spirit, declared,

'The Lord said to my Lord,
Sit at my right hand,
till I put thy enemies under thy feet.'

[37] David himself calls him Lord; so how is he his son?" And the great throng heard him gladly.

Lk. 20:41-44

[41] But he said to them, "How can they say that the Christ is David's son? [42] For David himself says in the Book of Psalms,

'The Lord said to my Lord,
Sit thou at my right hand,
[43] till I make thy enemies a stool for thy feet.'

[44] David thus calls him Lord; so how is he his son?"

John

§ 113. Jesus pronounces woes upon the scribes and Pharisees as hypocrites

Mt. 23:1-39

[1] Then said Jesus to the crowds and to his disciples, [2] "The scribes and the Pharisees sit on Moses' seat; [3] so practice and observe whatever they tell you, but not what they do;

Mk. 12:38-40

[38] And in his teaching he said, "Beware of the scribes, who like to go about in long robes, and to have salutations in the market places [39] and the best seats in the synagogues and the

Lk. 20:45-47

[45] And in the hearing of all the people he said to his disciples, [46] "Beware of the scribes, who like to go about in long robes, and love salutations in the market places and

John

[i] Or *himself, in.*
[j] Or *in the Spirit.*

Mt. 23:1-39

for they preach, but do not practice. [4] They bind heavy burdens, hard to bear,[k] and lay them on men's shoulders; but they themselves will not move them with their finger. [5] They do all their deeds to be seen by men; for they make their phylacteries broad and their fringes long, [6] and they love the place of honor at feasts and the best seats in the synagogues, [7] and salutations in the market places, and being called rabbi by men. [8] But you are not to be called rabbi, for you have one teacher, and you are all brethren. [9] And call no man your father on earth, for you have one Father, who is in heaven. [10] Neither be called masters, for you have one master, the Christ. [11] He who is greatest among you shall be your servant; [12] whoever exalts himself shall be humbled, and whoever humbles himself shall be exalted.

[13] "But woe to you, scribes and Pharisees,

Mk. 12:38-40

places of honor at feasts, [40] who devour widows' houses and for a pretense make long prayers. They will receive the greater condemnation."

Lk. 20:45-47

the best seats in the synagogues and the places of honor at feasts, [47] who devour widows' houses and for a pretense make long prayers. They will receive the greater condemnation."

John

[k] Some ancient authorities omit *hard to bear.*

Mt. 23:1-39 | Mk. 12 | Lk. 20 | John

hypocrites! because you shut the kingdom of
heaven against men; for you neither enter yourselves, nor allow those who would enter to go in.[l]
15 Woe to you, scribes and Pharisees, hypocrites!
for you traverse sea and land to make a single
proselyte, and when he becomes a proselyte, you
make him twice as much a child of hell[m] as yourselves.

16 "Woe to you, blind guides, who say, 'If any
one swears by the temple, it is nothing; but if any
one swears by the gold of the temple, he is bound
by his oath.' 17 You blind fools! For which is
greater, the gold or the temple that has made the
gold sacred? 18 And you say, 'If any one swears by
the altar, it is nothing; but if any one swears by
the gift that is on the altar, he is bound by his
oath.' 19 You blind men! For which is greater,
the gift or the altar that makes the gift sacred?
20 So he who swears by the altar, swears by it and
by everything on it; 21 and he who swears by the
temple, swears by it and by him who dwells in it;
22 and he who swears by heaven, swears by the
throne of God and by him who sits upon it.

23 "Woe to you, scribes and Pharisees, hypocrites!
for you tithe mint and dill and cummin, and have
neglected the weightier matters of the law, justice
and mercy and faith; these you ought to have done,
without neglecting the others. 24 You blind
guides, straining out a gnat and swallowing a
camel!

25 "Woe to you, scribes and Pharisees, hypocrites! for you cleanse the outside of the cup and
of the plate, but inside they are full of extortion
and rapacity. 26 You blind Pharisee! first cleanse
the inside of the cup and of the plate, that the
outside also may be clean.

27 "Woe to you, scribes and Pharisees, hypocrites! for you are like whitewashed tombs, which
outwardly appear beautiful, but within they are

[l] Some authorities add here (or after verse 12) verse 14, *Woe to you, scribes and Pharisees, hypocrites! for you devour widows' houses, and for a pretense you make long prayers; therefore you will receive the greater condemnation.*

[m] Greek *Gehenna.*

Mt. 23:1-39 | Mk. 12 | Lk. 20 | John

full of dead men's bones and all uncleanness. 28 So
you also outwardly appear righteous to men, but
within you are full of hypocrisy and iniquity.
29 "Woe to you, scribes and Pharisees, hypocrites! for you build the tombs of the prophets
and adorn the monuments of the righteous, 30 saying, 'If we had lived in the days of our fathers, we
would not have taken part with them in shedding
the blood of the prophets.' 31 Thus you witness
against yourselves, that you are sons of those who
murdered the prophets. 32 Fill up, then, the
measure of your fathers. 33 You serpents, you
brood of vipers, how are you to escape being
sentenced to hell?[m] 34 Therefore I send you
prophets and wise men and scribes, some of whom
you will kill and crucify, and some you will
scourge in your synagogues and persecute from
town to town, 35 that upon you may come all the
righteous blood shed on earth, from the blood of
innocent Abel to the blood of Zechariah the son
of Barachiah, whom you murdered between the
sanctuary and the altar. 36 Truly, I say to you, all
this will come upon this generation.
37 "O Jerusalem, Jerusalem, killing the prophets
and stoning those who are sent to you! How often
would I have gathered your children together as a
hen gathers her brood under her wings, and you
would not! 38 Behold, your house is forsaken and
desolate.[n] 39 For I tell you, you will not see me
again, until you say, 'Blessed be he who comes in
the name of the Lord.' "

(See also articles 82 and 88)

§ 114. Jesus comments on the widow's offering of two coins

Matt. | Mk. 12:41-44 | Lk. 21:1-4 | John

Mk. 12:41-44

41 And he sat down opposite
the treasury, and watched the
multitude putting money into
the treasury. Many rich people
put in large sums. 42 And a

Lk. 21:1-4

1 He looked up and saw the
rich putting their gifts into the
treasury; 2 and he saw a poor
widow put in two copper coins.
3 And he said, "Truly I tell you,

[m] Greek *Gehenna.*
[n] Some ancient authorities omit *and desolate.*

Matt.

Mk. 12:41-44

poor widow came, and put in
two copper coins, which make
a penny. 43 And he called his
disciples to him, and said to
them, "Truly, I say to you, this
poor widow has put in more
than all those who are contribut-
ing to the treasury. 44 For they
all contributed out of their
abundance; but she out of her
poverty has put in everything
she had, her whole living."

Lk. 21:1-4

this poor widow has put in
more than all of them; 4 for they
all contributed out of their
abundance, but she out of her
poverty put in all the living that
she had."

John

§ 115. Certain Greeks seek Jesus; the Jews reject him

Jn. 12:20-50

20 Now among those who went up to worship at the feast were some Greeks.
21 So these came to Philip, who was from Bethsaida in Galilee, and said to him,
"Sir, we wish to see Jesus." 22 Philip went and told Andrew; Andrew went with
Philip and they told Jesus. 23 And Jesus answered them, "The hour has come for
the Son of man to be glorified. 24 Truly, truly, I say to you, unless a grain of wheat
falls into the earth and dies, it remains alone; but if it dies, it bears much fruit.
25 He who loves his life loses it, and he who hates his life in this world will keep
it for eternal life. 26 If any one serves me, he must follow me; and where I am,
there shall my servant be also; if any one serves me, the Father will honor him.

27 "Now is my soul troubled. And what shall I say? 'Father, save me from this
hour'? No, for this purpose I have come to this hour. 28 Father, glorify thy name."
Then a voice came from heaven, "I have glorified it, and I will glorify it again."
29 The crowd standing by heard it and said that it had thundered. Others said,
"An angel has spoken to him." 30 Jesus answered, "This voice has come for your
sake, not for mine. 31 Now is the judgment of this world, now shall the ruler of this
world be cast out; 32 and I, when I am lifted up from the earth, will draw all men
to myself." 33 He said this to show by what death he was to die. 34 The crowd
answered him, "We have heard from the law that the Christ remains forever. How
can you say that the Son of man must be lifted up? Who is this Son of man?"
35 Jesus said to them, "The light is with you for a little longer. Walk while you
have the light, lest the darkness overtake you; who walks in the darkness does not
know where he goes. 36 While you have the light, believe in the light, that you
may become sons of light."

When Jesus had said this, he departed and hid himself from them. 37 Though
he had done so many signs before them, yet they did not believe in him; 38 it was
that the word spoken by the prophet Isaiah might be fulfilled:

"Lord, who has believed our report,
and to whom has the arm of the Lord been revealed?"

39 Therefore they could not believe. For Isaiah again said,

40 "He has blinded their eyes and hardened their heart,
lest they should see with their eyes and perceive with their heart,
and turn for me to heal them."

41 Isaiah said this because he saw his glory and spoke of him. 42 Nevertheless many
even of the authorities believed in him, but for fear of the Pharisees they did not
confess it, lest they should be put out of the synagogue; 43 for they loved the praise
of men more than the praise of God.
44 And Jesus cried out and said, "He who believes in me, believes not in me but
in him who sent me. 45 And he who sees me sees him who sent me. 46 I have come
as light into the world, that whoever believes in me may not remain in darkness.
47 If any one hears my sayings and does not keep them, I do not judge him; for
I did not come to judge the world but to save the world. 48 He who rejects me
and does not receive my sayings has a judge; the word that I have spoken will be
his judge on the last day. 49 For I have not spoken on my own authority; the
Father who sent me has himself given me commandment what to say and what to
speak. 50 And I know that his commandment is eternal life. What I say, therefore,
I say as the Father has bidden me."

§ 116. Jesus discourses on the destruction of Jerusalem, the close of the age, the coming of the Son of Man, and the judgment

a. Times and signs

Mt. 24:1-51

1 Jesus left the
temple and was going
away, when his dis-
ciples came to point
out to him the build-
ings of the temple.
2 But he answered
them, "You see all
these, do you not?
Truly, I say to you,
there will not be left
here one stone upon
another, that will not
be thrown down."
3 As he sat on the
Mount of Olives, the

Mk. 13:1-37

1 And as he came
out of the temple, one
of his disciples said to
him, "Look, Teacher,
what wonderful stones
and what wonderful
buildings!" 2 And Jesus
said to him, "Do you
see these great build-
ings? There will not
be left here one stone
upon another, that will
not be thrown down."
3 And as he sat on
the Mount of Olives
opposite the temple,

Lk. 21:5-38

5 And as some spoke
of the temple, how it
was adorned with
noble stones and offer-
ings, he said, 6 "As for
these things which you
see, the days will come
when there shall not be
left here one stone
upon another that will
not be thrown down."
7 And they asked him,
"Teacher, when will
this be, and what will
be the sign when this
is about to take place?"

John

Mt. 24:1-51	Mk. 13:1-37	Lk. 21:5-38	John

Mt. 24:1-51

disciples came to him privately, saying, "Tell us, when will this be, and what will be the sign of your coming and of the close of the age?" [4] And Jesus answered them, "Take heed that no one leads you astray. [5] For many will come in my name, saying, 'I am the Christ,' and they will lead many astray. [6] And you will hear of wars and rumors of wars; see that you are not alarmed; for this must take place, but the end is not yet. [7] For nation will rise against nation, and kingdom against kingdom, and there will be famines and earthquakes in various places: [8] all this is but the beginning of the sufferings.

[9] "Then they will deliver you up to tribulation, and put you to death; and you will be hated by all nations for my name's sake. [10] And then many will fall away,° and betray one another. [11] And many false prophets will arise and lead many astray. [12] And because wickedness is multiplied, most

° Or *stumble.*

Mk. 13:1-37

Peter and James and John and Andrew asked him privately, [4] "Tell us, when will this be, and what will be the sign when these things are all to be accomplished?" [5] And Jesus began to say to them, "Take heed that no one leads you astray. [6] Many will come in my name, saying, 'I am he!' and they will lead many astray. [7] And when you hear of wars and rumors of wars, do not be alarmed; this must take place, but the end is not yet. [8] For nation will rise against nation, and kingdom against kingdom; there will be earthquakes in various places, there will be famines; this is but the beginning of the sufferings.

[9] "But take heed to yourselves; for they will deliver you up to councils; and you will be beaten in synagogues; and you will stand before governors and kings for my sake, to bear testimony before them. [10] And the gospel must first be preached to all nations.

Lk. 21:5-38

[8] And he said, "Take heed that you are not led astray; for many will come in my name, saying, 'I am he!' and, 'The time is at hand!' Do not go after them. [9] And when you hear of wars and tumults, do not be terrified; for this must first take place, but the end will not be at once."

[10] Then he said to them, "Nation will rise against nation, and kingdom against kingdom; [11] there will be great earthquakes, and in various places famines and pestilences; and there will be terrors and great signs from heaven. [12] But before all this they will lay their hands on you and persecute you, delivering you up to the synagogues and prisons, and you will be brought before kings and governors for my name's sake. [13] This will be a time for you to bear testimony. [14] Settle it therefore in your minds, not to meditate beforehand how to answer; [15] for I will give you a mouth and wis-

Mt. 24:1-51

men's love will grow cold. 13 But he who endures to the end will be saved. 14 And this gospel of the kingdom will be preached throughout the whole world, as a testimony to all nations; and then the end will come.

15 "So when you see the desolating sacrilege spoken of by the prophet Daniel, standing in the holy place (let the reader understand), 16 then let those who are in Judea flee to the mountains; 17 let him who is on the housetop not go down to take what is in his house; 18 and let him who is in the field not turn back to take his mantle. 19 And alas for those who are with child and for those who give suck in those days! 20 Pray that your flight may not be in winter or on a sabbath. 21 For then there will be great tribulation, such as has not been from the beginning of the world until now, no, and never will be. 22 And if those days had not been shortened, no human being would be saved; but for the

Mk. 13:1-37

11 And when they bring you to trial and deliver you up, do not be anxious beforehand what you are to say; but say whatever is given you in that hour, for it is not you who speak, but the Holy Spirit. 12 And brother will deliver up brother to death, and the father his child, and children will rise against parents and have them put to death; 13 and you will be hated by all for my name's sake. But he who endures to the end will be saved.

14 "But when you see the desolating sacrilege set up where it ought not to be (let the reader understand), then let those who are in Judea flee to the mountains; 15 let him who is on the housetop not go down, nor enter his house, to take anything away; 16 and let him who is in the field not turn back to take his mantle. 17 And alas for those who are with child and for those who give suck in those days! 18 Pray that it may not happen in winter. 19 For in those days there will be such tribu-

Lk. 21:5-38

dom, which none of your adversaries will be able to withstand or contradict. 16 You will be delivered up even by parents and brothers and kinsmen and friends, and some of you they will put to death; 17 you will be hated by all for my name's sake. 18 But not a hair of your head will perish. 19 By your endurance you will gain your lives.

20 "But when you see Jerusalem surrounded by armies, then know that its desolation has come near. 21 Then let those who are in Judea flee to the mountains, and let those who are inside the city depart, and let not those who are out in the country enter it; 22 for these are days of vengeance, to fulfill all that is written. 23 Alas for those who are with child and for those who give suck in those days! For great distress shall be upon the earth and wrath upon this people; 24 they will fall by the edge of the sword, and be led captive among all nations; and Jeru-

John

Mt. 24:1-51

sake of the elect those
days will be shortened.
23 Then if any one says
to you, 'Lo, here is the
Christ!' or 'There he
is!' do not believe it.
24 For false Christs and
false prophets will arise
and show great signs
and wonders, so as to
lead astray, if possible,
even the elect. 25 Lo, I
have told you before-
hand. 26 So, if they say
to you, 'Lo, he is in the
wilderness,' do not go
out; if they say, 'Lo, he
is in the inner rooms,'
do not believe it. 27 For
as the lightning comes
from the east and
shines as far as the
west, so will be the
coming of the Son of
man. 28 Wherever the
body is, there the
eagles[p] will be gath-
ered together.

29 "Immediately after
the tribulation of those
days the sun will be
darkened, and the
moon will not give its
light, and the stars will
fall from heaven, and
the powers of the
heavens will be shaken;
30 then will appear the
sign of the Son of man
in heaven, and then all
the tribes of the earth

[p] Or *vultures*.

Mk. 13:1-37

lation as has not been
from the beginning of
the creation which God
created until now, and
never will be. 20 And
if the Lord had not
shortened the days, no
human being would be
saved; but for the sake
of the elect, whom he
chose, he shortened the
days. 21 And then if
any one says to you,
'Look, here is the
Christ!' or 'Look, there
he is!' do not believe it.
22 False Christs and
false prophets will arise
and show signs and
wonders, to lead astray,
if possible, the elect.
23 But take heed; I
have told you all things
beforehand.

24 "But in those days,
after that tribulation,
the sun will be
darkened, and the
moon will not give
its light, 25 and the
stars will be falling
from heaven, and the
powers in the heavens
will be shaken. 26 And
then they will see the
Son of man coming in
clouds with great
power and glory.
27 And then he will
send out the angels,
and gather his elect

Lk. 21:5-38

salem will be trodden
down by the Gentiles,
until the times of the
Gentiles are fulfilled.

25 "And there will be
signs in sun and moon
and stars, and upon the
earth distress of nations
in perplexity at the
roaring of the sea and
the waves, 26 men
fainting with fear and
with foreboding of
what is coming on the
world; for the powers
of the heavens will be
shaken. 27 And then
they will see the Son of
man coming in a cloud
with power and great
glory. 28 Now when
these things begin to
take place, look up and
raise your heads, be-
cause your redemption
is drawing near."

29 And he told them
a parable: "Look at the
fig tree, and all the
trees; 30 as soon as they
come out in leaf, you
see for yourselves and
know that the summer
is already near. 31 So
also, when you see
these things taking
place, you know that
the kingdom of God is
near. 32 Truly, I say to
you, this generation
will not pass away till

John

Mt. 24:1-51

will mourn, and they will see the Son of man coming on the clouds of heaven with power and great glory; 31 and he will send out his angels with a loud trumpet call, and they will gather his elect from the four winds, from one end of heaven to the other.

32 "From the fig tree learn its lesson: as soon as its branch becomes tender and puts forth its leaves, you know that summer is near. 33 So also, when you see all these things you know that he is near, at the very gates. 34 Truly, I say to you, this generation will not pass away till all these things take place. 35 Heaven and earth will pass away, but my words will not pass away.

36 "But of that day and hour no one knows, not even the angels of heaven, nor the Son, but the Father only. 37 As were the days of Noah, so will be the coming of the Son of man. 38 For as in those days before the flood they were eating and drinking, marrying and

Mk. 13:1-37

from the four winds, from the ends of the earth to the ends of heaven.

28 "From the fig tree learn its lesson: as soon as its branch becomes tender and puts forth its leaves, you know that summer is near. 29 So also, when you see these things taking place, you know that he is near, at the very gates. 30 Truly, I say to you, this generation will not pass away before all these things take place. 31 Heaven and earth will pass away, but my words will not pass away.

32 "But of that day or that hour no one knows, not even the angels in heaven, nor the Son, but only the Father. 33 Take heed, watch and pray,[q] for you do not know when the time will come. 34 It is like a man going on a journey, when he leaves home and puts his servants in charge, each with his work, and commands the doorkeeper to be on the watch. 35 Watch therefore—for you do

Lk. 21:5-38

all has taken place. 33 Heaven and earth will pass away, but my words will not pass away.

34 "But take heed to yourselves lest your hearts be weighed down with dissipation and drunkenness and cares of this life, and that day come upon you suddenly like a snare; 35 for it will come upon all who dwell upon the face of the whole earth. 36 But watch at all times, praying that you may have strength to escape all these things that will take place, and to stand before the Son of man."

37 And every day he was teaching in the temple, but at night he went out and lodged on the mount called Olivet. 38 And early in the morning all the people came to him in the temple to hear him.

John

[q] Some ancient authorities omit *and pray.*

Mt. 24:1-51

giving in marriage,
until the day when
Noah entered the ark,
39 and they did not
know until the flood
came and swept them
all away, so will be the
coming of the Son of
man. 40 Then two men
will be in the field; one
is taken and one is left.
41 Two women will be
grinding at the mill;
one is taken and one is
left. 42 Watch there-
fore, for you do not
know on what day your
Lord is coming. 43 But
know this, that if the
householder had known
in what part of the
night the thief was
coming, he would have
watched and would not
have let his house be
broken into. 44 There-
fore you also must be
ready; for the Son of
man is coming at an
hour you do not ex-
pect.

45 "Who then is the
faithful and wise serv-
ant, whom his mas-
ter has set over his
household, to give
them their food at the
proper time? 46 Blessed
is that servant whom
his master when he
comes will find so
doing. 47 Truly, I say

Mk. 13:1-37

not know when the
master of the house
will come, in the eve-
ning, or at midnight,
or at cockcrow, or in
the morning — 36 lest
he come suddenly and
find you asleep. 37 And
what I say to you I say
to all: Watch."

Lk. 21

John

Mt. 24:1-51	Mk. 13	Lk. 21	John
to you, he will set him over all his possessions. [48] But if that wicked servant says to himself, 'My master is delayed,' [49] and begins to beat his fellow servants, and eats and drinks with the drunken, [50] the master of that servant will come on a day when he does not expect him and at an hour he does not know, [51] and will punish[r] him and put him with the hypocrites; there men will weep and gnash their teeth."			

(See also article 94)

b. The parables of the ten maidens and of the talents

Mt. 25:1-30

[1] "Then the kingdom of heaven shall be compared to ten maidens who took their lamps and went to meet the bridegroom.[s] [2] Five of them were foolish, and five were wise. [3] For when the foolish took their lamps, they took no oil with them; [4] but the wise took flasks of oil with their lamps. [5] As the bridegroom was delayed, they all slumbered and slept. [6] But at midnight there was a cry, 'Behold, the bridegroom! Come out to meet him.' [7] Then all those maidens rose and trimmed their lamps. [8] And the foolish said to the wise, 'Give us some of your oil, for our lamps are going out.' [9] But the wise replied, 'Perhaps there will not be enough for us and for you; go rather to the dealers and buy for yourselves.' [10] And while they went to buy, the bridegroom came, and those who were ready went in with him to the marriage feast; and the door was shut. [11] Afterward the other maidens came also, saying, 'Lord, Lord, open to us.' [12] But he replied, 'Truly, I say to you, I do not know you.' [13] Watch therefore, for you know neither the day nor the hour.

[14] "For it will be as when a man going on a journey called his servants and entrusted to them his property; [15] to one he gave five talents,[t] to another two, to another one, to each according to his ability. Then he went away. [16] He who had received the five talents went at once and traded with them; and he made five talents

[r] Or *cut him in pieces.*
[s] Some ancient authorities add *and the bride.*
[t] See note on Matt. 18:24.

more. 17 So too, he who had the two talents made two talents more. 18 But he who
had received the one talent, went and dug in the ground and hid his master's money.
19 Now after a long time the master of those servants came and settled accounts with
them. 20 And he who had received the five talents came forward, bringing five talents
more, saying, 'Master, you delivered to me five talents; here I have made five talents
more.' 21 His master said to him, 'Well done, good and faithful servant; you have
been faithful over a little, I will set you over much; enter into the joy of your master.'
22 And he also who had the two talents came forward, saying, 'Master, you delivered
to me two talents; here I have made two talents more.' 23 His master said to him,
'Well done, good and faithful servant; you have been faithful over a little, I will set
you over much; enter into the joy of your master.' 24 He also who had received the
one talent came forward, saying, 'Master, I knew you to be a hard man, reaping
where you did not sow, and gathering where you did not winnow; 25 so I was afraid,
and I went and hid your talent in the ground. Here you have what is yours.' 26 But
his master answered him, 'You wicked and slothful servant! You knew that I reap
where I have not sowed, and gather where I have not winnowed? 27 Then you
ought to have invested my money with the bankers, and at my coming I should
have received what was my own with interest. 28 So take the talent from him, and
give it to him who has the ten talents. 29 For to every one who has will more be
given, and he will have abundance; but from him who has not, even what he has
will be taken away. 30 And cast the worthless servant into the outer darkness; there
men will weep and gnash their teeth.'

c. The great separation

Mt. 25:31-46

31 "When the Son of man comes in his glory, and all the angels with him, then he
will sit on his glorious throne. 32 Before him will be gathered all the nations, and
he will separate them one from another as a shepherd separates the sheep from the
goats, 33 and he will place the sheep at his right hand, but the goats at the left.
34 Then the King will say to those at his right hand, 'Come, O blessed of my
Father, inherit the kingdom prepared for you from the foundation of the world;
35 for I was hungry and you gave me food, I was thirsty and you gave me drink, I
was a stranger and you welcomed me, 36 I was naked and you clothed me, I was
sick and you visited me, I was in prison and you came to me.' 37 Then the righteous
will answer him, 'Lord, when did we see thee hungry and feed thee, or thirsty and
give thee drink? 38 And when did we see thee a stranger and welcome thee, or
naked and clothe thee? 39 And when did we see thee sick or in prison and visit thee?'
40 And the King will answer them, 'Truly, I say to you, as you did it to one of the
least of these my brethren, you did it to me.' 41 Then he will say to those at his
left hand, 'Depart from me, you cursed, into the eternal fire prepared for the devil
and his angels; 42 for I was hungry and you gave me no food, I was thirsty and you
gave me no drink, 43 I was a stranger and you did not welcome me, naked and you

did not clothe me, sick and in prison and you did not visit me.' [44] Then they also will answer, 'Lord, when did we see thee hungry or thirsty or a stranger or naked or sick or in prison, and did not minister to thee?' [45] Then he will answer them, 'Truly, I say to you, as you did it not to one of the least of these, you did it not to me.' [46] And they will go away into eternal punishment, but the righteous into eternal life."

§ 117. For thirty pieces of silver Judas Iscariot conspires with the rulers against Jesus

Mt. 26:1-5, 14-16

[1] When Jesus had finished all these sayings, he said to his disciples, [2] "You know that after two days the Passover is coming, and the Son of man will be delivered up to be crucified."

[3] Then the chief priests and the elders of the people gathered in the palace of the high priest, who was called Caiaphas, [4] and took counsel together in order to arrest Jesus by stealth and kill him. [5] But they said, "Not during the feast, lest there be a tumult among the people."

[14] Then one of the twelve, who was called Judas Iscariot, went to the chief priests [15] and said, "What will you give me if I deliver him to you?" And they paid him thirty pieces of silver. [16] And from that moment he sought an opportunity to betray him.

Mk. 14:1, 2, 10, 11

[1] It was now two days before the Passover and the feast of Unleavened Bread. And the chief priests and the scribes were seeking how to arrest him by stealth, and kill him; [2] for they said, "Not during the feast, lest there be a tumult of the people."

[10] Then Judas Iscariot, who was one of the twelve, went to the chief priests in order to betray him to them. [11] And when they heard it they were glad, and promised to give him money. And he sought an opportunity to betray him.

Lk. 22:1-6

[1] Now the feast of Unleavened Bread drew near, which is called the Passover. [2] And the chief priests and the scribes were seeking how to put him to death; for they feared the people.

[3] Then Satan entered into Judas called Iscariot, who was of the number of the twelve; [4] he went away and conferred with the chief priests and captains how he might betray him to them. [5] And they were glad, and engaged to give him money. [6] So he agreed, and sought an opportunity to betray him to them in the absence of the multitude.

John

§ 118. A woman of Bethany anoints Jesus; she is censured

Mt. 26:6-13

6 Now when Jesus
was at Bethany in the
house of Simon the
leper, 7 a woman came
up to him with an
alabaster jar of very
expensive ointment,
and she poured it on
his head, as he sat at
table. 8 But when the
disciples saw it, they
were indignant, saying,
"Why this waste? 9 For
this ointment might
have been sold for a
large sum, and given
to the poor." 10 But
Jesus, aware of this,
said to them, "Why do
you trouble the
woman? For she has
done a beautiful thing
to me. 11 For you al-
ways have the poor
with you, but you will
not always have me.
12 In pouring this oint-
ment on my body she
has done it to prepare
me for burial. 13 Truly,
I say to you, wherever
this gospel is preached
in the whole world,
what this woman has
done will be told in
memory of her."

Mk. 14:3-9

3 And while he was
at Bethany in the house
of Simon the leper, as
he sat at table, a
woman came with an
alabaster jar of oint-
ment of pure nard, very
costly, and she broke
the jar and poured it
over his head. 4 But
there were some who
said to themselves in-
dignantly, "Why was
the ointment thus
wasted? 5 For this oint-
ment might have been
sold for more than
three hundred denarii,[b]
and given to the poor."
And they reproached
her. 6 But Jesus said,
"Let her alone; why do
you trouble her? She
has done a beautiful
thing to me. 7 For you
always have the poor
with you, and when-
ever you will, you can
do good to them; but
you will not always
have me. 8 She has
done what she could;
she has anointed my
body beforehand for
burying. 9 And truly, I
say to you, wherever
the gospel is preached
in the whole world,
what she has done will

Luke

Jn. 12:1-11

1 Six days before
the Passover, Jesus
came to Bethany,
where Lazarus was,
whom Jesus had raised
from the dead. 2 There
they made him a sup-
per; Martha served,
but Lazarus was one of
those at table with
him. 3 Mary took a
pound[a] of costly oint-
ment of pure nard and
anointed the feet of
Jesus and wiped his
feet with her hair; and
the house was filled
with the fragrance of
the ointment. 4 But
Judas Iscariot, one of
his disciples (he who
was to betray him),
said, 5 "Why was this
ointment not sold for
three hundred denarii[b]
and given to the
poor?" 6 This he said,
not that he cared for
the poor but because
he was a thief, and as
he had the money box
he used to take what
was put into it. 7 Jesus
said, "Let her alone,
let her keep it for the
day of my burial. 8 The
poor you always have
with you, but you do
not always have me."

[a] Greek *litra.*
[b] See note on Matt. 18:28.

Mt. 26

Mk. 14:3-9

be told in memory of her."

Luke

Jn. 12:1-11

[9] When the great crowd of the Jews learned that he was there, they came, not only on account of Jesus but also to see Lazarus, whom he had raised from the dead. [10] So the chief priests planned to put Lazarus also to death, [11] because on account of him many of the Jews were going away and believing in Jesus.

Section N. Christ's Passion Week: His Last Supper, Trial, and Crucifixion

§ 119. Jesus and the twelve have the last supper together

a. Preparation for the passover

Mt. 26:17-19

[17] Now on the first day of Unleavened Bread the disciples came to Jesus, saying, "Where will you have us prepare for you to eat the passover?" [18] He said, "Go into the city to such a one, and say to him, 'The Teacher says, My time is at hand; I will keep the passover at your house with my disciples.'" [19] And the disciples did as Jesus had directed them, and they prepared the passover.

Mk. 14:12-16

[12] And on the first day of Unleavened Bread, when they sacrificed the passover lamb, his disciples said to him, "Where will you have us go and prepare for you to eat the passover?" [13] And he sent two of his disciples, and said to them, "Go into the city, and a man carrying a jar of water will meet you; follow him, [14] and wherever he enters, say to the householder, 'The Teacher says, Where is my guest room, where

Lk. 22:7-13

[7] Then came the day of Unleavened Bread, on which the passover lamb had to be sacrificed. [8] So Jesus[a] sent Peter and John, saying, "Go and prepare the passover for us, that we may eat it." [9] They said to him, "Where will you have us prepare it?" [10] He said to them, "Behold, when you have entered the city, a man carrying a jar of water will meet you; follow him into the house which he enters, [11] and tell the

John

[a] Greek *he*.

Mt. 26 | Mk. 14:12-16 | Lk. 22:7-13 | John

Mk. 14:12-16

I am to eat the pass-
over with my disciples?'
15 And he will show
you a large upper room
furnished and ready;
there prepare for us."
16 And the disciples set
out and went to the
city, and found it as he
had told them; and they
prepared the passover.

Lk. 22:7-13

householder, 'The
Teacher says to you,
Where is the guest
room, where I am to
eat the passover with
my disciples?' 12 And
he will show you a
large upper room fur-
nished; there make
ready." 13 And they
went, and found it as
he had told them; and
they prepared the pass-
over.

b. The washing of the disciples' feet

Jn. 13:1-20

1 Now before the feast of the Passover, when Jesus knew that his hour had
come to depart out of this world to the Father, having loved his own who were
in the world, he loved them to the end. 2 And during supper, when the devil had
already put it into the heart of Judas Iscariot, Simon's son, to betray him, 3 Jesus,
knowing that the Father had given all things into his hands, and that he had come
from God and was going to God, 4 rose from supper, laid aside his garments, and
girded himself with a towel. 5 Then he poured water into a basin, and began to
wash the disciples' feet, and to wipe them with the towel with which he was girded.
6 He came to Simon Peter; and Peter said to him, "Lord, do you wash my feet?"
7 Jesus answered him, "What I am doing you do not know now, but afterward you
will understand." 8 Peter said to him, "You shall never wash my feet." Jesus
answered him, "If I do not wash you, you have no part in me." 9 Simon Peter said
to him, "Lord, not my feet only but also my hands and my head!" 10 Jesus said
to him, "He who has bathed does not need to wash, except for his feet,[b] but he
is clean all over; and you are clean, but not all of you." 11 For he knew who was to
betray him; that was why he said, "You are not all clean."
12 When he had washed their feet, and taken his garments, and resumed his
place, he said to them, "Do you know what I have done to you? 13 You call me
Teacher and Lord; and you are right, for so I am. 14 If I then, your Lord and
Teacher, have washed your feet, you also ought to wash one another's feet.
15 For I have given you an example, that you also should do as I have done to you.
16 Truly, truly, I say to you, a servant[c] is not greater than his master; nor is he
who is sent greater than he who sent him. 17 If you know these things, blessed are

[b] Some ancient authorities omit *except for his feet.*
[c] Or *slave.*

you if you do them. [18] I am not speaking of you all; I know whom I have chosen; it is that the scripture may be fulfilled, 'He who ate my bread has lifted his heel against me.' [19] I tell you this now, before it takes place, that when it does take place you may believe that I am he. [20] Truly, truly, I say to you, he who receives any one whom I send receives me; and he who receives me receives him who sent me."

c. The meal and the betrayer

Mt. 26:20-25

[20] When it was evening, he sat at table with the twelve disciples;[d] [21] and as they were eating, he said, "Truly, I say to you, one of you will betray me." [22] And they were very sorrowful, and began to say to him one after another, "Is it I, Lord?" [23] He answered, "He who has dipped his hand in the dish with me, will betray me. [24] The Son of man goes as it is written of him, but woe to that man by whom the Son of man is betrayed! It would have been better for that man if he had not been born." [25] Judas, who betrayed him, said, "Is it I, Master?"[e] He said to him, "You have said so."

Mk. 14:17-21

[17] And when it was evening he came with the twelve. [18] And as they were at table eating, Jesus said, "Truly, I say to you, one of you will betray me, one who is eating with me." [19] They began to be sorrowful, and to say to him one after another, "Is it I?" [20] He said to them, "It is one of the twelve, one who is dipping bread in the same dish with me. [21] For the Son of man goes, as it is written of him, but woe to that man by whom the Son of man is betrayed! It would have been better for that man if he had not been born."

Luke

Jn. 13:21-35

[21] When Jesus had thus spoken, he was troubled in spirit, and testified, "Truly, truly, I say to you, one of you will betray me." [22] The disciples looked at one another, uncertain of whom he spoke. [23] One of his disciples, whom Jesus loved, was lying close to the breast of Jesus; [24] so Simon Peter beckoned to him and said, "Tell us who it is of whom he speaks." [25] So lying thus, close to the breast of Jesus, he said to him, "Lord, who is it?" [26] Jesus answered, "It is he to whom I shall give this morsel when I have dipped it." So when he had dipped the morsel, he gave it to Judas, the son of Simon Iscariot. [27] Then after the morsel, Satan entered into him. Jesus said to him, "What you are going

[d] Many authorities omit *disciples*.
[e] Or *Rabbi*.

Mt. 26	Mk. 14	Luke	Jn. 13:21-35

to do, do quickly."
28 Now no one at the
table knew why he
said this to him.
29 Some thought that,
because Judas had the
money box, Jesus was
telling him, "Buy what
we need for the feast";
or, that he should give
something to the poor.
30 So, after receiving
the morsel, he immedi-
ately went out; and it
was night.

31 When he had
gone out, Jesus said,
"Now is the Son of
man glorified, and in
him God is glorified;
32 if God is glorified in
him, God will also
glorify him in himself,
and glorify him at
once. 33 Little children,
yet a little while I am
with you. You will seek
me; and as I said to
the Jews so now I say
to you, 'Where I am
going you cannot
come.' 34 A new com-
mandment I give to
you, that you love one
another; even as I
have loved you, that
you also love one an-
other. 35 By this all
men will know that you
are my disciples, if you
have love for one an-
other."

d. The institution of the Lord's Supper

Mt. 26:26-29

26 Now as they were eating, Jesus took bread, and blessed, and broke it, and gave it to the disciples and said, "Take, eat; this is my body." 27 And he took a cup, and when he had given thanks he gave it to them, saying, "Drink of it, all of you; 28 for this is my blood of the[g] covenant, which is poured out for many for the forgiveness of sins. 29 I tell you I shall not drink again of this fruit of the vine until that day when I drink it new with you in my Father's kingdom."

Mk. 14:22-25

22 And as they were eating, he took bread, and blessed, and broke it, and gave it to them, and said, "Take; this is my body." 23 And he took a cup, and when he had given thanks he gave it to them, and they all drank of it. 24 And he said to them, "This is my blood of the[h] covenant, which is poured out for many. 25 Truly, I say to you, I shall not drink again of the fruit of the vine until that day when I drink it new in the kingdom of God."

Lk. 22:14-23

14 And when the hour came, he sat at table, and the apostles with him. 15 And he said to them, "I have earnestly desired to eat this passover with you before I suffer; 16 for I tell you I shall never eat it again[f] until it is fulfilled in the kingdom of God." 17 And he took a cup, and when he had given thanks he said, "Take this, and divide it among yourselves; 18 for I tell you that from now on I shall not drink of the fruit of the vine until the kingdom of God comes." 19 And he took bread, and when he had given thanks he broke it and gave it to them, saying, "This is my body.[i] 21 But behold the hand of him who betrays me is with me on the table. 22 For the Son of man goes as it has been determined; but woe to that man by whom he is betrayed!" 23 And they began to question one another, which of them it was that would do this.

John

[f] Some ancient authorities omit *again.*
[g] Many ancient authorities insert *new.*
[h] Some ancient authorities insert *new.*
[i] Many ancient authorities add *which is given for you. Do this in remembrance of me." 20 And likewise the cup after supper, saying, "This cup which is poured out for you is the new convenant in my blood.*

e. Contention as to the greatest disciple

Lk. 22:24-30

[24] A dispute also arose among them, which of them was to be regarded as the greatest. [25] And he said to them, "The kings of the Gentiles exercise lordship over them; and those in authority over them are called benefactors. [26] But not so with you; rather let the greatest among you become as the youngest, and the leader as one who serves. [27] For which is the greater, one who sits at table, or one who serves? Is it not the one who sits at table? But I am among you as one who serves.

[28] "You are those who have continued with me in my trials; [29] as my Father appointed a kingdom for me, so do I appoint for you [30] that you may eat and drink at my table in my kingdom, and sit on thrones judging the twelve tribes of Israel.

f. The forewarning of Peter and the other disciples

Mt. 26:30-35

[30] And when they had sung a hymn, they went out to the Mount of Olives. [31] Then Jesus said to them, "You will all fall away because of me this night; for it is written, 'I will strike the shepherd, and the sheep of the flock will be scattered.' [32] But after I am raised up, I will go before you to Galilee." [33] Peter declared to him, "Though they all fall away because of you, I will never fall away." [34] Jesus said to him, "Truly, I say to you, this very night, before the cock crows, you will deny me

Mk. 14:26-31

[26] And when they had sung a hymn, they went out to the Mount of Olives. [27] And Jesus said to them, "You will all fall away; for it is written, 'I will strike the shepherd, and the sheep will be scattered.' [28] But after I am raised up, I will go before you to Galilee." [29] Peter said to him, "Even though they all fall away, I will not." [30] And Jesus said to him, "Truly, I say to you, this very night, before the cock crows twice, you will deny me three times." [31] But he said vehe-

Lk. 22:31-38

[31] "Simon, Simon, behold, Satan demanded to have you, that he might sift you[j] like wheat, [32] but I have prayed for you that your faith may not fail; and when you have turned again, strengthen your brethren." [33] And he said to him, "Lord, I am ready to go with you to prison and to death." [34] He said, "I tell you, Peter, the cock will not crow this day, until you three times deny that you know me."

[35] And he said to them, "When I sent you out with no purse or bag

Jn. 13:36-38

[36] Simon Peter said to him, "Lord, where are you going?" Jesus answered, "Where I am going you cannot follow me now; but you shall follow afterward." [37] Peter said to him, "Lord, why cannot I follow you now? I will lay down my life for you." [38] Jesus answered, "Will you lay down your life for me? Truly, truly, I say to you, the cock will not crow, till you have denied me three times."

[j] The Greek word for *you* here is plural; in verse 32 it is singular.

Mt. 26:30-35

three times." [35] Peter said to him, "Even if I must die with you, I will not deny you." And so said all the disciples.

Mk. 14:26-31

mently, "If I must die with you, I will not deny you." And they all said the same.

Lk. 22:31-38

or sandals, did you lack anything?" They said, "Nothing." [36] He said to them, "But now, let him who has a purse take it, and likewise a bag. And let him who has no sword sell his mantle and buy one. [37] For I tell you that this scripture must be fulfilled in me, 'And he was reckoned with transgressors'; for what is written about me has its fulfillment." [38] And they said, "Look, Lord, here are two swords." And he said to them, "It is enough."

Jn. 13

§ 120. Jesus gives his farewell discourses and intercessory prayer

a. Discussion of faith, hope, love, and obedience

Jn. 14:1-15

[1] "Let not your hearts be troubled; believe in God, believe also in me. [2] In
my Father's house are many rooms; if it were not so, would I have told you that I
go to prepare a place for you? [3] And when I go and prepare a place for you, I
will come again and will take you to myself, that where I am you may be also.
[4] And you know the way where I am going."[k] [5] Thomas said to him, "Lord, we do
not know where you are going; how can we know the way?" [6] Jesus said to him,
"I am the way, and the truth, and the life; no one comes to the Father, but by me.
[7] If you had known me, you would have known my Father also; henceforth you know
him and have seen him."

[8] Philip said to him, "Lord, show us the Father, and we shall be satisfied."
[9] Jesus said to him, "Have I been with you so long, and yet you do not know me,
Philip? He who has seen me has seen the Father; how can you say, 'Show us the

[k] Some ancient authorities read *where I am going you know, and the way you know.*

Father'? 10 Do you not believe that I am in the Father and the Father in me? The
words that I say to you I do not speak on my own authority; but the Father who
dwells in me does his works. 11 Believe me that I am in the Father and the Father
in me; or else believe me for the sake of the works themselves.
12 "Truly, truly, I say to you, he who believes in me will also do the works that
I do; and greater works than these will he do, because I go to the Father. 13 Whatever you ask in my name, I will do it, that the Father may be glorified in the Son;
14 if you ask[l] anything in my name, I will do it.
15 "If you love me, you will keep my commandments.

b. Promise of the Counselor's coming

Jn. 14:16-31

16 "And I will pray the Father, and he will give you another Counselor, to be with
you forever, 17 even the Spirit of truth, whom the world cannot receive, because
it neither sees him nor knows him; you know him, for he dwells with you, and will
be in you.
18 "I will not leave you desolate; I will come to you. 19 Yet a little while, and the
world will see me no more, but you will see me; because I live, you will live also.
20 In that day you will know that I am in my Father, and you in me, and I in you.
21 He who has my commandments and keeps them, he it is who loves me; and he
who loves me will be loved by my Father, and I will love him and manifest myself
to him." 22 Judas (not Iscariot) said to him, "Lord, how is it that you will manifest
yourself to us, and not to the world?" 23 Jesus answered him, "If a man loves me,
he will keep my word, and my Father will love him, and we will come to him and
make our home with him. 24 He who does not love me does not keep my words;
and the word which you hear is not mine but the Father's who sent me.
25 "These things I have spoken to you, while I am still with you. 26 But the
Counselor, the Holy Spirit, whom the Father will send in my name, he will teach
you all things, and bring to your remembrance all that I have said to you. 27 Peace
I leave with you; my peace I give to you; not as the world gives do I give to you.
Let not your hearts be troubled, neither let them be afraid. 28 You heard me say
to you, 'I go away, and I will come to you.' If you loved me, you would have
rejoiced, because I go to the Father; for the Father is greater than I. 29 And now
I have told you before it takes place, so that when it does take place, you may
believe. 30 I will no longer talk much with you, for the ruler of this world is coming.
He has no power over me; 31 but I do as the Father has commanded me, so that
the world may know that I love the Father. Rise, let us go hence."

c. Allegory of the vine and the branches; the command to love one another

Jn. 15:1-17

1 "I am the true vine, and my Father is the vinedresser. 2 Every branch of mine
that bears no fruit, he takes away, and every branch that does bear fruit he prunes,

[l] Many ancient authorities add *me.*

that it may bear more fruit. [3] You are already made clean by the word which I
have spoken to you. [4] Abide in me, and I in you. As the branch cannot bear fruit
by itself, unless it abides in the vine, neither can you unless you abide in me.
[5] I am the vine, you are the branches. He who abides in me, and I in him, he it is
that bears much fruit, for apart from me you can do nothing. [6] If a man does
not abide in me, he is cast forth as a branch and withers; and the branches are
gathered, thrown into the fire and burned. [7] If you abide in me, and my words
abide in you, ask whatever you will, and it shall be done for you. [8] By this my
Father is glorified, that you bear much fruit, and so prove to be my disciples.
[9] As the Father has loved me, so have I loved you; abide in my love. [10] If you
keep my commandments, you will abide in my love, just as I have kept my Father's
commandments and abide in his love. [11] These things I have spoken to you, that
my joy may be in you, and that your joy may be full.

[12] "This is my commandment, that you love one another as I have loved you.
[13] Greater love has no man than this, that a man lay down his life for his friends.
[14] You are my friends if you do what I command you. [15] No longer do I call you
servants,[m] for the servant[n] does not know what his master is doing; but I have called
you friends, for all that I have heard from my Father I have made known to you.
[16] You did not choose me, but I chose you and appointed you that you should go
and bear fruit and that your fruit should abide; so that whatever you ask the Father
in my name, he may give it to you. [17] This I command you, to love one another."

d. Warning of persecution for his witnesses

Jn. 15:18—16:4a

[18] "If the world hates you, know that it has hated me before it hated you. [19] If
you were of the world, the world would love its own; but because you are not of
the world, but I chose you out of the world, therefore the world hates you.
[20] Remember the word that I said to you, 'A servant[o] is not greater than his
master.' If they persecuted me, they will persecute you; if they kept my word,
they will keep yours also. [21] But all this they will do to you on my account, because
they do not know him who sent me. [22] If I had not come and spoken to them,
they would not have sin; but now they have no excuse for their sin. [23] He who
hates me hates my Father also. [24] If I had not done among them the works which
no one else did, they would not have sin; but now they have seen and hated both
me and my Father. [25] It is to fulfill the word that is written in their law, 'They
hated me without a cause.' [26] But when the Counselor comes, whom I shall send
to you from the Father, even the Spirit of truth, who proceeds from the Father,
he will bear witness to me; [27] and you also are witnesses because you have been
with me from the beginning.

[1] "I have said all this to you to keep you from falling away. [2] They will put you
out of the synagogues; indeed, the hour is coming when whoever kills you will

[m] Or *slaves.*
[n] Or *slave.*
[o] Or *slave.*

think he is offering service to God. 3 And they will do this because they have not
known the Father, nor me. 4a But I have said these things to you, that when their
hour comes you may remember that I told you of them."

e. Words of comfort for the disciples concerning his going

Jn. 16:4b-33

4b "I did not say these things to you from the beginning, because I was with you.
5 But now I am going to him who sent me; yet none of you asks me, 'Where are
you going?' 6 But because I have said these things to you, sorrow has filled your
hearts. 7 Nevertheless I tell you the truth: it is to your advantage that I go away,
for if I do not go away, the Counselor will not come to you; but if I go, I will send
him to you. 8 And when he comes, he will convince the world of sin and of
righteousness and of judgment: 9 of sin, because they do not believe in me; 10 of
righteousness, because I go to the Father, and you will see me no more; 11 of
judgment, because the ruler of this world is judged.

12 "I have yet many things to say to you, but you cannot bear them now.
13 When the Spirit of truth comes, he will guide you into all the truth; for he will
not speak on his own authority, but whatever he hears he will speak, and he will
declare to you the things that are to come. 14 He will glorify me, for he will take
what is mine and declare it to you. 15 All that the Father has is mine; therefore I
said that he will take what is mine and declare it to you.

16 "A little while, and you will see me no more; again a little while, and you
will see me." 17 Some of his disciples said to one another, "What is this that he
says to us, 'A little while, and you will not see me, and again a little while, and you
will see me'; and, 'because I go to the Father'?" 18 They said, "What does he
mean by 'a little while'? We do not know what he means." 19 Jesus knew that they
wanted to ask him; so he said to them, "Is this what you are asking yourselves, what
I meant by saying, 'A little while, and you will not see me, and again a little while,
and you will see me'? 20 Truly, truly, I say to you, you will weep and lament, but
the world will rejoice; you will be sorrowful, but your sorrow will turn into joy.
21 When a woman is in travail she has sorrow, because her hour has come; but
when she is delivered of the child, she no longer remembers the anguish, for joy
that a child[p] is born into the world. 22 So you have sorrow now, but I will see you
again and your hearts will rejoice, and no one will take your joy from you. 23 On
that day you will ask me no questions. Truly, truly, I say to you, if you ask anything of the Father, he will give it to you in my name. 24 Hitherto you have asked
nothing in my name; ask, and you will receive, that your joy may be full.

25 "I have said this to you in figures; the hour is coming when I shall no longer
speak to you in figures but tell you plainly of the Father. 26 In that day you will ask
in my name; and I do not say to you that I shall pray the Father for you; 27 for the
Father himself loves you, because you have loved me and have believed that I came

[p] Greek *a human being.*

from the Father. 28 I came from the Father and have come into the world; again
I am leaving the world and going to the Father."

29 His disciples said, "Ah, now you are speaking plainly, not in any figure!
30 Now we know that you know all things, and need none to question you; by this
we believe that you came from God." 31 Jesus answered them, "Do you now
believe? 32 The hour is coming, indeed it has come, when you will be scattered,
every man to his home, and will leave me alone; yet I am not alone, for the Father
is with me. 33 I have said this to you, that in me you may have peace. In the world
you have tribulation; but be of good cheer, I have overcome the world.

f. Prayer for his own

Jn. 17:1-26

1 When Jesus had spoken these words, he lifted up his eyes to heaven and said,
Father, the hour has come; glorify thy Son that the Son may glorify thee, 2 since
thou hast given him power over all flesh, so that he might give eternal life to all
whom thou hast given him. 3 And this is eternal life, that they know thee the only
true God, and Jesus Christ whom thou hast sent. 4 I glorified thee on earth,
having accomplished the work which thou gavest me to do; 5 and now, Father,
glorify thou me in thy own presence with the glory which I had with thee before
the world was made.

6 "I have manifested thy name to the men whom thou gavest me out of the
world; thine they were, and thou gavest them to me, and they have kept thy word.
7 Now they know that everything that thou hast given me is from thee; 8 for I have
given them the words which thou gavest me, and they have received them and
know in truth that I came from thee; and they have believed that thou didst send
me. 9 I am praying for them; I am not praying for the world but for those whom
thou hast given me, for they are thine; 10 all mine are thine, and thine are mine,
and I am glorified in them. 11 And now I am no more in the world, but they are
in the world, and I am coming to thee. Holy Father, keep them in thy name which
thou hast given me, that they may be one, even as we are one. 12 While I was with
them, I kept them in thy name which thou hast given me; I have guarded them, and
none of them is lost but the son of perdition, that the scripture might be fulfilled.
13 But now I am coming to thee; and these things I speak in the world, that they
may have my joy fulfilled in themselves. 14 I have given them thy word; and the
world has hated them because they are not of the world, even as I am not of the
world. 15 I do not pray that thou shouldst take them out of the world, but that thou
shouldst keep them from the evil one.[q] 16 They are not of the world, even as I am
not of the world. 17 Consecrate them in the truth; thy word is truth. 18 As thou
didst send me into the world, so I have sent them into the world. 19 And for their
sake I consecrate myself, that they also may be consecrated in truth.

20 "I do not pray for these only, but also for those who are to believe in me
through their word, 21 that they may all be one; even as thou, Father, art in me,

[q] Or *from evil.*

and I in thee, that they also may be in us, so that the world may believe that thou hast sent me. 22 The glory which thou hast given me I have given to them, that they may be one even as we are one, 23 I in them and thou in me, that they may become perfectly one, so that the world may know that thou hast sent me and hast loved them even as thou hast loved me. 24 Father, I desire that they also, whom thou hast given me, may be with me where I am, to behold my glory which thou hast given me in thy love for me before the foundation of the world. 25 O righteous Father, the world has not known thee, but I have known thee; and these know that thou hast sent me. 26 I made known to them thy name, and I will make it known, that the love with which thou hast loved me may be in them, and I in them."

§ 121. Jesus prays in Gethsemane; is betrayed and arrested

Mt. 26:36-56

36 Then Jesus went with them to a place called Gethsemane, and he said to his disciples, "Sit here, while I go yonder and pray." 37 And taking with him Peter and the two sons of Zebedee, he began to be sorrowful and troubled. 38 Then he said to them, "My soul is very sorrowful, even to death; remain here, and watch[r] with me." 39 And going a little farther he fell on his face and prayed, "My Father, if it be possible, let this cup pass from me; nevertheless, not as I will, but as thou wilt." 40 And he

Mk. 14:32-52

32 And they went to a place which was called Gethsemane; and he said to his disciples, "Sit here, while I pray." 33 And he took with him Peter and James and John, and began to be greatly distressed and troubled. 34 And he said to them, "My soul is very sorrowful, even to death; remain here, and watch."[r] 35 And going a little farther, he fell on the ground and prayed that if it were possible, the hour might pass from him. 36 And he said, "Abba, Father, all things are possible to

Lk. 22:39-53

39 And he came out, and went, as was his custom, to the Mount of Olives; and the disciples followed him. 40 And when he came to the place he said to them, "Pray that you may not enter into temptation." 41 And he withdrew from them about a stone's throw, and knelt down and prayed, 42 saying, "Father, if thou art willing, remove this cup from me; nevertheless not my will, but thine, be done." 43 And there appeared to him an angel from heaven, strengthening him. 44 And being in an agony he prayed

Jn. 18:1-12

1 When Jesus had spoken these words, he went forth with his disciples across the Kidron valley, where there was a garden, which he and his disciples entered. 2 Now Judas, who betrayed him, also knew the place; for Jesus often met there with his disciples. 3 So Judas, procuring a band of soldiers and some officers from the chief priests and the Pharisees, went there with lanterns and torches and weapons. 4 Then Jesus, knowing all that was to befall him, came forward and said to

[r] Or *keep awake*.

Mt. 26:36-56

came to the disciples and found them sleeping; and he said to Peter, "So, could you not watch[r] with me one hour? 41 Watch[r] and pray that you may not enter into temptation; the spirit indeed is willing, but the flesh is weak." 42 Again, for the second time, he went away and prayed, "My Father, if this cannot pass unless I drink it, thy will be done." 43 And again he came and found them sleeping, for their eyes were heavy. 44 So, leaving them again, he went away and prayed for the third time, saying the same words. 45 Then he came to the disciples and said to them, "Are you still sleeping and taking your rest? Behold, the hour is at hand, and the Son of man is betrayed into the hands of sinners. 46 Rise, let

Mk. 14:32-52

thee; remove this cup from me; yet not what I will, but what thou wilt." 37 And he came and found them sleeping, and he said to Peter, "Simon, are you asleep? Could you not watch[r] one hour? 38 Watch[r] and pray that you may not enter into temptation; the spirit indeed is willing, but the flesh is weak." 39 And again he went away, and prayed, saying the same words. 40 And again he came and found them sleeping, for their eyes were very heavy; and they did not know what to answer him. 41 And he came the third time, and said to them, "Are you still sleeping and taking your rest? It is enough; the hour has come; the Son of man is betrayed into the hands of sinners. 42 Rise, let us be going; see, my betrayer is at hand."

Lk. 22:39-53

more earnestly; and his sweat became like great drops of blood falling down upon the ground.[*] 45 And when he rose from prayer, he came to the disciples and found them sleeping for sorrow, 46 and he said to them, "Why do you sleep? Rise and pray that you may not enter into temptation."

47 While he was still speaking, there came a crowd, and the man called Judas, one of the twelve, was leading them. He drew near to Jesus to kiss him; 48 but Jesus said to him, "Judas, would you betray the Son of man with a kiss?" 49 And when those who were about him saw what would follow, they said, "Lord, shall we strike with the sword?" 50 And one of them struck the slave of the high priest and cut off his right

Jn. 18:1-12

them, "Whom do you seek?" 5 They answered him, "Jesus of Nazareth." Jesus said to them, "I am he." Judas, who betrayed him, was standing with them. 6 When he said to them, "I am he," they drew back and fell to the ground. 7 Again he asked them, "Whom do you seek?" And they said, "Jesus of Nazareth." 8 Jesus answered, "I told you that I am he; so, if you seek me, let these men go." 9 This was to fulfill the word which he had spoken, "Of those whom thou gavest me I lost not one." 10 Then Simon Peter, having a sword, drew it and struck the high priest's slave and cut off his right ear. The slave's name was Malchus. 11 Jesus said to Peter, "Put your sword into its sheath; shall I not drink the cup

[r] Or *keep awake.*
[*] Many ancient authorities omit verses 43 and 44.

Mt. 26:36-56

us be going; see, my betrayer is at hand."

47 While he was still speaking, Judas came, one of the twelve, and with him a great crowd with swords and clubs, from the chief priests and the elders of the people. 48 Now the betrayer had given them a sign, saying, "The one I shall kiss is the man; seize him." 49 And he came up to Jesus at once and said, "Hail, Master!"[t] And he kissed him. 50 Jesus said to him, "Friend, why are you here?"[u] Then they came up and laid hands on Jesus and seized him. 51 And behold, one of those who were with Jesus stretched out his hand and drew his sword, and struck the slave of the high priest, and cut off his ear. 52 Then Jesus said to him, "Put your sword back into its place;

Mk. 14:32-52

43 And immediately, while he was still speaking, Judas came, one of the twelve, and with him a crowd with swords and clubs, from the chief priests and the scribes and the elders. 44 Now the betrayer had given them a sign, saying, "The one I shall kiss is the man; seize him and lead him away safely." 45 And when he came, he went up to him at once, and said, "Master!"[t] And he kissed him. 46 And they laid hands on him and seized him. 47 But one of those who stood by drew his sword, and struck the slave of the high priest and cut off his ear. 48 And Jesus said to them, "Have you come out as against a robber, with swords and clubs to capture me? 49 Day after day I was with you in the temple teach-

Lk. 22:39-53

ear. 51 But Jesus said, "No more of this!" And he touched his ear and healed him. 52 Then Jesus said to the chief priests and captains of the temple and elders, who had come out against him, "Have you come out as against a robber, with swords and clubs? 53 When I was with you day after day in the temple, you did not lay hands on me. But this is your hour, and the power of darkness."

Jn. 18:1-12

which the Father has given me?" 12 So the band of soldiers and their captain and the officers of the Jews seized Jesus and bound him.

[t] Or *Rabbi.*

[u] Or *do that for which you have come.*

Mt. 26:36-56

for all who take the sword will perish by the sword. 53 Do you think that I cannot appeal to my Father, and he will at once send me more than twelve legions of angels? 54 But how then should the scriptures be fulfilled, that it must be so?" 55 At that hour Jesus said to the crowds, "Have you come out as against a robber with swords and clubs to capture me? Day after day I sat in the temple teaching, and you did not seize me. 56 But all this has taken place, that the scriptures of the prophets might be fulfilled." Then all the disciples forsook him and fled.

Mk. 14:32-52

ing, and you did not seize me. But let the scriptures be fulfilled." 50 And they all forsook him, and fled.

51 And a young man followed him, with nothing but a linen cloth about his body; and they seized him, 52 but he left the linen cloth and ran away naked.

Lk. 22

Jn. 18

§ 122. Jesus is tried and condemned; Peter denies; Judas dies

a. Investigation before the Jewish authorities; arraignment before Annas and Caiaphas; Peter's denial; condemnation of Jesus

Mt. 26:57—27:1

57 Then those who had seized Jesus led him to Caiaphas the high

Mk. 14:53-72

53 And they led Jesus to the high priest; and all the chief priests and

Lk. 22:54-71

54 Then they seized him and led him away bringing him into the

Jn. 18:13-27

13 First they led him to Annas; for he was the father-in-law of Caia-

Mt. 26:57—27:1

priest, where the scribes and the elders had gathered. 58 But Peter followed him at a distance, as far as the courtyard of the high priest, and going inside he sat with the guards to see the end. 59 Now the chief priests and the whole council sought false witness against Jesus, that they might put him to death, 60 but they found none, though many witnesses came forward. At last two came forward 61 and said, "This fellow said, 'I am able to destroy the temple of God, and to build it in three days.' " 62 And the high priest stood up and said, "Have you no answer to make? What is it that these men testify against you?" 63 But Jesus was silent. And the high priest said to him, "I adjure you by the living God, tell us if you

Mk. 14:53-72

the elders and the scribes were assembled. 54 And Peter had followed him at a distance, right into the courtyard of the high priest; and he was sitting with the guards, and warming himself at the fire. 55 Now the chief priests and the whole council sought testimony against Jesus, to put him to death; but they found none. 56 For many bore false witness against him, and their witness did not agree. 57 And some stood up and bore false witness against him, saying, 58 "We heard him say, 'I will destroy this temple that is made with hands, and in three days I will build another, not made with hands.' " 59 Yet not even so did their testimony agree. 60 And the high priest stood up in the midst, and asked Jesus,

Lk. 22:54-71

high priest's house. Peter followed at a distance; 55 and when they had kindled a fire in the middle of the courtyard and sat down together, Peter sat among them. 56 Then a maid, seeing him as he sat in the light and gazing at him, said, "This man also was with him." 57 But he denied it, saying, "Woman, I do not know him." 58 And a little later some one else saw him and said, "You also are one of them." But Peter said, "Man, I am not." 59 And after an interval of about an hour still another insisted, saying, "Certainly this man also was with him; for he is a Galilean." 60 But Peter said, "Man, I do not know what you are saying." And immediately, while he was still speaking, the cock crowed. 61 And

Jn. 18:13-27

phas, who was high priest that year. 14 It was Caiaphas who had given counsel to the Jews that it was expedient that one man should die for the people.

15 Simon Peter followed Jesus, and so did another disciple. As this disciple was known to the high priest, he entered the court of the high priest along with Jesus, 16 while Peter stood outside at the door. So the other disciple, who was known to the high priest, went out and spoke to the maid who kept the door, and brought Peter in. 17 The maid who kept the door said to Peter, "Are not you also one of this man's disciples?" He said, "I am not." 18 Now the servants* and officers had made a charcoal fire, be-

* Or *slaves.*

Mt. 26:57—27:1

are the Christ, the Son of God." [64] Jesus said to him, "You have said so. But I tell you, hereafter you will see the Son of man seated at the right hand of Power, and coming on the clouds of heaven." [65] Then the high priest tore his robes, and said, "He has uttered blasphemy. Why do we still need witnesses? You have now heard his blasphemy. [66] What is your judgment?" They answered, "He deserves death." [67] Then they spat in his face, and struck him; and some slapped him, [68] saying, "Prophesy to us, you Christ! Who was it that struck you?"

[69] Now Peter was sitting outside in the courtyard. And a maid came up to him, and said, "You also were with Jesus the Galilean." [70] But he denied it before them all, saying, "I

Mk. 14:53-72

"Have you no answer to make? What is it that these men testify against you?" [61] But he was silent and made no answer. Again the high priest asked him, "Are you the Christ, the Son of the Blessed?" [62] And Jesus said, "I am; and you will see the Son of man sitting at the right hand of Power, and coming with the clouds of heaven." [63] And the high priest tore his mantle, and said, "Why do we still need witnesses? [64] You have heard his blasphemy. What is your decision?" And they all condemned him as deserving death. [65] And some began to spit on him, and to cover his face, and to strike him, saying to him, "Prophesy!" And the guards received him with blows.

[66] And as Peter was below in the courtyard, one of

Lk. 22:54-71

the Lord turned and looked at Peter. And Peter remembered the word of the Lord, how he had said to him, "Before the cock crows today, you will deny me three times." [62] And he went out, and wept bitterly.

[63] Now the men who were holding Jesus mocked him and beat him; [64] they also blindfolded him and asked him, "Prophesy! Who is it that struck you?" [65] And they spoke many other words against him, reviling him.

[66] When day came, the assembly of the elders of the people gathered together, both chief priests and scribes; and they led him away to their council, and they said, [67] "If you are the Christ, tell us." But he said to them, "If I tell you, you will not believe; [68] and if I ask you, you

Jn. 18:13-27

cause it was cold, and they were standing and warming themselves; Peter also was with them, standing and warming himself.

[19] The high priest then questioned Jesus about his disciples and his teaching. [20] Jesus answered him, "I have spoken openly to the world; I have always taught in synagogues and in the temple, where all Jews come together; I have said nothing secretly. [21] Why do you ask me? Ask those who have heard me, what I said to them; they know what I said." [22] When he had said this, one of the officers standing by struck Jesus with his hand, saying, "Is that how you answer the high priest?" [23] Jesus answered him, "If I have spoken wrongly, bear witness to the wrong; but if I

Mt. 26:57—27:1

do not know what you mean." 71 And when he went out to the porch, another maid saw him, and she said to the bystanders, "This fellow was with Jesus of Nazareth." 72 And again he denied it with an oath, "I do not know the man." 73 After a little while the bystanders came up and said to Peter, "Certainly you are also one of them, for your accent betrays you." 74 Then he began to invoke a curse on himself and to swear, "I do not know the man." And immediately the cock crowed. 75 And Peter remembered the saying of Jesus, "Before the cock crows, you will deny me three times." And he went out and wept bitterly.

1 When morning came, all the chief priests and the elders of the people took counsel

Mk. 14:53-72

the maids of the high priest came; 67 and seeing Peter warming himself, she looked at him, and said, "You also were with the Nazarene, Jesus." 68 But he denied it, saying, "I neither know nor understand what you mean." And he went out into the gateway.** 69 And the maid saw him, and began again to say to the bystanders, "This man is one of them." 70 But again he denied it. And after a little while again the bystanders said to Peter, "Certainly you are one of them; for you are a Galilean." 71 But he began to invoke a curse on himself and to swear, "I do not know this man of whom you speak." 72 And immediately the cock crowed a second time. And Peter remembered how Jesus had said to him, "Before the

Lk. 22:54-71

will not answer. 69 But from now on the Son of man shall be seated at the right hand of the power of God." 70 And they all said, "Are you the Son of God, then?" And he said to them, "You say that I am." 71 And they said, "What further testimony do we need? We have heard it ourselves from his own lips."

Jn. 18:13-27

have spoken rightly, why do you strike me?" 24 Annas then sent him bound to Caiaphas the high priest.

25 Now Simon Peter was standing and warming himself. They said to him, "Are not you also one of his disciples?" He denied it and said, "I am not." 26 One of the servants* of the high priest, a kinsman of the man whose ear Peter had cut off, asked, "Did I not see you in the garden with him?" 27 Peter again denied it; and at once the cock crowed.

* Or *slaves.*
** Or *fore-court.* Some ancient authorities add *and the cock crowed.*

Mt. 26:57—27:1

against Jesus to put him to death;

Mk. 14:53-72

cock crows twice, you will deny me three times." And he broke down and wept.

Lk. 22

Jn. 18

b. Beginning of trial before Pilate; the charge and examination

Mt. 27:2, 11-14

2 And they bound him and led him away and delivered him to Pilate the governor.

11 Now Jesus stood before the governor; and the governor asked him, "Are you the King of the Jews?" Jesus said to him, "You have said so." 12 But when he was accused by the chief priests and elders, he made no answer. 13 Then Pilate said to him, "Do you not hear how many things they testify against you?" 14 But he gave him no answer, not even to a single charge; so that the governor wondered greatly.

Mk. 15:1-5

1 And as soon as it was morning the chief priests, with the elders and scribes, and the whole council held a consultation; and they bound Jesus and led him away and delivered him to Pilate. 2 And Pilate asked him, "Are you the King of the Jews?" And he answered him, "You have said so." 3 And the chief priests accused him of many things. 4 And Pilate again asked him, "Have you no answer to make? See how many charges they bring against you." 5 But Jesus made no further answer, so that Pilate wondered.

Lk. 23:1-5

1 Then the whole company of them arose, and brought him before Pilate. 2 And they began to accuse him, saying, "We found this man perverting our nation, and forbidding us to give tribute to Caesar, and saying that he himself is Christ a king." 3 And Pilate asked him, "Are you the King of the Jews?" And he answered him, "You have said so." 4 And Pilate said to the chief priests and the multitudes, "I find no crime in this man." 5 But they were urgent, saying, "He stirs up the people, teaching throughout all Judea, from Galilee even to this place."

Jn. 18:28-38a

28 Then they led Jesus from the house of Caiaphas to the praetorium. It was early. They themselves did not enter the praetorium, so that they might not be defiled, but might eat the passover. 29 So Pilate went out to them and said, "What accusation do you bring against this man?" 30 They answered him, "If this man were not an evildoer, we would not have handed him over." 31 Pilate said to them, "Take him yourselves and judge him by your own law." The Jews said to him, "It is not lawful for us to put any man to death." 32 This was to fulfill the

Mt. 27 | Mk. 15 | Lk. 23 | Jn. 18:28-38a

word which Jesus had spoken to show
by what death he was to die.
33 Pilate entered the praetorium
again and called Jesus, and said to
him, "Are you the King of the Jews?"
34 Jesus answered, "Do you say this
of your own accord, or did others say
it to you about me?" 35 Pilate answered, "Am I a Jew? Your own
nation and the chief priests have
handed you over to me; what have
you done?" 36 Jesus answered, "My
kingship is not of this world; if my
kingship were of this world, my
servants would fight, that I might not
be handed over to the Jews; but my
kingship is not from the world."
37 Pilate said to him, "So you are a
king?" Jesus answered, "You say that
I am a king. For this I was born, and
for this I have come into the world,
to bear witness to the truth. Every
one who is of the truth hears my
voice." 38a Pilate said to him, "What
is truth?"

c. Judas' suicide

Mt. 27:3-10

3 When Judas, his betrayer, saw that he was condemned, he repented and
brought back the thirty pieces of silver to the chief priests and the elders, 4 saying,
"I have sinned in betraying innocent blood." They said, "What is that to us? See
to it yourself." 5 And throwing down the pieces of silver in the temple, he departed;
and he went and hanged himself. 6 But the chief priests, taking the pieces of silver,
said, "It is not lawful to put them into the treasury, since they are blood money."
7 So they took counsel and bought with them the potter's field, to bury strangers in.
8 Therefore that field has been called the Field of Blood to this day. 9 Then was
fulfilled what had been spoken by the prophet Jeremiah, saying, "And they took the
thirty pieces of silver, the price of him on whom a price had been set by some of
the sons of Israel, 10 and they gave them for the potter's field, as the Lord directed me."

d. Mockery before Herod

Lk. 23:6-12

6 When Pilate heard this, he asked whether the man was a Galilean. 7 And when he learned that he belonged to Herod's jurisdiction, he sent him over to Herod, who was himself in Jerusalem at that time. 8 When Herod saw Jesus, he was very glad, for he had long desired to see him, because he had heard about him, and he was hoping to see some sign done by him. 9 So he questioned him at some length; but he made no answer. 10 The chief priests and the scribes stood by, vehemently accusing him. 11 And Herod with his soldiers treated him with contempt and mocked him; then, arraying him in gorgeous apparel, he sent him back to Pilate. 12 And Herod and Pilate became friends with each other that very day, for before this they had been at enmity with each other.

e. Continuation of trial before Pilate; the tumult of the people; the release of Barabbas

Mt. 27:15-26

15 Now at the feast the governor was accustomed to release for the crowd any one prisoner whom they wanted. 16 And they had then a notorious prisoner, called Barabbas.[u] 17 So when they had gathered, Pilate said to them, "Whom do you want me to release for you, Barabbas[u] or Jesus who is called Christ?" 18 For he knew that it was out of envy that they had delivered him up. 19 Besides, while he was sitting on the judgment seat,

Mk. 15:6-15

6 Now at the feast he used to release for them any one prisoner whom they asked. 7 And among the rebels in prison, who had committed murder in the insurrection, there was a man called Barabbas. 8 And the crowd came up and began to ask Pilate to do as he was wont to do for them. 9 And he answered them, "Do you want me to release for you the King of the Jews?" 10 For he perceived that it was out of envy that the chief priests had de-

Lk. 23:13-25

13 Pilate then called together the chief priests and the rulers and the people, 14 and said to them, "You brought me this man as one who was perverting the people; and after examining him before you, behold, I did not find this man guilty of any of your charges against him; 15 neither did Herod, for he sent him back to us. Behold, nothing deserving death has been done by him; 16 I will therefore chastise him and release him."[v]

Jn. 18:38b-40

38b After he had said this, he went out to the Jews again, and told them, "I find no crime in him. 39 But you have a custom that I should release one man for you at the Passover; will you have me release for you the King of the Jews?" 40 They cried out again, "Not this man, but Barabbas!" Now Barabbas was a robber.

[u] Some ancient authorities read *Jesus Barabbas.*

[v] Here, or after verse 19, some ancient authorities add verse 17, *Now he was obliged to release one man to them at the festival.*

Mt. 27:15-26

his wife sent word
to him, "Have
nothing to do with
that righteous man,
for I have suffered
much over him to-
day in a dream."
20 Now the chief
priests and the
elders persuaded
the people to ask
for Barabbas and
destroy Jesus.
21 The governor
again said to them,
"Which of the
two do you want
me to release for
you?" And they
said, "Barabbas."
22 Pilate said to
them, "Then what
shall I do with
Jesus who is called
Christ?" 23 They
all said, "Let him
be crucified." And
he said, "Why,
what evil has he
done?" But they
shouted all the
more, "Let him be
crucified."

24 So when Pi-
late saw that he
was gaining noth-
ing, but rather that
a riot was begin-
ning, he took
water and washed
his hands before
the crowd, saying,

Mk. 15:6-15

livered him up.
11 But the chief
priests stirred up
the crowd to have
him release for
them Barabbas in-
stead. 12 And Pi-
late again said to
them, "Then what
shall I do with
the man whom
you call the King
of the Jews?"
13 And they cried
out again, "Crucify
him." 14 And Pi-
late said to them,
"Why, what evil
has he done?" But
they shouted all
the more, "Crucify
him." 15 So Pilate,
wishing to satisfy
the crowd, released
for them Barab-
bas; and having
scourged Jesus, he
delivered him to
be crucified.

Lk. 23:13-25

18 But they all
cried out together,
"Away with this
man, and release to
us Barabbas" ——
19 a man who had
been thrown into
prison for an in-
surrection started
in the city, and for
murder. 20 Pilate
addressed them
once more, desir-
ing to release
Jesus; 21 but they
shouted out,
"Crucify, crucify
him!" 22 A third
time he said to
them, "Why, what
evil has he done?
I have found in
him no crime de-
serving death; I
will therefore chas-
tise him and re-
lease him." 23 But
they were urgent,
demanding with
loud cries that he
should be crucified.
And their voices
prevailed. 24 So Pi-
late gave sentence
that their demand
should be granted.
25 He released the
man who had been
thrown into prison
for insurrection
and murder, whom
they asked for; but

Jn. 18

Mt. 27:15-26

"I am innocent of this man's blood;[s] see to it yourselves." 25 And all the people answered, "His blood be on us and on our children!" 26 Then he released for them Barabbas, and having scourged Jesus, delivered him to be crucified.

Mk. 15

Lk. 23:13-25

Jesus he delivered up to their will.

Jn. 18

f. Conclusion of trial before Pilate; the mocking of Jesus; his final condemnation

Mt. 27:27-31

27 Then the soldiers of the governor took Jesus into the praetorium, and they gathered the whole battalion before him. 28 And they stripped him and put a scarlet robe upon him, 29 and plaiting a crown of thorns they put it on his head, and put a reed in his right hand. And kneeling before him they mocked him, saying, "Hail, King of the Jews!" 30 And they spat upon him, and took the reed and struck him on the head. 31 And when they had mocked him, they stripped him of the robe, and put his own clothes on him,

Mk. 15:16-20

16 And the soldiers led him away inside the palace (that is, the praetorium); and they called together the whole battalion. 17 And they clothed him in a purple cloak, and plaiting a crown of thorns they put it on him. 18 And they began to salute him, "Hail, King of the Jews!" 19 And they struck his head with a reed, and spat upon him, and they knelt down in homage to him. 20 And when they had mocked him, they stripped him of the purple cloak, and put his own clothes on him. And they led him out to crucify him.

Luke

Jn. 19:1-16

1 Then Pilate took Jesus and scourged him. 2 And the soldiers plaited a crown of thorns, and put it on his head, and arrayed him in a purple robe; 3 they came up to him, saying, "Hail, King of the Jews!" and struck him with their hands. 4 Pilate went out again, and said to them, "Behold, I am bringing him out to you, that you may know that I find no crime in him." 5 So Jesus came out, wearing the crown of thorns and the purple robe. Pilate said to them, "Here is the man!" 6 When the chief priests and the

[s] Some authorities read *this righteous blood* or *this righteous man's blood.*

Mt. 27:27-31 | Mk. 15 | Luke | Jn. 19:1-16

and led him away to crucify him.

officers saw him, they cried out, "Crucify him, crucify him!" Pilate said to them, "Take him yourselves and crucify him, for I find no crime in him."
[7] The Jews answered him, "We have a law, and by that law he ought to die, because he has made himself the Son of God."
[8] When Pilate heard these words, he was the more afraid; [9] he entered the praetorium again and said to Jesus, "Where are you from?" But Jesus gave no answer.
[10] Pilate therefore said to him, "You will not speak to me? Do you not know that I have power to release you, and power to crucify you?" [11] Jesus answered him, "You would have no power over me unless it had been given you from above; therefore he who delivered me to you has the greater sin."

[12] Upon this Pilate sought to release him, but the Jews cried out, "If you release this man, you are not Caesar's friend; every

Mt. 27	Mk. 15	Luke	Jn. 19:1-16
			one who makes himself a king sets himself against Caesar." 13 When Pilate heard these words, he brought Jesus out and sat down on the judgment seat at a place called The Pavement, and in Hebrew, Gabbatha. 14 Now it was the day of Preparation for the Passover; it was about the sixth hour. He said to the Jews, "Here is your King!" 15 They cried out, "Away with him, away with him, crucify him!" Pilate said to them, "Shall I crucify your King?" The chief priests answered, "We have no king but Caesar." 16 Then he handed him over to them to be crucified.

§ 123. Jesus is crucified on Golgotha. The "seven words"

Mt. 27:32-56

32 As they were marching out, they came upon a man of Cyrene, Simon by name; this man they compelled to carry his cross. 33 And when they came to a place called Golgotha, which means the place of a skull, 34 they offered him wine to drink, mingled with gall; but when he tasted it, he would not drink it. 35 And when they had crucified him, they divided his garments among them by casting lots; 36 then they sat down and kept

Mk. 15:21-41

21 And they compelled a passer-by, Simon of Cyrene, who was coming in from the country, the father of Alexander and Rufus, to carry his cross. 22 And they brought him to the place called Golgotha (which means the place of a skull). 23 And they offered him wine mingled with myrrh; but he did not take it. 24 And they crucified him, and divided his garments among them, casting lots for them, to decide what each should take. 25 And it was

Lk. 23:26-49

26 And as they led him away, they seized one Simon of Cyrene, who was coming in from the country, and laid on him the cross, to carry it behind Jesus. 27 And there followed him a great multitude of the people, and of women who bewailed and lamented him. 28 But Jesus turning to them said, "Daughters of Jerusalem, do not weep for me, but weep for yourselves and for your children. 29 For behold, the days are coming

Jn. 19:17-37

17 So they took Jesus, and he went out, bearing his own cross, to the place called the place of a skull, which is called in Hebrew Golgotha. 18 There they crucified him, and with him two others, one on either side, and Jesus between them. 19 Pilate also wrote a title and put it on the cross; it read, "Jesus of Nazareth, the King of the Jews." 20 Many of the Jews read this title, for the place where Jesus was

Mt. 27:32-56

watch over him there. 37 And over his head they put the charge against him, which read, "This is Jesus the King of the Jews." 38 Then two robbers were crucified with him, one on the right and one on the left. 39 And those who passed by derided him, wagging their heads 40 and saying, "You who would destroy the temple and build it in three days, save yourself! If you are the Son of God, come down from the cross." 41 So also the chief priests, with the scribes and elders, mocked him, saying, 42 "He saved others; he cannot save himself. He is the King of Israel; let him come down now from the cross, and we will believe in him. 43 He trusts in God; let God deliver him now, if he desires him;

Mk. 15:21-41

the third hour, when they crucified him. 26 And the inscription of the charge against him read, "The King of the Jews." 27 And with him they crucified two robbers, one on his right and one on his left.[a] 29 And those who passed by derided him, wagging their heads, and saying, "Aha! You who would destroy the temple and build it in three days, 30 save yourself, and come down from the cross!" 31 So also the chief priests mocked him to one another with the scribes, saying, "He saved others; he cannot save himself. 32 Let the Christ, the King of Israel, come down now from the cross, that we may see and believe." Those who were crucified with him also reviled him.

33 And when the

Lk. 23:26-49

when they will say, 'Blessed are the barren, and the wombs that never bore, and the breasts that never gave suck!' 30 Then they will begin to say to the mountains, 'Fall on us'; and to the hills, 'Cover us.' 31 For if they do this when the wood is green, what will happen when it is dry?"

32 Two others also, who were criminals, were led away to be put to death with him. 33 And when they came to the place which is called The Skull, there they crucified him, and the criminals, one on the right and one on the left. 34 And Jesus said, "Father, forgive them; for they know not what they do."[b] And they cast lots to divide his garments. 35 And the people stood by, watching; but the

Jn. 19:17-37

crucified was near the city; and it was written in Hebrew, in Latin, and in Greek. 21 The chief priests of the Jews then said to Pilate, "Do not write, 'The King of the Jews,' but, 'This man said, I am King of the Jews.'" 22 Pilate answered, "What I have written I have written."

23 When the soldiers had crucified Jesus they took his garments and made four parts, one for each soldier. But his tunic was without seam, woven from top to bottom; 24 so they said to one another, "Let us not tear it, but cast lots for it to see whose it shall be." This was to fulfill the scripture,

"They parted my
garments among
them,
and for my clothing they cast
lots."

25 So the soldiers

[a] Many ancient authorities insert verse 28, *And the scripture was fulfilled which says, "He was reckoned among the transgressors."*
[b] Some ancient authorities omit the sentence *And Jesus . . . . what they do.*

Mt. 27:32-56

for he said, 'I am the Son of God.'" 44 And the robbers who were crucified with him also reviled him in the same way.

45 Now from the sixth hour there was darkness over all the land[c] until the ninth hour. 46 And about the ninth hour Jesus cried with a loud voice, "Eli, Eli, lama sabachthani?" that is, "My God, my God, why hast thou forsaken me?" 47 And some of the bystanders hearing it said, "This man is calling Elijah." 48 And one of them at once ran and took a sponge, filled it with vinegar, and put it on a reed, and gave it to him to drink. 49 But the others said, "Wait, let us see whether Elijah will come to save him."[e] 50 And Jesus cried again with a loud voice

Mk. 15:21-41

sixth hour had come, there was darkness over the whole land[c] until the ninth hour. 34 And at the ninth hour Jesus cried with a loud voice, "Eloi, Eloi, lama sabachthani?" which means, "My God, my God, why hast thou forsaken me?" 35 And some of the bystanders hearing it said, "Behold, he is calling Elijah." 36 And one ran and, filling a sponge full of vinegar, put it on a reed and gave it to him to drink, saying, "Wait, let us see whether Elijah will come to take him down." 37 And Jesus uttered a loud cry, and breathed his last. 38 And the curtain of the temple was torn in two, from top to bottom. 39 And when the centurion, who stood facing him, saw that he thus[f]

Lk. 23:26-49

rulers scoffed at him, saying, "He saved others; let him save himself, if he is the Christ of God, his Chosen One!" 36 The soldiers also mocked him, coming up and offering him vinegar, 37 and saying, "If you are the King of the Jews, save yourself!" 38 There was also an inscription over him,[d] "This is the King of the Jews."

39 One of the criminals who were hanged railed at him, saying, "Are you not the Christ? Save yourself and us!" 40 But the other rebuked him, saying, "Do you not fear God, since you are under the same sentence of condemnation? 41 And we indeed justly; for we are receiving the due reward of our deeds; but this man has done nothing wrong."

Jn. 19:17-37

did this; but standing by the cross of Jesus were his mother, and his mother's sister, Mary the wife of Clopas, and Mary Magdalene. 26 When Jesus saw his mother, and the disciple whom he loved standing near, he said to his mother, "Woman, behold your son!" 27 Then he said to the disciple, "Behold your mother!" And from that hour the disciple took her to his own home.

28 After this Jesus, knowing that all was now finished, said (to fulfill the scripture), "I thirst." 29 A bowl full of sour wine stood there; so they put a sponge full of the wine on hyssop and held it to his mouth. 30 When Jesus had received the wine, he said, "It is

[c] Or *earth*.
[d] Many ancient authorities add *in letters of Greek and Latin and Hebrew*.
[e] Many ancient authorities insert *And another took a spear and pierced his side, and out came water and blood*.
[f] Many ancient authorities insert *cried out and*.

Mt. 27:32-56

and yielded up his spirit.

51 And behold, the curtain of the temple was torn in two, from top to bottom; and the earth shook, and the rocks were split; 52 the tombs also were opened, and many bodies of the saints who had fallen asleep were raised, 53 and coming out of the tombs after his resurrection they went into the holy city and appeared to many. 54 When the centurion and those who were with him, keeping watch over Jesus, saw the earthquake and what took place, they were filled with awe, and said, "Truly this was a son of God!"

55 There were also many women there, looking on from afar, who had followed Jesus from Galilee, ministering to him; 56 among whom

Mk. 15:21-41

breathed his last, he said, "Truly this man was a son of God."

40 There were also women looking on from afar, among whom were Mary Magdalene, and Mary the mother of James the younger and of Joses, and Salome, 41 who, when he was in Galilee, followed him, and ministered to him; and also many other women who came up with him to Jerusalem.

Lk. 23:26-49

42 And he said, "Jesus, remember me when you come in your kingly power."[g] 43 And he said to him, "Truly, I say to you, today you will be with me in Paradise."

44 It was now about the sixth hour, and there was darkness over the whole land[h] until the ninth hour, 45 while the sun's light failed;[i] and the curtain of the temple was torn in two. 46 Then Jesus, crying with a loud voice, said, "Father, into thy hands I commit my spirit!" And having said this he breathed his last. 47 Now when the centurion saw what had taken place, he praised God, and said, "Certainly this man was innocent!" 48 And all the multitudes who assembled to see the sight, when they saw what had

Jn. 19:17-37

finished"; and he bowed his head and gave up his spirit.

31 Since it was the day of Preparation, in order to prevent the bodies from remaining on the cross on the sabbath (for that sabbath was a high day), the Jews asked Pilate that their legs might be broken, and that they might be taken away. 32 So the soldiers came and broke the legs of the first, and of the other who had been crucified with him; 33 but when they came to Jesus and saw that he was already dead, they did not break his legs. 34 But one of the soldiers pierced his side with a spear, and at once there came out blood and water. 35 He who saw it has borne witness — his testimony is

[g] Greek *kingdom.*
[h] Or *earth.*
[i] Or *the sun was eclipsed.* Many ancient authorities read *the sun was darkened.*

Mt. 27:32-56

were Mary Magdalene, and Mary the mother of James and Joseph, and the mother of the sons of Zebedee.

Mk. 15:21-41

Lk. 23:26-49

taken place, returned home beating their breasts. 49 And all his acquaintances and the women who had followed him from Galilee stood at a distance and saw these things.

Jn. 19:17-37

true, and he knows that he tells the truth — that you also may believe. 36 For these things took place that the scripture might be fulfilled, "Not a bone of him shall be broken." 37 And again another scripture says, "They shall look on him whom they have pierced."

§ 124. Joseph and Nicodemus bury Jesus in the tomb of Joseph of Arimathea; soldiers seal and guard the burial place

Mt. 27:57-66

57 When it was evening, there came a rich man from Arimathea, named Joseph, who also was a disciple of Jesus. 58 He went to Pilate and asked for the body of Jesus. Then Pilate ordered it to be given to him. 59 And Joseph took the body, and wrapped it in a clean linen shroud, 60 and laid it in his own new tomb, which he had hewn in the rock;

Mk. 15:42-47

42 And when evening had come, since it was the day of Preparation, that is, the day before the sabbath, 43 Joseph of Arimathea, a respected member of the council, who was also himself looking for the kingdom of God, took courage and went to Pilate, and asked for the body of Jesus. 44 And Pilate wondered if he were already dead; and summoning the cen-

Lk. 23:50-56

50 Now there was a man named Joseph from the Jewish town of Arimathea. He was a member of the council, a good and righteous man, 51 who had not consented to their purpose and deed, and he was looking for the kingdom of God. 52 This man went to Pilate and asked for the body of Jesus. 53 Then he took it down and wrapped it in a linen shroud, and

Jn. 19:38-42

38 After this Joseph of Arimathea, who was a disciple of Jesus, but secretly, for fear of the Jews, asked Pilate that he might take away the body of Jesus; and Pilate gave him leave. So he came and took away his body. 39 Nicodemus also, who had at first come to him by night, came bringing a mixture of myrrh and aloes, about a hundred pounds[f]

[f] Greek *litras.*

Mt. 27:57-66

and he rolled a great stone to the entrance of the tomb, and departed. 61 And Mary Magdalene and the other Mary were there, sitting opposite the tomb.

62 Next day, that is, after the day of Preparation, the chief priests and the Pharisees gathered before Pilate 63 and said, "Sir, we remember how that impostor said, while he was still alive, 'After three days I will rise again.' 64 Therefore order the tomb to be made secure until the third day, lest his disciples go and steal him away, and tell the people, 'He has risen from the dead,' and the last fraud will be worse than the first." 65 Pilate said to them, "You have a guard[m] of soldiers; go, make it as secure as you can."[n] 66 So they

Mk. 15:42-47

turion, he asked him whether he was already dead.[k] 45 And when he learned from the centurion that he was dead, he granted the body to Joseph. 46 And he bought a linen shroud, and taking him down, wrapped him in the linen shroud, and laid him in a tomb which had been hewn out of the rock; and he rolled a stone against the door of the tomb. 47 Mary Magdalene and Mary the mother of Joses saw where he was laid.

Lk. 23:50-56

laid him in a rock-hewn tomb, where no one had ever yet been laid. 54 It was the day of Preparation, and the sabbath was beginning.[l] 55 The women who had come with him from Galilee followed, and saw the tomb, and how his body was laid; 56 then they returned, and prepared spices and ointments.

On the sabbath they rested according to the commandment.

Jn. 19:38-42

weight. 40 They took the body of Jesus, and bound it in linen cloths with the spices, as is the burial custom of the Jews. 41 Now in the place where he was crucified there was a garden, and in the garden a new tomb where no one had ever been laid. 42 So because of the Jewish day of Preparation, as the tomb was close at hand, they laid Jesus there.

[k] Some ancient authorities read *whether he had been some time dead.*
[l] Greek *was dawning.*
[m] Or *Take a guard.*
[n] Greek *know.*

Mt. 27:57-66

went and made the tomb secure by sealing the stone and setting a guard.

Mk. 15

Lk. 23

Jn. 19

Section O. Christ's Resurrection, Subsequent Appearances, and Ascension

§ 125. Jesus arises

a. The women visit the tomb and find it empty

Mt. 28:1-7

[1] Now after the sabbath, toward the dawn of the first day of the week, Mary Magdalene and the other Mary went to see the tomb. [2] And behold, there was a great earthquake; for an angel of the Lord descended from heaven and came and rolled back the stone, and sat upon it. [3] His appearance was like lightning, and his raiment white as snow. [4] And for fear of him the guards trembled and became like dead men. [5] But the angel said to the women, "Do

Mk. 16:1-8

[1] And when the sabbath was past, Mary Magdalene, and Mary the mother of James, and Salome, bought spices, so that they might go and anoint him. [2] And very early on the first day of the week they went to the tomb when the sun had risen. [3] And they were saying to one another, "Who will roll away the stone for us from the door of the tomb?" [4] And looking up, they saw that the stone was rolled back; for it was very large. [5] And entering the tomb, they saw a young

Lk. 24:1-12

[1] But on the first day of the week, at early dawn, they went to the tomb, taking the spices which they had prepared. [2] And they found the stone rolled away from the tomb, [3] but when they went in they did not find the body.[a] [4] While they were perplexed about this, behold, two men stood by them in dazzling apparel; [5] and as they were frightened and bowed their faces to the ground, the men said to them, "Why do you seek the living among the dead?[b] [6] Remember how

Jn. 20:1, 2

[1] Now on the first day of the week Mary Magdalene came to the tomb early, while it was still dark, and saw that the stone had been taken away from the tomb. [2] So she ran, and went to Simon Peter and the other disciple, the one whom Jesus loved, and said to them, "They have taken the Lord out of the tomb, and we do not know where they have laid him."

[a] Some ancient authorities add *of the Lord Jesus.*
[b] Some ancient authorities add *He is not here, but has risen.*

Mt. 28:1-7

not be afraid; for I know that you seek Jesus who was crucified. [6] He is not here; for he has risen, as he said. Come, see the place where he[c] lay. [7] Then go quickly and tell his disciples that he has risen from the dead, and behold, he is going before you to Galilee; there you will see him. Lo, I have told you."

Mk. 16:1-8

man sitting on the right side, dressed in a white robe; and they were amazed. [6] And he said to them, "Do not be amazed; you seek Jesus of Nazareth, who was crucified. He has risen, he is not here; see the place where they laid him. [7] But go, tell his disciples and Peter that he is going before you to Galilee; there you will see him, as he told you." [8] And they went out and fled from the tomb; for trembling and astonishment had come upon them; and they said nothing to any one, for they were afraid.[e]

Lk. 24:1-12

he told you, while he was still in Galilee, [7] that the Son of man must be delivered into the hands of sinful men, and be crucified, and on the third day rise." [8] And they remembered his words, [9] and returning from the tomb they told all this to the eleven and to all the rest. [10] Now it was Mary Magdalene and Joanna and Mary the mother of James and the other women with them who told this to the apostles; [11] but these words seemed to them an idle tale, and they did not believe them.[d]

Jn. 20

[c] Some ancient authorities read *the Lord.*

[d] Some ancient authorities add verse 12, *But Peter rose and ran to the tomb; stooping and looking in, he saw the linen cloths by themselves: and he went home wondering at what had happened.*

[e] Some texts and versions add as 16:9-20 the following passage:

[9] *Now when he rose early on the first day of the week, he appeared first to Mary Magdalene, from whom he had cast out seven demons.* [10] *She went and told those who had been with him, as they mourned and wept.* [11] *But when they heard that he was alive and had been seen by her, they would not believe it.*

[12] *After this he appeared in another form to two of them, as they were walking into the country.* [13] *And they went back and told the rest, but they did not believe them.*

[14] *Afterward he appeared to the eleven themselves as they sat at table; and he upbraided them for their unbelief and hardness of heart, because they had not believed those who saw him after he had risen.* [15] *And he said to them, "Go into all the world and preach the gospel to the whole creation.* [16] *He who believes and is baptized will be saved; but he who does not believe will be condemned.* [17] *And these signs will accompany those who believe: in my name they will cast out demons; they will speak in new tongues;* [18] *they will pick up serpents, and if they drink any deadly things, it will not hurt them; they will lay their hands on the sick, and they will recover."*

[19] *So then the Lord Jesus, after he had spoken to them, was taken up into heaven, and sat down at the right hand of God.* [20] *And they went forth and preached everywhere, while the Lord worked with them and confirmed the message by the signs that attended it. Amen.*

Other ancient authorities add after verse 8 the following: *But they reported briefly to Peter and those with him all that they had been told. And after this, Jesus himself sent out by means of them, from east to west, the sacred and imperishable proclamation of eternal salvation.*

b. Peter and another disciple run to the tomb

Jn. 20:3-10

3 Peter then came out with the other disciple, and they went toward the tomb.
4 They both ran, but the other disciple outran Peter and reached the tomb first;
5 and stooping to look in, he saw the linen cloths lying there, but he did not go
in. 6 Then Simon Peter came, following him, and he went into the tomb; he saw
the linen cloths lying, 7 and the napkin, which had been on his head, not lying with
the linen cloths but rolled up in a place by itself. 8 Then the other disciple, who
reached the tomb first, also went in, and he saw and believed; 9 for as yet they
did not know the scripture, that he must rise from the dead. 10 Then the disciples
went back to their homes.

c. Mary Magdalene and the other women see and hear the risen Lord

Mt. 28:8-10

8 So they departed quickly
from the tomb with fear and
great joy, and ran to tell his disciples. 9 And behold, Jesus met
them and said, "Hail!" And
they came up and took hold of
his feet and worshiped him.
10 Then Jesus said to them, "Do
not be afraid; go and tell my
brethren to go to Galilee, and
there they will see me."

Mark

Luke

Jn. 20:11-18

11 But Mary stood weeping
outside the tomb, and as she
wept she stooped to look into
the tomb; 12 and she saw two
angels in white, sitting where
the body of Jesus had lain, one
at the head and one at the
feet. 13 They said to her,
"Woman, why are you weep-
ing?" She said to them, "Because they have taken away
my Lord, and I do not know
where they have laid him."
14 Saying this, she turned
round and saw Jesus standing,
but she did not know that it
was Jesus. 15 Jesus said to her,
"Woman, why are you weep-
ing? Whom do you seek?"
Supposing him to be the
gardener, she said to him, "Sir,
if you have carried him away,
tell me where you have laid
him, and I will take him away."
16 Jesus said to her, "Mary."
She turned and said to him in
Hebrew, "Rabboni!" (which
means Teacher). 17 Jesus said

Mt. 28	Mark	Luke	Jn. 20:11-18
			to her, "Do not hold me, for I have not yet ascended to the Father; but go to my brethren and say to them, I am ascending to my Father and your Father, to my God and your God." 18 Mary Magdalene went and said to the disciples, "I have seen the Lord"; and she told them that he had said these things to her.

d. The guard reports

Mt. 28:11-15

11 While they were going, behold, some of the guard went into the city and told
the chief priests all that had taken place. 12 And when they had assembled with the
elders and taken counsel, they gave a sum of money to the soldiers 13 and said, "Tell
people, 'His disciples came by night and stole him away while we were asleep.' 14 And
if this comes to the governor's ears, we will satisfy him and keep you out of trouble."
15 So they took the money and did as they were directed; and this story has been
spread among the Jews to this day.

§ 126. Jesus appears to Cleopas and a companion walking to Emmaus

Lk. 24:13-35

13 That very day two of them were going to a village named Emmaus, about seven
miles[f] from Jerusalem, 14 and talking with each other about all these things that had
happened. 15 While they were talking and discussing together, Jesus himself drew
near and went with them. 16 But their eyes were kept from recognizing him. 17 And
he said to them, "What is this conversation which you are holding with each other
as you walk?" And they stood still, looking sad. 18 Then one of them, named Cleopas,
answered him, "Are you the only visitor to Jerusalem who does not know the things
that have happened there in these days?" 19 And he said to them, "What things?"
And they said to him, "Concerning Jesus of Nazareth, who was a prophet mighty
in deed and word before God and all the people, 20 and how our chief priests and
rulers delivered him up to be condemned to death and crucified him. 21 But we had
hoped that he was the one to redeem Israel. Yes, and besides all this, it is now the
third day since this happened. 22 Moreover, some women of our company amazed
us. They were at the tomb early in the morning 23 and did not find his body; and
they came back saying that they had even seen a vision of angels, who said that he
was alive. 24 Some of those who were with us went to the tomb, and found it just

[f] Greek *sixty stadia.*

as the women had said; but him they did not see." 25 And he said to them, "O foolish
men, and slow of heart to believe all that the prophets have spoken! 26 Was it not
necessary that the Christ should suffer these things and enter into his glory?" 27 And
beginning with Moses and all the prophets, he interpreted to them in all the scriptures
the things concerning himself.
28 So they drew near to the village to which they were going; and he made as
though he would go further, 29 but they constrained him, saying, "Stay with us, for
it is toward evening and the day is now far spent." So he went in to stay with them.
30 When he was at table with them, he took the bread and blessed, and broke it,
and gave it to them. 31 And their eyes were opened and they recognized him; and
he vanished out of their sight. 32 They said to each other, "Did not our hearts burn
within us while he talked to us on the road, while he opened to us the scriptures?"
33 And they rose that same hour and returned to Jerusalem; and they found the eleven
gathered together and those who were with them, 34 who said, "The Lord has risen
indeed, and has appeared to Simon!" 35 Then they told what had happened on the
road, and how he was known to them in the breaking of the bread.

§ 127. Jesus appears to the disciples in Jerusalem, Thomas being absent

Jn. 20:19-25

19 On the evening of that day, the first day of the week, the doors being shut
where the disciples were, for fear of the Jews, Jesus came and stood among them
and said to them, "Peace be with you." 20 When he had said this, he showed them
his hands and his side. Then the disciples were glad when they saw the Lord.
21 Jesus said to them again, "Peace be with you. As the Father has sent me, even
so I send you." 22 And when he had said this, he breathed on them, and said to
them, "Receive the Holy Spirit. 23 If you forgive the sins of any, they are forgiven;
if you retain the sins of any, they are retained."
24 Now Thomas, one of the twelve, called the Twin, was not with them when
Jesus came. 25 So the other disciples told him, "We have seen the Lord." But he
said to them, "Unless I see in his hands the print of the nails, and place my finger
in the mark of the nails, and place my hand in his side, I will not believe."

§ 128. Jesus appears to Thomas with the other disciples

Matt.	Mark	Lk. 24:36-49	Jn. 20:26-29
		36 As they were saying this, Jesus himself stood among them.[g] 37 But they were startled and frightened, and supposed that they saw a spirit. 38 And he said to them, "Why are you troubled, and why do question-	26 Eight days later, his dis- ciples were again in the house, and Thomas was with them. The doors were shut, but Jesus came and stood among them, and said, "Peace be with you." 27 Then he said to Thomas,

[g] Some ancient authorities add *and said to them, "Peace to you!"*

Matt.	Mark	Lk. 24:36-49	Jn. 20:26-29
		ings rise in your hearts? [39] See my hands and my feet, that it is I myself; handle me, and see; for a spirit has not flesh and bones as you see that I have.[h] [41] And while they still disbelieved for joy, and wondered, he said to them, "Have you anything here to eat?" [42] They gave him a piece of broiled fish, [43] and he took it and ate before them. [44] Then he said to them, "These are my words which I spoke to you, while I was still with you, that everything written about me in the law of Moses and the prophets and the psalms must be fulfilled." [45] Then he opened their minds to understand the scriptures, [46] and said to them, "Thus it is written, that the Christ should suffer and on the third day rise from the dead, [47] and that repentance and forgiveness of sins should be preached in his name to all nations,[i] beginning from Jerusalem. [48] You are witnesses of these things. [49] And behold, I send the promise of my Father upon you; but stay in the city, until you are clothed with power from on high."	"Put your finger here, and see my hands; and put out your hand, and place it in my side; do not be faithless, but believing." [28] Thomas answered him, "My Lord and my God!" [29] Jesus said to him, "Have you believed because you have seen me? Blessed are those who have not seen and yet believe."

§ 129. Seven disciples see Jesus by the Sea of Tiberias; have large catch of fish; Peter expresses his love and is restored to favor

Jn. 21:1-23

[1] After this Jesus revealed himself again to the disciples by the Sea of Tiberias; and he revealed himself in this way. [2] Simon Peter, Thomas called the Twin, Nathanael of Cana in Galilee, the sons of Zebedee, and two others of his disciples

[h] Some ancient authorities add verse 40, *And when he had said this, he showed them his hands and his feet.*

[i] Or *nations. Beginning from Jerusalem you are witnesses.*

were together. 3 Simon Peter said to them, "I am going fishing." They said to
him, "We will go with you." They went out and got into the boat; but that night
they caught nothing.

4 Just as day was breaking, Jesus stood on the beach; yet the disciples did not
know that it was Jesus. 5 Jesus said to them, "Children, have you any fish?" They
answered him, "No." 6 He said to them, "Cast the net on the right side of the
boat, and you will find some." So they cast it, and now they were not able to
haul it in, for the quantity of fish. 7 That disciple whom Jesus loved said to Peter,
"It is the Lord!" When Simon Peter heard that it was the Lord, he put on his
clothes, for he was stripped for work, and sprang into the sea. 8 But the other
disciples came in the boat, dragging the net full of fish, for they were not far
from the land, but about a hundred yards[y] off.

9 When they got out on land, they saw a charcoal fire there, with fish lying
on it, and bread. 10 Jesus said to them, "Bring some of the fish that you have
just caught." 11 So Simon Peter went aboard and hauled the net ashore, full of
large fish, a hundred and fifty-three of them; and although there were so many,
the net was not torn. 12 Jesus said to them, "Come and have breakfast." Now
none of the disciples dared ask him, "Who are you?" They knew it was the Lord.
13 Jesus came and took the bread and gave it to them, and so with the fish. 14 This
was now the third time that Jesus was revealed to the disciples after he was raised
from the dead.

15 When they had finished breakfast, Jesus said to Simon Peter, "Simon, son
of John, do you love me more than these?" He said to him, "Yes, Lord; you
know that I love you." 16 He said to him, "Feed my lambs." A second time he
said to him, "Simon, son of John, do you love me?" He said to him, "Yes, Lord;
you know that I love you." He said to him, "Tend my sheep." 17 He said to him
the third time, "Simon, son of John, do you love me?" Peter was grieved because
he said to him the third time, "Do you love me?" And he said to him, "Lord, you
know everything; you know that I love you." Jesus said to him, "Feed my sheep.
18 Truly, truly, I say to you, when you were young, you girded yourself and
walked where you would; but when you are old, you will stretch out your hands,
and another will gird you and carry you where you do not wish to go." 19 (This
he said to show by what death he was to glorify God.) And after this, he said to
him, "Follow me."

20 Peter turned and saw following them the disciple whom Jesus loved, who had
lain close to his breast at the supper and had said, "Lord, who is it that is going
to betray you?" 21 When Peter saw him, he said to Jesus, "Lord, what about this
man?" 22 Jesus said to him, "If it is my will that he remain until I come, what is
that to you? Follow me!" 23 The saying spread abroad among the brethren that
the disciple was not to die; yet Jesus did not say to him that he was not to die,
but, "If it is my will that he remain until I come, what is that to you?"

[y] Greek *two hundred cubits.*

§ 130. Jesus appears to the eleven on a mountain in Galilee; gives the "great commission"

Mt. 28:16-20

16 Now the eleven disciples went to Galilee, to the mountain to which Jesus had
directed them. 17 And when they saw him they worshiped him; but some doubted.
18 And Jesus came and said to them, "All authority in heaven and on earth has been
given to me. 19 Go therefore and make disciples of all nations, baptizing them in the
name of the Father and of the Son and of the Holy Spirit, 20 teaching them to observe
all that I have commanded you; and lo, I am with you always, to the close of the age."

§ 131. Jesus ascends

Lk. 24:50-53

50 Then he led them out as far as Bethany, and lifting up his hands he blessed them.
51 While he blessed them, he parted from them.[k] 52 And they[l] returned to Jerusalem
with great joy, 53 and were continually in the temple blessing God.

§ 132. The purpose and the conclusion of John's Gospel

Jn. 20:30, 31; 21:24, 25

30 Now Jesus did many other signs in the presence of the disciples, which are not
written in this book; 31 but these are written that you may believe that Jesus is the
Christ, the Son of God, and that believing you may have life in his name.

24 This is the disciple who is bearing witness to these things, and who has written
these things; and we know that his testimony is true.

25 But there are also many other things which Jesus did; were every one of them
to be written, I suppose that the world itself could not contain the books that
would be written.

[k] Many ancient authorities add *and was carried up into heaven.*

[l] Many ancient authorities add *worshiped him, and.*

INDEX TO PRINCIPAL PARABLES

TITLE	REFERENCE			
Article	Matthew	Mark	Luke	Page
The two debtors	----------	----------	7:41-43	54
The soils	13:1-9	4:1-9	8:4-8	58
The weeds	13:24-30	----------	----------	61
The virile seed and the fertile earth	----------	4:26-29	----------	62
The mustard seed	13:31,32	4:30-32	(13:18,19)	62
The leaven	13:33	----------	(13:20,21)	63
The hidden treasure	13:44	----------	----------	63
The pearl of great value	13:45,46	----------	----------	63
The net	13:47-50	----------	----------	63
The treasures old and new	13:51,52	----------	----------	63
The unforgiving servant	18:23-35	----------	----------	98
The good Samaritan	----------	----------	10:25-37	108
The friend calling at midnight	----------	----------	11:5-8	109
The foolish rich man	----------	----------	12:13-21	112
The watchful servants	----------	----------	12:42-48	113
The unfruitful fig tree	----------	----------	13:6-9	114
The great banquet	----------	----------	14:15-24	116
The lost sheep	----------	----------	15:1-7	117
The lost coin	----------	----------	15:8-10	117
The lost son	----------	----------	15:11-32	118
The dishonest steward	----------	----------	16:1-13	118
The rich man and Lazarus	----------	----------	16:19-31	119
The widow and the judge	----------	----------	18:1-5	121
The Pharisee and the tax collector	----------	----------	18:9-14	122
The laborers in a vineyard	20:1-16	----------	----------	126
The pounds	----------	----------	19:11-27	129
The two sons	21:28-32	----------	----------	140
The wicked tenants	21:33-41	12:1-9	20:9-19	141
The wedding feast of the king's son	22:1-14	----------	----------	142
The ten maidens	25:1-13	----------	----------	158
The talents	25:14-30	----------	----------	158

INDEX TO PRINCIPAL MIRACLES

TITLE	REFERENCE				
Article	Matthew	Mark	Luke	John	Page
Water made wine	—	—	—	2:1-12	22
An official's son	—	—	—	4:46-54	26
A great catch of fish	—	—	5:1-11	—	28
A man with an unclean spirit	—	1:23-28	4:33-37	—	30
Simon Peter's mother-in-law	8:14-17	1:30,31	4:38,39	—	31
A leper	8:1-4	1:40-45	5:12-16	—	32
A paralytic carried by four friends	9:2-8	2:1-12	5:17-26	—	33
An invalid man at a pool	—	—	—	5:1-16	37
A man with a withered hand	12:9-14	3:1-6	6:6-11	—	40
A centurion's slave	8:5-13	—	7:1-10	—	50
A widow's only son	—	—	7:11-17	—	51
A blind and dumb demoniac	12:22	—	(11:14)	—	55
The calming of the storm	8:23-27	4:35-41	8:22-25	—	63
A Gerasene demoniac	8:28-34	5:1-20	8:26-39	—	64
Jairus' daughter	9:18-26	5:22-43	8:49-56	—	67
A woman with hemorrhage	9:20-22	5:25-34	8:43-48	—	67
Two blind men	9:27-31	—	—	—	70
A dumb demoniac	9:32-34	—	—	—	70
The feeding of five thousand	14:15-21	6:34-44	9:12-17	6:5-13	77
Walking on the sea	14:22-32	6:47-51	—	6:16-21	79
A Syrophoenician woman's daughter	15:21-28	7:24-30	—	—	85
A deaf mute	—	7:31-37	—	—	86
The feeding of four thousand	15:32-38	8:1-9	—	—	86
A blind man near Bethsaida	—	8:22-26	—	—	89
An epileptic boy	17:14-20	9:14-29	9:37-43a	—	93
The half-shekel tax	17:24-27	—	—	—	95
A man blind from birth	—	—	—	9:1-41	103
A stooped woman	—	—	13:10-17	—	114
A man with dropsy	—	—	14:1-6	—	116
Ten lepers	—	—	17:11-19	—	120
Blind Bartimaeus	20:29-34	10:46-52	18:35-43	—	128
The raising of Lazarus	—	—	—	11:1-44	130
A great catch of fish	—	—	—	21:1-11	197

INDEX TO GOSPEL PASSAGES

MATTHEW

Passage	Article	Passage	Article	Passage	Article	Passage	Article
1:1	1a	9:2-8	30	14:22-36	53	22:1-14	111c
1:2-17	1c	9:9-13	31	15:1-20	55	22:15-22	112a
1:18-25	6	9:14-17	32	15:21-28	56	22:23-33	112b
2:1-12	10	9:18-26	48b	15:29-31	57	22:34-40	112c
2:13-23	11	9:27-34	48c	15:32-39	58	22:41-46	112d
3:1-3	14a	9:35–10:4	50a	16:1-12	59	23:1-39	113
3:4-6	14b	10:5-15	50b	16:13-20	61	24:1-51	116a
3:7-10	14c	10:16-33	50c	16:21-23	62	25:1-30	116b
3:11,12	14d	10:34–11:1	50d	16:24-28	63	25:31-46	116c
3:13-17	15	11:2-15	42a	17:1-13	64	26:1-5,14-16	117
4:1-11	16	11:16-19	42b	17:14-21	65	26:6-13	118
4:12-17	26	11:20-24	42c	17:22,23	66	26:17-19	119a
4:18-22	28	11:25-30	42d	17:24-27	67	26:20-25	119c
4:23-25	29d	12:1-8	35	18:1-14	68	26:26-29	119d
5:1-12	39a	12:9-14	36	18:15-35	69	26:30-35	119f
5:13-16	39b	12:15-21	37	19:1,2	75	26:36-56	121
5:17-19	39c	12:22-30	45b	19:3-12	96	26:57–27:1	122a
5:20-48	39d	12:31-45	45c	19:13-15	97	27:2,11-14	122b
6:1-18	39e	12:46-50	45d	19:16-30	98	27:3-10	122c
6:19-34	39f	13:1-9	46a	20:1-16	99	27:15-26	122e
7:1-12	39g	13:10-23	46b	20:17-19	100	27:27-31	122f
7:13-23	39h	13:24-30	46c	20:20-28	101	27:32-56	123
7:24-29	39i	13:31-33	46e	20:29-34	102	27:57-66	124
8:1-4	29e	13:34,35	46f	21:1-11	107	28:1-7	125a
8:5-13	40	13:36-43	46c	21:12-17	109	28:8-10	125c
8:14-17	29c	13:44-52	46g	21:18-22	108	28:11-15	125d
8:18,23-27	47	13:53-58	49	21:23-27	110	28:16-20	130
8:19-22	76	14:1-12	51	21:28-32	111a		
8:28–9:1	48a	14:13-21	52	21:33-46	111b		

MARK

Passage	Article	Passage	Article	Passage	Article	Passage	Article
1:1	1a	1:35-39	29d	3:28-30	45c	6:6b-7	50a
1:2-4	14a	1:40-45	29c	3:31-35	45d	6:8-11	50b
1:5,6	14b	2:1-12	30	4:1-9	46a	6:12,13	50d
1:7,8	14d	2:13-17	31	4:10-25	46b	6:14-29	51
1:9-11	15	2:18-22	32	4:26-29	46d	6:30-44	52
1:12,13	16	2:23-28	35	4:30-32	46e	6:45-56	53
1:14,15	26	3:1-6	36	4:33,34	46f	7:1-23	55
1:16-20	28	3:7-12	37	4:35-41	47	7:24-30	56
1:21,22	29a	3:13-19a	38	5:1-20	48a	7:31-37	57
1:23-28	29b	3:19b-21	45a	5:21-43	48b	8:1-10	58
1:29-34	29c	3:22-27	45b	6:1-6a	49		

MARK

Passage	Article	Passage	Article	Passage	Article	Passage	Article
8:11-21	59	10:13-16	97	12:13-17	112a	14:22-25	119d
8:22-26	60	10:17-31	98	12:18-27	112b	14:26-31	119f
8:27-30	61	10:32-34	100	12:28-34	112c	14:32-52	121
8:31-33	62	10:35-45	101	12:35-37	112d	14:53-72	122a
8:34–9:1	63	10:46-52	102	12:38-40	113	15:1-5	122b
9:2-13	64	11:1-11	107	12:41-44	114	15:6-15	122e
9:14-29	65	11:12-14	108	13:1-37	116a	15:16-20	122f
9:30-32	66	11:15-19	109	14:1,2,10,11	117	15:21-41	123
9:33-50	68	11:20-25	108	14:3-9	118	15:42-47	124
10:1	75	11:27-33	110	14:12-16	119a	16:1-8	125a
10:2-12	96	12:1-12	111b	14:17-21	119c		

LUKE

Passage	Article	Passage	Article	Passage	Article	Passage	Article
1:1-4	1a	6:12-19	38	9:57-62	76	18:35-43	102
1:5-25	2	6:20-26	39a	10:1-24	77	19:1-10	103
1:26-38	3	6:27-36	39d	10:25-37	78	19:11-28	104
1:39-56	4	6:37-42	39g	10:38-42	79	19:29-44	107
1:57-80	5	6:43-45	39h	11:1-13	80	19:45-48	109
2:1-7	6	6:46-49	39i	11:14-36	81	20:1-8	110
2:8-20	7	7:1-10	40	11:37-54	82	20:9-19	111
2:21	8	7:11-17	41	12:1-12	83a	20:20-26	112a
2:22-40	9	7:18-30	42a	12:13-21	83b	20:27-38	112b
2:41-50	12	7:31-35	42b	12:22-34	83c	20:39,40	112c
2:51,52	13	7:36-50	43	12:35-48	83d	20:41-44	112d
3:1-6	14a	8:1-3	44	12:49-59	83e	20:45-47	113
3:7-14	14c	8:4-8	46a	13:1-9	84	21:1-4	114
3:15-18	14d	8:9-18	46b	13:10-17	85	21:5-38	116a
3:19,20	14e	8:19-21	45d	13:18-21	86	22:1-6	117
3:21,22	15	8:22-25	47	13:22-30	87	22:7-13	119a
3:23-38	1c	8:26-39	48a	13:31-35	88	22:14-23	119d
4:1-13	16	8:40-56	48b	14:1-24	89	22:24-30	119e
4:14,15	25	9:1,2	50a	14:25-35	90	22:31-38	119f
4:16-30	27	9:3-5	50b	15:1-7	91a	22:39-53	121
4:31,32	29a	9:6	50d	15:8-10	91b	22:54-71	122a
4:33-37	29b	9:7-9	51	15:11-32	91c	23:1-5	122b
4:38-41	29c	9:10-17	52	16:1-18	91d	23:6-12	122d
4:42-44	29d	9:18-20	61	16:19-31	91e	23:13-25	122e
5:1-11	28	9:21,22	62	17:1-10	92	23:26-49	123
5:12-16	29e	9:23-27	63	17:11-19	93	23:50-56	124
5:17-26	30	9:28-36	64	17:20–18:8	94	24:1-12	125a
5:27-32	31	9:37-43a	65	18:9-14	95	24:13-35	126
5:33-39	32	9:43b-45	66	18:15-17	97	24:36-49	128
6:1-5	35	9:46-50	68	18:18-30	98	24:50-53	131
6:6-11	36	9:51-56	75	18:31-34	100		

JOHN

Passage	Article	Passage	Article	Passage	Article	Passage	Article
1:1-18	.... 1b	5:19-47	 34	11:45-57	 106	18:13-27	.... 122a
1:19-34	 17	6:1-14	 52	12:1-11	 118	18:28-38a	.... 122b
1:35-51	 18	6:15-24	 53	12:12-19	 107	18:38b-40	.....122e
2:1-12	 19	6:25-71	 54	12:20-50	 115	19:1-16	.... 122f
2:13-25	 20	7:1-15	.... 70a	13:1-20	.... 119b	19:17-37	 123
3:1-21	 21	7:16-24	.... 70b	13:21-35	.... 119c	19:38-42	 124
3:22-36	 22	7:25-52	.... 70c	13:36-38	.... 119f	20:1,2	.... 125a
4:1-15	.... 23a	8:12-30	.... 71a	14:1-15	.... 120a	20:3-10	.... 125b
4:16-26	.... 23b	8:31-38	.... 71b	14:16-31	.... 120b	20:11-18	.... 125c
4:27-38	.... 23c	8:39-59	.... 71c	15:1-17	.... 120c	20:19-25	 127
4:39-42	.... 23d	9:1-41	 72	15:18–16:4a	.... 120d	20:26-29	 128
4:43-45	 24	10:1-21	 73	16:4b-33	.... 120e	20:30,31	 132
4:46-54	 25	10:22-42	 74	17:1-26	.... 120f	21:1-23	 129
5:1-18	 33	11:1-44	 105	18:1-12	 121	21:24,25	 132